It has taken 30 years to find the courage to write this book. You were right Tracey, it has made me feel better. You are my rock and without you, I probably wouldn't be here right now. I love you with all my heart.

Thanks to everyone who has worked (for nothing) alongside me over the past 30 years. We did make a difference!

To John Anderson who has never stopped believing in me and has been my dear friend for more than 30 years and to Beth Anderson who has put up with both of us all this time.

To Robert McCusker, thanks mate! You've always been there for me and are a true, dear friend.

To Bev Creagh, thanks for your patience, hard work and belief. We got there!

And, to Bob Brian for reading and liking my first draft and to Charlie, for always being last to the bar!

*FOR MY CHILDREN
AND ALL THE WORLD'S CHILDREN.*

If you could change the world, would you?

FORWARD

I Ran the World is not a book about sport or running. It is a book about an era in time and one man's dream to change the world.

People talk about the 60s as a time of unrest and social change. The 80s were a time of global consciousness and a willingness of individuals to take responsibility for others, no matter where they were or the conditions they faced. It was a time of global events to raise awareness and funds for people in need.

The movement began with Bob Geldof and Live Aid. It continued with Sport Aid, Hands Across America, Canada's Northern Lights and The First Earth Run. It was a time when people removed responsibility from the hands of charitable and non-governmental organizations and took action themselves - individually and collectively.

The movement started with music - Live Aid, *Tears Are Not Enough*, *We Are the World*, *Do They Know It's Christmas*?

But Chris Long had a vision and a dream. He believed that people could do more than listen to music and make donations - they could actively engage in the cause - and what better vehicle than sport?

I Ran the World is his story.

It is the story of how one man mobilised a team of 130 young volunteers in a small office in London, secured the support of huge organizations like Band Aid and UNICEF and then mobilised 20 million people around the world to run and demand action for Africa.

1

It is the story of these young tireless volunteers working long into the night every day for months, refusing to take no for an answer.

It is how Chris Long convinced Jim Grant, the Executive Director of UNICEF, to make Sport Aid a centrepiece in bringing the message of the people to the UN Special Session on Africa in May 1986. It is the story of how all of this happened and what the results and consequences of Sport Aid really were.

Finally, it is a challenge to the young people of today to pick up the torch and run with it, finding their own way to change and affect the world in which they live.

I Ran the World tells the story of Chris' passion to make a difference and how it led him to his vision for Sport Aid. It describes the challenges of getting Bob Geldof, Band Aid and UNICEF, the British Royals, British Airways, various governments and hundreds of road running organizations to support his vision. It tells the story of the challenges and ultimate heartbreak of Sport Aid '88. But it also tells the story of hope with Earthdive and Chris's continuing struggle to make a difference - this time through citizen scientists protecting our oceans and reefs.

Finally, it provides a blue print for the next global event - using our latest communication technology and recognizing the short attention spans and lifestyles of young people today.

It is a passionate, at times funny and often insightful look at how one man and a group of like-minded people truly made a difference to the world in which they lived.

John C Anderson Ph.D.
President/CEO
International Strategic Marketing Inc.

2

CONTENTS

PRELUDE

The British Airways Jumbo thumped the runway at Heathrow. I looked up, half asleep and gazed out of the window. Rivulets of rain were pushing across the glass in an uncharted fashion as they tried to make their way to the bottom. It reminded me a lot of my journey over the past year.

It was cold, grey and overcast - a fairly typical warm welcome to London. The plane braked hard and then veered off the runway to find its nominated stand space among its brothers and sisters.

I was exhausted . . . knackered . . . fucked.

This was my second New York roundtrip of the week and everything I had worked so hard for rested on the next few hours.

I had gone over the pitch a thousand times during the very short night but still felt really nervous.

This has to work.

I had no luggage - just a small briefcase containing my notes, toothbrush and prized Filofax - so headed straight out of the terminal to grab a taxi to Bob Geldof's house in Chelsea. My new erstwhile friend Simon had been with me on both trips to New York. He had worked with UNICEF before and it was largely down to him that I had that first meeting with its boss, Jim Grant.

I will never forget that day at the offices of the United Nations. Dressed in faded jeans scruffy t-shirt and old trainers I pitched my big idea.

"Do you want to do a project with Geldof and Band Aid?"

"Sure. How?"

"Easy, just get each of your 63 field offices and national committees to organise a fun run."

"But we're development specialists, not race organisers."

"Don't worry, I'll show you how to do it."

"What's the deal?"

"50/50."

"OK, we're in."

Of course, the meeting in reality was much more than that but that was the essence of it UNICEF – a major UN agency - had just committed 63 countries to my project - the Race Against Time.

It felt like ages since that first meeting and yet it was only two days since I'd met Bob Geldof at Madame Tussauds to give him what I thought was great news. His wax work dummy was being made while we talked. I preferred that version of him - the one that didn't answer back!

"UNICEF have promised their 63 country offices to stage races for us - that's 63 countries just for a start Bob."

"What's the deal?"

"50/50."

"Tell 'em to fock off!"

With that, I headed straight back to the airport and New York to give UNICEF the news and pass on Bob's signature expletive. That lyrical "fock" had brightened up more than one live media interview and was now aimed at the United Nations.

It was going to be a challenge but Lady Luck was smiling on me for the first time in a long while.

Jim was the first to greet us at UNICEF's headquarters, just across the road from the UN tower on First Avenue. He had some news of his own and he looked very excited.

"There's going to be a Special Session on Africa at the UN."

"You serious . . . when?"

"May 26 to 30."

"What? Can we have the UN as a stage on May 25?"

"Yes. Yes, you can. I'll get it for you. I'll deliver the UN."

Well that's it. It's got to be on.

"Is Bob happy with the 50/50 deal?"

"Yeah, he's fine."

We headed straight back to JFK and caught the next 'red eye' flight home. Now the fate of my baby rested on the next few hours.

Traffic started to increase as we got closer to London and I could feel the nerves building. The rain eased a little and there was an eerie silence in the cab. We were both apprehensive, nervous, excited. We had sat up all night, hatching our plan to help change the world.

This has to work.

I stared out the window and started to think beyond the next few hours for the first time in over a week.

Shit, what if he says yes? Can I really pull this off? How do I manage Bob Geldof and UNICEF? It'll be a fucking nightmare. Can I really make all this happen?

I felt sick.

The cab finally pulled up outside Bob's home. He lived in a really nice town house just off Sloane Square in Chelsea. It made my rented flat above a shop in

Wembley seem a bit shit in comparison and I started to doubt myself all over again.

Don't. This has to work.

I hit the bell and waited.

Bob let us in and ushered us into the front room. It was quite dark and almost gothic if I recall correctly. Deep red seemed to be the dominant colour and I remember thinking this must be how rock'n'roll stars live. I sat down, with Simon by my side. I could hear Paula upstairs with Fifi but she didn't come down. Bob sat opposite with an expectant look on his face and I realised suddenly that the stage was all mine.

I took a deep breath.

"Bob, UNICEF are giving us the UN as a stage on May 25. The following week is going to be the very first UN Special Session on Africa. Heads of state and policymakers from all over the world are coming to the UN to discuss the plight of Africa for the very first time - it's amazing, Bob. What we're going to do, one week before, is get an African runner to light a torch from the burning embers of a refugee camp fire in Africa. Then we're going to take that runner on a journey through the streets of Europe to meet heads of state and policy makers to demand action."

Bob looked interested and I felt the confidence beginning to build inside me. I was on a roll and soon words were coming from my mouth that not even I had heard before.

"Then we're going to fly him to Greece. We're going to light the Olympic torch in Olympia - for the very first time outside of the Olympic Games - then merge the torch of Africa with the torch of Sport Aid at the Parthenon."

I was winging it.

"Then we'll build that momentum during the week as he meets world leaders, the Pope, Kings and Queens. Finally, on May 25 – on the eve of the very first UN Special Session on Africa - our African runner will run down First Avenue to the United Nations. Bob, you will be there to receive that torch – the torch of Africa. You'll pass it over to president Abdou Diouf, who's chairing the UN Special Session. So, Bob, it'll be like you passing on the responsibility to the governments of the world, telling them to sort out this fucking problem once and for all. This could be your swan-song."

I looked at him.

This has to work.

"You'll then light a cauldron outside the UN. We'll connect with the whole world via TV and satellite and that will be the starting signal for the whole world to run."

Nearly there.

I took a final deep breath, like a conjurer revealing the rabbit from a hat for the very first time.

"We'll put a camera above your head and lift the image to another camera in a hot air balloon… and then to a satellite and then, at that single moment in time Bob, the whole fucking world will run for Africa."

There was silence and then he smiled.

"Now you've got a fockin' show!"

50/50 was never mentioned again and one week later, Sport Aid and Run the World was launched to the world's press.

INTRODUCTION

It's more than 30 years since that day. The day that changed my life, the day it really all started - when I had just 100 days to organise the biggest mass participation event the world has ever seen.

What followed were years of blood, sweat and tears, exultation, happiness, triumph, depression and then despair when it all came crashing down to earth.

The best days of my life, the worst days of my life.

So, why write about it at all?

I've thought about writing this book a million times and a million times I've found a reason not to.

At first, I screamed in frustration and anger at the nonsense of all that had happened. I so wanted to say something, but just couldn't.

You can't tell the truth.

Then, Live 8 came. Bob back up where he belonged, leading another line-up of bands on a global stage. Live 8 was a string of benefit concerts that took place on July 2, 2005. They were timed to precede the G8 conference and summit held at Gleneagles. It also coincided with the 20th anniversary of Live Aid. It was designed to lobby policymakers at the G8.

Four days later, the IOC announced London had won the 2012 Olympic games. One day after that, the London bombings occurred.

Live 8 seemed forgotten.

I couldn't help but think back to my time and wonder what might have been.

Why now when you had this opportunity all those years ago?

It pissed me off.

Almost everyone remembers Band Aid.

Many remember Live Aid.

Few remember Sport Aid and Run the World.

Does that bother me?

You bet the fuck it does.

It bothers me that so few remember just how much a handful of young people helped to change the world back then.

It bothers me that 30 years on, an entire generation has no living memory of it and yet exists in an increasingly divisive world that should seek change now more than ever.

Populations grow, wars and hostility rage, refugees are constantly displaced and religion continues to divide us. Stubborn disbelievers ignore the reality of climate change, melting glaciers and warming oceans.

We live in dangerous times, or so it feels.

Not just a feeling.

My children . . . your children . . . our grandchildren . . . face unprecedented global crises within their lifetimes as humanity continues to live on the edge.

Finding a remedy is a matter of survival and that solution lies with all of us, not just our elected representatives - the policymakers of our world.

We can and must change the world in which we live.

That's why I decided to write this book.

CHAPTER 1
Greece

My story starts in Greece.

I fell in love with the place during a holiday and moved there in 1980. I was just 25 at the time and I specialised in the Nutrient Film Technique (NFT).

It sounds grand but it really wasn't.

NFT was a method of growing plants in re-circulating water. Their roots were in plastic channels, water containing nutrients was pumped up to a header pipe and gravity facilitated its flow past the roots. At the end of the cycle, the water was monitored, nutrients added if needed and then pumped back to begin the cycle again.

I worked for Soil-less Cultivation Systems Limited (SCS) and had secured an NFT project for the company in the Peloponnese. I was their marketing man, among other things.

My days in Greece consisted of driving backwards and forwards between Varda - a lovely little place on the Ionian coastline just south of Patras - and Athens. I looked after the operation of the project and managed our ex-pat growers.

I never tired of the journey.

On one trip, I got stopped for speeding by a very cool policeman on a motorbike. He wore Ray-Bans, a flashy uniform and looked like Tom Cruise with a moustache. He asked me to produce my passport.

"Engleesh?"

Break the ice.

"Yes, English - like Bobby Charlton."

A big grin appeared across his face.

"You. You know Babby Sharlton."

"Oh? Well I don't really..."

"YOU KNOW Babby Sharlton!"

He threw his arms around me, greeting me like the super star I wasn't and squeezed me tight in a bear hug.

"You know Babby Sharlton."

I didn't. But by then, it didn't really matter. He had torn up the ticket, returned my passport and waved me off into the sunset.

It was my first lesson in the value of using celebrities. I didn't know it then but I was to meet 'Babby Sharlton' a couple of years later, when I told him the story.

I lived in Athens and chased new opportunities for sales. It was a nice life for a while but Athens was a difficult place in which to live and work and it brought some challenges. The Greek government was offering sizeable grants to local companies who would invest in high-tech agricultural projects. I had seen this as a major opportunity for SCS and set about finding a local company to form a joint venture.

SCS was my brother-in-law Michael's company - or at least it used to be. It was now a wholly owned subsidiary of Dunlop Irrigation.

Michael was tall, good-looking, dark-haired, blue-eyed and intelligent. He owned a Mini Cooper S and ended up marrying Diana - the only girl I really fancied from school. I probably should have hated him but I didn't.

Michael had completed a thesis on hydroponics at Chelsea Design School. His father owned a plastic pipe manufacturing company in Italy and together they designed and produced a cultivation system to grow salad crops by NFT.

I had a good job at ICI Plant Protection when I first met him but Michael and his father used their Italian charm and promised much to prise me away. My wife and in-laws also pushed hard. The sun shone out of Michael's arse and they thought I should follow the sunbeams.

"Michael is a leader – he's going places. You're more of a number two."

It was my father-in-law who said that. I never warmed to him much and I think the feeling was mutual. He was an artist and an intellectual. I was working class and liked beer and football.

I worked with Michael and his father for nearly four years before I felt the need to do my own thing.

SCS should, I thought, have grown crops, not just sold the equipment to grow them.

Most growers in the world could put together a basic NFT system and they were doing it more and more frequently.

So I decided that's what I would do.

My plan was to go to Greece and build an NFT project in Crete. I would grow lettuce and strawberries on an elevated system overlooking the Aegean Sea. My wife could swim, drink wine and enjoy the sun. My daughter and I could play together and eat all the strawberries.

A great plan.
My Greek dream.

I'd bought my first house when I was at ICI and had already sold it to buy a better one in Haslemere in Surrey. It was the early 1970s and house prices had started to climb. I leveraged the equity in the house to get a loan and left the UK to chase my dream.

I travelled to Athens quite a bit over the next months, staying with friends, meeting bankers and trying to put together my plan. My other sister-in-law Julia had friends in Crete. She was an actress and had starred in a BBC series called *The Lotus Eaters*. It had been filmed in Crete and she knew it well. Her friends lived in Chania so I headed off to stay with them for a week.

"When you get to the airport, get a cab. They only live 10 minutes away."

It was my first time in Crete. I collected my luggage from an ageing, squeaky conveyor belt and headed out of the airport.

The heat was incredible.

I never got fed up with the sumptuous feeling of being enveloped in that hot blanket of welcomeness. Especially in July and August. I loved the intense heat and I loved Greece. The smell of pine, the ouzo, the endless sound of crickets.

I grabbed a cab and showed the driver the address I had scribbled on a piece of scrap paper.

He smiled and greeted me.

"Chania?

"Yes."

I smiled back.

We headed out of the airport with me in the back of a taxi that had seen better days. All the windows were open because they were broken and hot air hit me like a hair dryer on full blast. After 10 minutes, there was no sign of any sea and instead we appeared to be headed uphill for the mountains. Nervously, I tapped the driver on the shoulder.

"Chania?"

"Nai, Nai, i Chaniá eínai étsi."

I had no idea what he said but vaguely heard the word, Chania. He seemed very happy and I could only pray we were going in the right direction.

After another 10 minutes, we stopped outside a little Greek taverna with a bright blue front door. The door opened and two women and a child walked out. One woman was very old and dressed completely in black. The taxi driver leapt out of the car and opened the front offside door.

The old lady got in.

The back door then opened and the other lady and the child squeezed in beside me. They were very excited and very noisy.

"Geia sas, efcharistó, sas efcharistó."

What the…

I tapped the driver on the shoulder one more time and stared at him intensely in his rear-view mirror.

"Excuse me, what's going on? Chania? Yes? We go?"

I pointed to my crumpled piece of paper once more. "Nai, Nai, Chaniá, yes, yes."

He was still very happy and convinced we were going in the right direction and so I sat back, squeezed in the seat alongside my new travelling companions. I had no idea where we were, where we were going or who these people were.

Was I being hijacked? Was this the Greek mafia?

The little girl with jet black hair and a beautiful face smiled back at me.

I sat it out a little longer.

Two hours and 5,000 drachmae later we arrived in Chania. During my trip, the story unfolded. I had flown to Heraklion Airport – in the middle of the island. I should have flown to Chania Airport in the west of the Island, 140 km away. The taxi driver, believing Christmas had come early, decided to pick up his mother, wife and child and give them a day out and a picnic at my expense.

I eventually said goodbye to Stelios, his wife, mother and little Sofia. It was emotional in the way only a Greek farewell could be. We were now old friends. They got out of the taxi and ushered me off in the right direction.

Hopefully.

My first Cretan friends.

I can see the funny side now but back then it was an unmitigated disaster. The money I had set aside to explore the island of Crete had all been blown on one fucking taxi ride. It was clear I needed more cash and when I got back to the UK, I placed an advert in the Financial Times.

'SEEKING INVESTMENT FOR GREEK HYDROPONIC PROJECT.'

Someone noticed and responded.

A few phone calls later, two guys arrived at my house to receive my proposal.

Early on in life I'd developed an interest in art and graphic presentation so I prepared an A3 portfolio with photographs, drawings and very smart Letraset headings. It looked really good and I was pleased with it.

Both men were middle-aged, dressed in suits and carried expensive briefcases.

They looked the part.

I drove them to see an NFT greenhouse in action. They liked it and my presentation and after a series of meetings and many more discussions, they agreed to back my project.

I met with my bank manager to give him the news. He was the father of a school friend and I'd known him for some years. His son worked in a garage and I think he enjoyed supporting me and my unconventional ideas.

He was getting nervous though.

I asked a solicitor to look over the deal.

"Be careful. What happens if the exchange rate moves? Where's the money coming from? Is it the Middle East? Are they money laundering?"

This was the most difficult decision of my life thus far and I stressed over it for days.

I was at home one day pondering the deal when there was a knock at the door. A friend, whose children babysat my daughter from time to time, had come to see us. She desperately needed somewhere to live. She was our neighbour and apparently the people who owned the house she was renting wanted it back at short notice.

She heard we were going abroad.

It made my mind up.

She was a friend and needed help. We needed income and I needed to do the best for everyone so I rented our house, turned my back on the deal of a lifetime and headed off to Greece to work for SCS again.

It had felt satisfying to get the Peloponnese project. It wasn't my Greek dream or the joint venture I had been seeking but it was a start and helped restore some belief that I'd made the right decision.

In between my trips to the Peloponnese I chased a much bigger prize in Athens - a joint venture with a company that owned supermarkets and a huge pharmaceutical company.

Slowly and painfully I helped steward a grant application through the Greek government system.

It took forever to process.

Each time I got close to an approval the application was met either with political change, objections, unrest or even corruption.

After three years of sheer bloody-mindedness the project was finally passed for investment.

I cried like a baby that day.

I was in Dunlop's office in downtown Athens when I got the news. The office was inside the main Athens bus station on the edge of the motorway than ran from Athens to Thessaloniki.

Fumes from the buses as well as the famous Athens smog seeped into my gas chamber of an office. My eyes would water most days from the bus fumes alone but on this day, I didn't mind the tears.

They were happy tears.

Unadulterated relief tears.

But had it really been worth it?

My Greek dream had not turned out as I had planned and had come at a huge cost. My wife had decided Greece was not for her. She had returned with our (now) two daughters, to live back in England.

Another problem was we no longer had a house.

The lady who had rented ours wasn't what she had seemed. She never once paid rent. Instead, she locked herself away with 16 cats and slowly let our home crumble around her. It took two years to get her out following court orders and many trips back to the UK.

The bank had been patient because they had no choice. Eventually we sold it and barely covered our debts.

The stress was just too much and my marriage fell apart.

I so nearly called it a day but stayed.

I had invested heavily in Greece both financially and emotionally and desperately needed to see something come from it.

SCS advertised for an experienced NFT grower to run the new joint venture project. Someone working with hydroponics in the UAE got the job and he and his wife upped sticks and moved to Greece.

They had only been living in Athens for about six weeks when all of a sudden, my world came crashing down again.

The giant Sumitomo Corporation of Japan bought out Dunlop.

It was totally unexpected and a huge surprise. An even bigger one came a week later, when Dunlop Irrigation's board director turned up in Athens to tell us both they were shutting down the irrigation division and we were out of a job.

"It's over. Pack your bags and come back to England."

Fuck. You are kidding me.

I was devastated.

Everything I had worked for was snuffed out in an instant.

Justification for everything, gone.

The grower from the UAE was beside himself with worry. He'd just moved his family – much against his wife's wishes, apparently - to take up the new job.

Compared to me mate, you're smelling of roses.

I suggested we try to restructure the deal without Dunlop and somehow hold on to the government grant. We all put in a little seed money to see if we could do it.

The Greek partner contributed a free office, telephones, telex and administration support. The guy from the UAE put in three grand. He was nervous his wife might think he was throwing good money after bad but he did it anyway.

"Can I tell her it's a loan?"

Tell her what you like mate.

I put in the same and we tried to resurrect the project.

It was a desperate fight and probably doomed from the outset but too much had been sacrificed to not at least try.

A few months later it was confirmed.

The grant had been sanctioned on the basis that Dunlop was the joint venture partner and not SCS.

It was dead in the water.

My Greek dream, finally over.

I was really depressed, emotionally drained and even slightly suicidal. I started drinking heavily and things spiralled onwards and downwards.

I'd hit the bars around Glyfada, a suburb situated in the southern part of Athens. It stretched from the foot of Hymettus mountain to the Saronic Gulf. Glyfada was also home to a large US Airforce base and I got to know many people who liked to party.

I spent a shit-load of cash I didn't really have and had to leave my lovely flat overlooking the Aegean Sea. I ended up in a one-bed cupboard and stayed out for days drinking and smoking myself into oblivion.

On one occasion, I forgot where I parked my car and it took me over a week to find it. When I did, I took a drive to Sounion to clear my head. Cape Sounion was home to the ruins of the Greek temple of Poseidon. It was a spiritual place and sometimes it just helped to be there.

I never made it this time.

I came to a bend in the road and didn't turn the wheel.

Fuck it, I don't care anymore.

As I left the road and headed towards the cliff edge, something inside me screamed 'stop!'

I hit the brake just before the huge drop into the sea. The car skidded on gravel and the noise intensified the horror and stupidity of what I had nearly done.

It scared the shit out of me.

I gripped the steering wheel with white knuckles as my heart pounded in my chest.

I'm ill. I need to go home.

I missed my kids and headed back to England.

CHAPTER 2
London

Martin and Elsa put me up in their London flat just off Regents Park Road. Martin also worked for SCS and I had known him before leaving for Greece. He was one of life's nice guys and I liked him. He was a big man with a big personality and a moustache that never seemed to move when he smiled. He'd picked up the baton where I left off and was now the one who supported Michael.

Elsa was just lovely. A beautiful Portuguese girl who'd moved to England years before to become a nanny. She had looked after Julia's children and that's how the two of them first met.

"You can stay with us."

"Thanks mate."

I was in a bad way when I got back to London and Martin and Elsa were my lifeline. They fed me and put a roof over my head. They offered me an ear when I needed it and shut up when I didn't. They were my friends.

We are here for you.

I spent my days trying to work out my next steps and seeing my girls. They were the one thing in my life that kept me sane. They now lived in Barnes so getting to see them wasn't too difficult.

"Stay in London and work for SCS."

That was both Martin and Michael's suggestion.

Michael had bought SCS back from Dunlop/Sumitomo.

I couldn't go back though.

It would be like going back in time.

Everything had changed and yet nothing had changed.

I still needed to do my own thing.

I just didn't know what.

SCS had secured a project in Canada with a company called Sprung Instant Structures. Michael was travelling back and forth to Calgary and needed someone in London to support the project and help run SCS alongside Martin. He'd developed a central service core for all the NFT pumping and monitoring equipment. It was very futuristic and actually looked amazing.

He's a good designer. Maybe he's on to something.

In the end, I gave in and went back. I wasn't sure but I desperately needed an income and I had already overstayed my welcome with Martin and Elsa.

The company was based in Dover Street in London. It looked very posh but was actually a serviced office block. SCS had one room and a shared boardroom.

I quickly fell back into the old routine and life began to pass me by once more. Occasionally I'd get to go to Calgary to work on the project for a few days at a time.

I enjoyed that but something was missing.

It was late October and the clocks were going back at the weekend. I headed off early one day to make use of the precious light while I still had it.

I really missed Greece.

I turned on the TV and the six-o'clock news had just started.

What happened next was to change my life forever.

"In Ethiopia seven million people are threatened by starvation. Thousands have already died. The famine caused by drought is the worst in living memory."

It was the BBC News and what followed was a report by Michael Buerk.

"Dawn, and as the sun breaks through the piercing chill of night on the plain outside Korem it lights up a biblical famine, now, in the 20th century. This place, say workers here, is the closest thing to hell on earth. Thousands of wasted people are coming here for help. Many find only death. They flood in every day from villages hundreds of miles away, dulled by hunger, driven beyond the point of desperation. Fifteen thousand children here now, suffering, confused, lost. Death is all around. A child or an adult dies every 20 minutes. Korem, an insignificant town, has become a place of grief."

It went on.

I stood and watched.

Frozen to the spot.

Like many, that report affected me deeply. I thought about it all night and for most of the next few days.

What could I do to help?

Relief organisations set up appeals and I sent some money but it wasn't much.

Hydroponics! You can grow food with hydroponics and you don't need much water.

Maybe, just maybe this was my fate.

Perhaps my destiny was not Greece but Africa instead.

They have a drought.

They can't grow food.

I can help them.

I got to the office early the next morning.

I felt energised.

I hadn't felt like that in a long, long time and I couldn't wait for Michael and Martin to arrive.

"Did you see it?"

"What?"

"The news. The news last night. The famine."

"Oh yeah. Terrible, isn't it?"

"We could help. They need food but they haven't got water."

We had been working on a system for growing wheat in ISO freight containers using a clever little plastic granule, technically called a polyacrylamide hydrophilic. We could plug in the container to a solar energy source and produce wheat shoots and thick root mat in just days. No set-up. Just ship the container, plug in and grow.

Michael looked interested and suggested we speak with the aid agencies to see if we could get funding for it. For now, Canada was his priority and he needed to leave for the airport.

Martin seemed more interested and we talked about it over the next few days.

"Let's look at it."

I started some research and spent most of November looking into the famine; the scale of it, the logistics of producing food and how we might do it. It wasn't as simple as I first thought.

The harvest in Ethiopia had looked very poor all year. There had not been the usual spring rains and disease had destroyed the crops in Sidamo, Ethiopia's traditional breadbasket region. In March, the Ethiopian Government had already warned that five million people were at risk from starvation because the country could only produce 6.2 million tonnes of grain a year, one million less than they needed.

As I looked into it more, I discovered that tens of thousands had already died of starvation and related diseases. Aid agencies were reporting that seven million people were at immediate risk.

Why have we waited 'til now?

It appeared that western governments had been reluctant to get involved. Ethiopia had been a Marxist state since the overthrow of Emperor Haile Selassie in September 1974. The West feared it would bear the cost of drought aid while the military government of Mengistu Haile Mariam spent money buying weapons and cementing a Marxist-Leninist regime.

But if the West did not help, millions of people would just die.

"Seven million people are threatened with starvation."

It still rang in my ears.

That's a shit load of containers!

A few days later Band Aid was announced and shortly after that the record, *Do they know it's Christmas*, was released.

Bob Geldof - lead singer of the Boomtown Rats - and Midge Ure, from the group Ultravox, had put together a charity record. Ure had taken Geldof's lyrics and created a melody and a backing track. Geldof had assembled a host of popular British pop performers and persuaded them to give up their time for free.

His method of selection?

How famous they were.

He just wanted to maximise sales. Raise as much money as they could.

A recording studio gave Band Aid free space to record and mix the song. It took place at SARM Studios in Notting Hill and the entire event was filmed by director Nigel Dick for a pop video.

Every stage and every detail of the process was reported in the media.

It was big news.

The first tracks recorded were of the group and choir choruses, which were also filmed by the British and international press. Footage was rushed to newsrooms where it aired while the remainder of the recording process continued to produce a video.

Phil Collins brought his own drums.

Tony Hadley of Spandau Ballet was the first to record a vocal, while a section sung by Status Quo was deemed unusable and replaced with a piece comprising Paul Weller, Sting, and Glenn Gregory from Heaven 17. Simon Le Bon from Duran Duran sang between contributions from George Michael and Sting. Paul Young's opening lines had been written for David Bowie, but he wasn't able to make the recording. Boy George arrived late to record his solo part after Geldof had apparently woken him up by phone in New York, ordering him to get on Concorde. Culture Club was in the middle of a US tour.

They were huge at the time.

As soon as it was finished, Geldof appeared on the Radio One breakfast show with Mike Read.

He promised that every penny would go to Ethiopia and Sudan.

It was a huge statement and led to a stand-off with the Government who refused to waive VAT on the sales of the single. Geldof stood up to Margaret Thatcher and, sensing the strength of public feeling, the

Government backed down and donated the tax back to the charity.

It was fucking amazing.

The record went straight to Number One, outselling all the others in the UK chart put together. It was the fastest-selling single of all time, racking up a million copies in the first week alone. It was to stay at Number One for another five weeks.

I drove my daughters to my Mum and Dad's house that Christmas. The girls loved to play music in the car and to sing along out loud. The Band Aid single got a huge amount of airplay and Radio One was playing it every hour.

I drummed the steering wheel while the girls sang in the back. We were all tone deaf but what we lacked in performance we made up with passion.

'It's Christmastime, there's no need to be afraid.
At Christmastime, we let in light and we banish shade.
And in our world of plenty we can spread a smile of joy.
Throw your arms around the world at Christmastime.'

We learned every word.

Band Aid was everywhere that Christmas and £8 million had been raised before it was even over.

It was incredible. Brilliant. Amazing!

I was utterly inspired.

I was sad so many people were dying but I was so happy Band Aid were trying to help.

I want to help too.

CHAPTER 3
Band Aid and Geldof

After Christmas, all I could talk about was Band Aid and what we could do to help.

"Maybe we can raise some money."

Michael was more focused on how SCS could help with NFT.

I wasn't so sure anymore.

I didn't think the wheat production idea was practical and the last thing the people of Ethiopia and Sudan needed right now was a nice salad.

Keep it to yourself.

"Why don't we speak to Geldof?"

"And say what?"

"Tell him what we do and say we want to help – see where it goes."

My sister-in-law Julia, the actress, knew Trudie Styler who was also Sting's girlfriend.

"Let's see if we can get Geldof's number."

It worked.

Julia called Trudie and phoned us with Bob's number. A few days later, I gave him a call.

My very first meeting with Bob Geldof was at the SCS office in Dover Street. We had booked the board room in order to impress.

Geldof arrived alone.

I was expecting a gruff, no-nonsense, messy-haired punk rocker and he was all of that, and more.

Bob listened.

We explained what we did and that we wanted to help. He told us what he had done and how the Band

Aid Trust had been set up to ensure that every single penny it raised would get to Africa and would benefit Africa. He explained the need for immediate famine relief and that millions and millions of Africans faced starvation.

It was Bob Geldof and he was sitting next to me.

I like him.

Over the next few days we all thought long and hard about that meeting.

Michael was beginning to accept that the prospect of SCS getting anything out of this was fading fast. His interest was waning too. In fairness, he had a lot on his plate with the Canadian project.

Martin and I, however, were shifting our interest up another gear.

"Let's raise some money."

"How?"

"Sport!"

I played football as a kid and was all right at it. I played for my county and for South East England. I played basketball. I did athletics. I ran to keep fit. I liked running.

"We're not stupid. Let's put on something."

Shit, that's it.

"Let's put on a sponsored fun run."

Running, jogging, whatever you called it, was very popular. The method of getting sponsored per mile was well understood and maybe, just maybe, this could be a good mechanism to raise even more money for Band Aid.

Martin and I batted the idea around and very soon we had come up with the idea of staging 10 sponsored fun runs around the UK.

"Let's call it the Race Against Time."

"We can have a race in London, Edinburgh, Cardiff, Newcastle, Birmingham – all the major cities. We can have famous people running in each race. We could get TV involved."

It was a great idea and I was hooked.

I did some more research and made a call to the head of BBC and ITV Sport.

The head of ITV Sport came to our offices and we set out our grand plan of the Race Against Time. I had no real idea what I was doing but just made it up as I went along.

"Who's committed?"

"What do you mean?"

"Celebrities, famous sportsmen and women. Who's committed?

"Well, nobody yet…"

It was a short meeting and a quick lesson in what TV really wanted. A mass fun run in 10 cities wasn't going to cut the ice with them. Geldof was a great start but they wanted names.

Big names.

Sporting legends.

Celebrities.

Around this time an American benefit record was also released. Harry Belafonte and US fundraiser Ken Kragen had put together a US song for Africa. Michael Jackson and Lionel Richie had written it and it was called *We Are the World*.

It was music doing even more and it brought together the most famous artists in the American music industry at the time.

It also became a worldwide commercial success, topping music charts around the globe and becoming the fastest-selling American pop single in history.

The first ever single to be certified multi-platinum.

We Are the World received a quadruple platinum certification from the Recording Industry Association of America - which only served to increase the momentum and raise the bar even higher.

The music industry was on its A game.

The weeks unfolded and it became clear this was not going to be as easy as it first sounded. Michael was back, we were busy and I was giving less and less time to the project that had just re-booted my soul.

I felt uneasy and also needed somewhere to live.

I found a flat listed in the Evening Standard. It was in Wembley, near Sudbury Town tube station. It was a big flat over a shop. Not pretty but spacious and I could just afford the rent.

I went to see it.

"It's only a company let. We can't rent to individuals. Is that OK?"

"Sure, no problem. I'll get you a letter or something."

Shouldn't be a problem.

When I got back to the office I told the guys about my 'new' home. I was excited about getting some independence back and I needed some space away from SCS.

"Michael, it's a company let. If I write a letter can you sign it for me?"

"What do you mean?"

"It's a company let. I pay the rent and am responsible for the place. It's just they won't do a personal let.

"I can't do that."

And he didn't.

Fuck it.

That afternoon, I made my way to Wembley and blagged my way into a new flat.

It was the straw that broke the camel's back and finally made up my mind. I was going to leave SCS and make Sport Aid happen.

I told Martin first.

I think he wanted to come with me, but couldn't.

"I can't risk it."

I understood and to be fair, I was relieved. Both of us leaving would have been a crushing blow to SCS.

I needed to find the right time to let Michael down gently but, more importantly, I needed to speak to Mr Bob Geldof one more time.

I called Bob and he came to the office in Dover Street again.

He had news of his own.

"We're doing this concert at Wembley Stadium on July 13. We're going to link it live to another, huge concert in New York. The best bands in the world are playing. It's going to be called Live Aid. That's on the Saturday and the week before we're holding loads of other events. David Bailey might be doing Photo Aid on Monday and Yves St Laurent might do Fashion Aid on Tuesday."

"What's happening Thursday?"

"Nothing yet."

"Put me down for Sport Aid."

Bob liked the concept of the Race Against Time and well, that was that.

All I had to do now was make it happen.

I chose my moment and told Michael I was leaving. I think he half expected it and seemed prepared. It was painful but, at least this time, I hoped he understood.

I was never going to be a number two.

Over the next few months the buzz around Live Aid just grew and grew. The New York concert was dropped and replaced with the John F Kennedy Stadium in Philadelphia.

Bands were being announced every day. Elton John, Queen, Alison Moyet, Paul McCartney and The Who. In the US: Tom Petty, The Rolling Stones and Duran Duran. The great Jack Nicholson was going to host the US concert.

Live Aid was going to be the most ambitious international satellite television venture that had ever been attempted. The TV feed was going to be supplied by the BBC in the UK and ABC in the USA. It was going to be broadcast to more than a billion people!

The BBC agreed to cover the event, clearing their schedules to run the 16-hour concert in its entirety on BBC One, BBC Two and Radio One.

Newspapers displayed double-page spreads of complicated graphics on how the most complex TV show in the world was going to be done.

I didn't know it at the time but the one I was to do a year later was to eclipse it by a mile.

Michael Jackson refused to take part and that made even bigger news.

Positive or negative, the hype just kept growing.

Harvey Goldsmith told the story of how he'd called all the staging guys putting together the Bruce Springsteen concert at Wembley into his office. Live Aid was going to use the Springsteen concert staging.

"I've got some good news and bad news. You are all helping to put on the biggest rock show the world will ever see. The bad news? You're not being paid. Anyone got a problem with that you can fuck off."

I loved it.

The whole thing just built and built until the entire country was immersed in Live Aid fever.

As the day drew closer and closer, there was no mention of Fashion Aid, Photo Aid or indeed my beloved Sport Aid. Live Aid had now earned solo-status and centre-stage in a global press frenzy and there was no room for anything else.

I called Harvey Goldsmith's office and asked for tickets.

"You have to pay for them. Everyone has to pay for them."

"Of course, no problem."

"Pick them up at the box office on the day."

I was so excited, I couldn't sleep.

CHAPTER 4
Live Aid

I stood in the crowd at Live Aid just in front of the mixing tower to the right. The view was great and the atmosphere even better. It was a hot, sunny day and the place was buzzing.

This was supposed to be the culmination of a week of fundraising events for Africa. That had been Bob's plan when we met back in February and I was supposed to have put on 10 sponsored runs last Thursday.

It didn't happen.

I was glad.

Sport can do more than a few sponsored runs in the UK.

I look back now with such fondness on what was one of that decade's most incredible events and one that changed my life forever.

July 13, 1985 was one of the hottest days in the year.

The Coldstream Guards band opened the show with *God Save the Queen* and then came Status Quo with *Rockin' All Over the World*.

We were only 10 minutes into the day and the place was already on fire.

Next Style Council finishing a set with *Walls Come Tumbling Down*.

Then on came Bob with the Boomtown Rats singing *I Don't Like Mondays*.

He stopped just after the line '*the lesson today is how to die*'. It was such a poignant moment and the crowd went mad. I clapped so hard I thought my hands would fall off. He finished the song, leaving us all to sing the final words.

Next Adam Ant, Ultravox and Spandau Ballet with *True*.

Elvis Costello sang a version of The Beatles' *All You Need Is Love*, which he introduced by asking the audience to join in.

And so we did.

Then Nik Kershaw and Sade followed by Phil Collins and Sting.

U2 played a 14 minute rendition of *Bad,* during which Bono jumped off the stage to dance with a girl. The poor kid was being crushed by the throngs of people pushing forwards. Bono saw her and gestured frantically at security to help.

It was a two-song masterclass on how to command a crowd and 30 second lesson in first aid.

Then came Dire Straits with *Money for Nothing* and *Sultans of Swing*.

Queen then took to the stage.

I hadn't heard much of them before but for Queen, Live Aid was a magnificent relaunch, recasting their legacy in a 20-minute eruption of magnificence and passion before a spellbound Wembley crowd – and me.

Freddie Mercury took the day to yet another level.

Their fast-moving afternoon set covered the breadth of the band's catalogue, cramming a whole concert's worth of highlights into an amazing performance that included *Bohemian Rhapsody, Radio Ga Ga*, *Hammer to Fall*, *Crazy Little Thing Called Love* and the grand finale of *We Are the Champions*.

Then, Bowie. A performance that was described by Rolling Stone as his last triumph of the 1980s. He gave up part of his amazing set for a special video. It had been put together by CBC and, as he said at the time:

"The subject speaks for itself."

What followed was an image of a small African child, lying next to her mother in a refugee camp in Africa. As the soundtrack played the entire audience watched in total silence as the tiny tot, ravaged by famine, tried to simply stand up. The video was directed by 23-year-old Timothy Hutton, who had won an Oscar for his role in the movie *Ordinary People*. Hutton wanted to direct at the time, so when Ric Ocasek of The Cars suggested it, Hutton had jumped at the chance.

I just cried.

I cried along with 70,000 people and there wasn't a dry eye in the house. It was a truly incredible moment and I decided then that Sport Aid was going to be huge and it was going to be global.

If music can do this, sport can do so, so much more.

The Who played with Kenney Jones on drums, their first performance since they'd officially disbanded after their 1982 'farewell' tour. The set included a chaotic and blistering version of *Won't Get Fooled Again*.

Towards the end of the show, Paul McCartney's microphone failed as he sang *Let it be*. For the first two minutes, you couldn't hear a thing and it didn't matter. Bob, David Bowie, Alison Moyet and Pete Townshend came to his aid to sing along with him. We all joined in, while technicians frantically tried to repair his mic in the background.

At the end, Bob was raised onto the shoulders of Pete Townshend and Paul McCartney and the crowd went mad.

It was just perfect.

But despite its enormity, its glamour, its bands - the best in the world - for me, Live Aid was still a concert of superstars on two rich continents, raising money for poor African people who couldn't help themselves.

But they can help themselves.

Some of the best runners in the world came from the Sudan and Ethiopia and I made a pledge there and then that I would empower them to help themselves.

I just didn't know how yet.

Brian May was quoted as saying:

"It was the greatest day of our lives."

It was mine as well.

I walked home from Wembley Stadium that night with the music still ringing in my ears. I wasn't sure where my next steps were going to take me but I was excited and scared shitless all at the same time.

The response to Live Aid was huge.

Within just a few weeks, Live Aid had raised triple the £10 million expected. A single donor from the ruling family of Dubai had given £1 million alone.

In the US, 22,000 pledges were received within five minutes of the Beach Boys taking to the stage.

It was amazing.

The world had been fired up and governments had begun a global relief operation.

Something very special had happened and it seemed to embrace the whole world.

The buzz continued into the following weeks and only served to heighten my anxiety even more.

I was on my own now.

I had no money and I was going to make the Race Against Time a global event.

Somehow.

I started to research organisations and networks who might help in organising runs in different countries and I found AIMS.

The Association of International Marathons (AIMS) had been established in 1982 with its first Congress in London. During the previous two years, some of the world's leading marathon race directors had held informal discussions with a view to setting up an association.

It was still in its infancy.

I decided to pitch my idea to them.

If I could get race organisers to buy in to the concept, maybe they could organise races for me in all the major cities. In return, they could raise their profile and possibly help themselves.

There was no internet or email in 1985 and only a very patchy facsimile network, so I sent off letters and awaited a response.

I made a few phone calls to AIMS headquarters in an effort to help speed things along but, inevitably, my resources were very limited and I simply had to wait.

It was a frustrating time and the bar had been set very high.

You can do this.

CHAPTER 5
Birmingham

A few weeks later, BBC News threw me a lifeline.

Birmingham had been selected from a number of UK cities to bid to host the 1992 Olympic Games. The campaign was being led by Denis Howell, the Minister for Sport. Birmingham's bid was estimated at £500 million and the National Exhibition Centre was sold as the ideal location, with excellent transport links including the railway station and motorway network.

It hit me like a thunderbolt.

Yes!

I couldn't believe my luck.

What better way for Birmingham and the NEC to show off their resources and capabilities to the world than to host Sport Aid?

Maybe I could get them to host different sporting events at different venues.

They could show off their facilities.

My mind was racing.

I put a call through to the City Council offices and said it was Bob Geldof.

Then, in my best Irish accent. . .

"How would you like to stage Sport Aid?"

Unsurprisingly, I got a meeting and headed up to Birmingham the next day to pitch my idea.

This was going to be the ultimate 'elevator pitch.' You know, when you've got about 10 seconds to sell it or they call security and you're out on your arse.

They were expecting Bob Geldof and he wasn't coming.

A number of councillors and senior members of the NEC management team had been assembled for the meeting and when I walked into the room everyone looked over my shoulder expecting Bob Geldof the Live Aid star to sweep into the room behind me.

He didn't and the door slammed shut.

"You've seen Live Aid. Sport Aid is going to be bigger and better. It's a week-long series of international sporting events culminating in a global simultaneous fun run called the Race Against Time. Billions will watch it on TV in awe of what you guys have done. There is no better way for Birmingham to show off its Olympic credentials than by staging it. Host Sport Aid and you'll win the Olympic Games."

Good elevator pitch.

"Who are you?"

"My name is Chris Long. I'm chairman of Sport Aid."

"Where's Mr Geldof."

"Sorry, he couldn't make it. Something came up."

They all looked at each other, slightly uncomfortable. A murmur spread among the white-collared crowd.

Then a short pause.

"What do we have to do?"

And that was it.

We talked more about detail but, in that single moment, they had all made up their minds.

Birmingham and the NEC were now hosting Sport Aid.

Within a week, I had a portakabin outside hall six. A reporter from the Birmingham Post & Mail was seconded to the project along with a secretary from the NEC.

I suddenly had resources but more importantly, a big partner with a shit-load to lose.

Barry Clevedon was the events manager at the NEC and Terry Golding was his chief executive. Barry was a really nice guy. He was hugely energetic, enthusiastic and fired up at the prospect of what Sport Aid might bring to the NEC.

I dealt with Barry on a day-to-day basis.

I was able to make much more progress with AIMS now that I had someone paying for the telephone and telex.

Bob Bright, one of its founding members and head of the Chicago Marathon, had been in touch and seemed very supportive. In addition, Ray Oliu from Barcelona, Fred Lebow from New York and Hyon Joon Yoo from Seoul had also registered interest.

It soon became obvious that a marathon wasn't practical but I didn't just want a token mile.

Sport Aid had to be about making a point.

Millions were starving in Africa and I wanted people to run and to hurt - at least a little.

This was about raising money but it was also about showing that people really cared and that they wanted something to be done. I decided 10 kilometres was going to be the distance.

Its only six miles...

My 'experts' at AIMS agreed.

Barry and I explored other events that could take place during Sport Aid week. He was very keen on getting an ice rink into the NEC and asked if we could consider an ice skating event.

Why not?

Jayne Torvill and Christopher Dean had been adored by the British public since winning gold at the winter Olympics the year before. The pair became the highest scoring figure skaters of all time, receiving 12 perfect 6.0s and six 5.9s. They danced to *Bolero* and were watched by a British television audience of more than 24 million.

I called them.

I met Chris and Jayne along with Barry for breakfast at a hotel in Birmingham a few days later.

I was really nervous.

These guys were true superstars who had achieved the ultimate in their chosen sport. They would be a great asset to Sport Aid and I thought I would have to pitch really hard to get their support.

I didn't.

They were amazing.

Gracious.

Supportive.

They had been caught up in the whole Band Aid vibe.

"Of course we will help."

Before I could eat my second sausage they had not only agreed to take part but had also agreed to try and convince Katerina Witt, Brian Orser, Robin Cousins, John Curry, the famous Protopopovs and others to join a Sport Aid ice spectacular at the NEC. They were completely carried away with the concept of Sport Aid and wanted skating to be in on the act.

Barry almost wet himself.

He had just discovered the real power of Sport Aid and he liked it - a lot.

I kept Bob informed of the main developments. His interest and knowledge of sport seemed to be at the other end of the spectrum to music but he came up with a couple of great ideas.

"Let's have the Birmingham race around Spaghetti Junction."

Crazy, but I loved it.

I attended a high-powered meeting of officials from Birmingham's police force, council, highways' management and others to explore the possibility of shutting down the M6.

"You're mad. Do you know how difficult it is to shut down the M6 and Spaghetti Junction? It's the UK's busiest arterial road."

"Do you know how difficult it is to watch 18 million African people die when you could have fucking saved them?"

It was as simple as that and it wasn't as simple as that.

I could visualise the delivery of a poignant message to the world. Aerial cameras showing thousands and thousands of people running in protest around Britain's busiest road network while cars queued up from London to Penrith.

Now, that's a fucking statement.

But the police bombarded me with red tape and problems and, ultimately, it wasn't to be. I only had so much energy and I needed to focus on the battles I could win.

A few weeks later, I set up a meeting with Ron Dennis, of McLaren Racing. McLaren had merged with Ron's Project Four Racing and he had taken over as team principal. I arrived at the high-tech office in Surrey and was escorted to Ron's office.

"Can you put on a Formula One race up the M1?"

Bob loved the idea.

He wanted pit stops at all the motorway service stations and sponsors' logos on all the bridges. The problem was, we didn't understand Formula One.

"The cars will blow up. They're not designed for straight lines. It'll be a procession. It won't be a race. It'll cost a load of money and I can't see the teams doing it."

"Yeah, but it'll be a fucking vibe."

Ron couldn't really disagree with that but the practical and financial problems were real and were, ultimately, to get in the way of that one too.

The next few weeks continued in the same vein. Exploring sports, exploring radical ideas. Trying to create a week-long series of world class sporting events.

"Let's do cricket at Edgbaston."

England were playing Australia in the 5th Test here and I decided to go along to see if I could meet Ian Botham.

Ian was in the team along with David Gower, Mike Gatting, Gooch etc. They were playing a formidable Australian team made up of the likes of Border, Wood, Hilditch and Richie. England won by an innings and 118 runs in the end but even while they were batting, getting to meet the players proved difficult during the game. But that day a dialogue started that was going to end with cricket playing its part.

"What about football?"

Football was the world's biggest sport and had to play a big part in Sport Aid.

I had mapped out all the mega events of the next year and it looked more and more likely that the Race Against Time was now going to be in the Spring. The FIFA World Cup finals were taking place in Mexico from May to June.

Maybe we can get FIFA to put on a match?

I needed someone to help me champion the cause and I couldn't think of anyone better than the great 'Babby Sharlton'.

I tracked him down and called his office.

Bobby was going to the FIFA World Cup final draw in Mexico City. I explained what I was trying to do and he invited me to join him.

"Maybe we can get FIFA to put on a match?"

Bobby paid for my air ticket and my hotel and suggested we talk to FIFA in Mexico.

"It's best you go there. Everyone will be there."

I met Bobby for the first time at Birmingham International Airport as we boarded a plane for Mexico City. I had watched him win the World Cup when I was 12.

Football was my thing.

Bobby was my hero.

He was my hero then and he was my hero now. He didn't have to do what he was doing for me and I was so happy to be sitting next to an icon and a thoroughly nice bloke.

On the flight over, we talked about the World Cup, his career, that plane crash. I was in awe and ever so slightly star-struck. This was the great Bobby Charlton.

I was his travelling companion and he had saved me a speeding ticket.

Bobby now ran his world-famous Bobby Charlton Soccer Schools. He had seen a young lad there called

David Beckham who apparently showed some promise. Bobby was also branching out into travel and hospitality packages. He had actually taken a punt on some hotel rooms in Mexico in the hope that England would play there. He wanted to put together some travel packages for the World Cup.

Bobby was combining his business trip with Sport Aid and I was very, very grateful.

When we arrived in Mexico, Bobby drew crowds wherever he went. Every man, woman and child remembered that amazing thirty yard goal that sunk Mexico in the 1966 World Cup.

"… and Charlton flooded into the space and kept going, feinting and shimmying as he went, before transferring the ball on to his right foot and thundering his shot across Calderon and rattling towards the left stanchion with unstoppable force and swerve. He runs towards the right corner flag and leaps 4 feet and thrashes the air in jubilation. What a goal. What a man."

What a man indeed! I remember it to this day.

And so did all of Mexico.

The day before the World Cup draw, Bobby and I attended an exhibition match organised by our host, the Mexican Football Federation. It was Mexico v Hungary.

I eagerly awaited the kick-off as I took my seat alongside Bobby in what was a star-studded VIP section of the ground.

I'm sitting next to Bobby Charlton.

I think the occasion and events leading up to it had started to take their toll as it was at least 10 minutes into the game before I plucked up enough courage to say anything.

"Great pass."

"Yes, very good."

The response came from the other side of me and I recognised it instantly. I hadn't noticed before but I was sitting between Bobby Charlton and the great Franz Beckenbauer. Franz, as I was now about to call him, had just validated my technical observation.

My mate Franz.

I just laughed.

An incredible moment and a story I was to dine out on for years. I was to meet Franz a few years later as well but I didn't know that then.

I shook his hand and said goodbye.

Mexico won 2-0.

The next day, the draw for the World Cup Finals was held in a beautiful theatre in downtown Mexico City.

The president of FIFA was Joao Havelange, a Brazilian, and the secretary was Sepp Blatter. It was a busy time for both of them and Bobby thought it better that we meet up with them after all the formalities had finished.

I agreed and so, for the meantime, I was taking part in all the events.

I was like a kid in a sweet shop.

Bobby and I took our seats in the main stalls about midway between the stage and rear exits. The boxes and circle, which wrapped all around the theatre up to the stage, were full of cameras and commentators from all over the world. The event was being transmitted live and it had a huge global audience.

The tension built as the balls were picked out from various containers on stage. The first ball decided team locations and the second was to discover their opponents in this, the world's biggest soccer event.

It was getting closer and closer to England's announcement and Mr Charlton was getting nervous.

The cameras had picked up on this and would swing round to his direction to try to catch a reaction.

Blatter picked out a ball.

"England."

"Will play in…"

"Monterrey."

"*Shit.*"

That wasn't what Bobby had hoped for and he looked a bit disappointed.

Cameras panned round and captured his response.

"…and Charlton looks disappointed… maybe it's the heat in Monterrey, the humidity? Not the best venue for England? Why?"

The investigation continued. You could see the BBC guys in the gantry, looking down.

Speculating.

Bobby did look disappointed.

But he was probably thinking what the hell am I going do with all these hotel rooms in Mexico City, more than he was speculating on England's fate.

I laughed out loud which must have added to the confusion even more.

Soon the formalities ended and the VIP audience made its way out of the little theatre into the bright sunshine of the day.

England were going to play Morocco and Poland in Monterrey and then Paraguay at the Aztec Stadium, in Mexico City.

"Would you like to see it?"

The next day Bobby took me to the Aztec Stadium. The Estadio Azteca, as the Spanish call it, is the iconic football stadium located in the suburb of Santa Ursula in Mexico City.

Since its opening in 1966 it had become the official home of the Mexico national football team.

It was the largest stadium in Mexico and sat at an altitude of 7,200 ft above sea level. It was regarded as one of the most famous and iconic in the world. It was the first to host two FIFA World Cup Finals in 1970 and 1986.

My England team were going to play here but, for now, I was standing on the centre circle with the great Bobby Charlton.

It was empty but still imposing.

Roughly 108,000 seats surrounded us and seemed to go up and up forever. I could feel the Azteca as the intimidating fortress it must have been on match days. An amazing atmosphere created by the passionate fans of the home side with opposing teams wilting under the pressure - to say nothing of the heat, altitude and smog of the city.

I stood in silence with Bobby.

Me, dreaming of what could have been.

Him, just remembering what he had done.

From the Aztec stadium, we drove to the area around the General Hospital.

A week before we had flown out, Mexico had been hit by a huge earthquake. The event caused the deaths of at least 5,000 as well as serious damage to the Greater Mexico City area. The epicentre was along the middle America Trench, more than 350 km away. The event caused between three and four billion US dollars in damage. Four hundred buildings collapsed and another 3,000 were seriously damaged.

The earthquake had damaged the Gynaecology Unit and the Medical Residence tower was completely destroyed. More than 295 people died there, including patients, residents, and medical staff.

Most of the earthquake damage was to buildings.

Two reasons were the resonance in lakebed sediments and the long duration of the shaking. The buildings most damaged were from six to 15 stories in height. These resonated most with the energetic frequency band of the lakebed motions. Strangely, in many damaged buildings, just one floor had collapsed. In some cases, the damage was caused by the top of a lower, adjacent building banging against the walls and supporting columns of a neighbour. Eventually, the columns just gave way. In other cases, the first few floors were designed as parking garages, open lobbies or large shopping areas. These were particularly flexible and just collapsed.

It was a mess.

I couldn't help thinking back to my first year in Athens.

We had just moved from a hotel to our first flat in Kalamaki. Our home was on the sixth floor of an apartment block. In the middle of the night everything started shaking violently. I rushed into my daughter's bedroom and grabbed her. We stood under a doorway arch until the shaking eventually stopped – a good two minutes later.

It was terrifying.

That quake measured 6.6 on the Richter scale and we slept outside in the car for the rest of the night. The one that hit Mexico was 7.5. I could only imagine the terror those poor people must have felt.

"We should raise money for Africa and these people."

Bobby agreed and we headed back to our hotel.

Tomorrow we were meeting with Havelange and Blatter.

We presented our idea of an all-stars match ahead of the World Cup finals. It could easily precede the opening ceremony and world football could make its own personal gift to Africa, together with a donation to the Mexican earthquake victims.

The World Cup was to start on May 31.

A week before would be great.

All the teams would be in Mexico by then.

It would make it easy to arrange.

Wrong.

Havelange and Blatter poured scorn on the idea, blaming players, managers and football associations.

"They will not release players before the World Cup. What about injuries?"

"We're not asking them to kick the shit out of each other."

Just one match.

It was clear they were going to make it difficult. We left the meeting with them promising to do something but both knowing, in our hearts, they probably wouldn't.

It seemed like FIFA only cared about FIFA and well, that was that.

It was really disappointing.

The world's richest and biggest sport was going to contribute nothing.

Up to that day, I loved football.

Now, not so much.

I got back from Mexico and tried to put the disappointment of FIFA behind me but it had left its mark.

Just one match and it didn't really have to be competitive. They could have held hands for an hour and a half for all I cared.

They should have done something.

My idea of the week-long series of sporting events was designed for professional sports men and women to inspire ordinary people to get off their backsides and run for Africa.

What kind of example were these overpaid prima donnas going to show to the world?

I also felt sorry for Bobby.

Why weren't they all like him?

I had contacted the British Gymnastics Association before I left and their chief executive officer had been in touch.

The BGA was interested in hosting a multi-nation gymnastics display at the NEC for Sport Aid.

I had also been thinking rugby and maybe an international sevens tournament.

Barry conceded that rugby could go to Cardiff Arms Park.

There were not enough hours in the days and they were getting longer and longer.

I signed up more race cities and focused on other sports that might form part of the week. Dealing with race cities meant difficult hours and I would be working at the NEC into the early hours, speaking to different countries. Early morning, Australia and Asia. Evening, the Americas.

It was getting tiring and I needed more help.

Foolishly, I had thought that in the bow wave of Live Aid's success it would be easy to get sponsorship and support.

It wasn't.

"Oh, sorry, we already did something for Live Aid."

"We've done our bit."

"We've already given a load of stuff to Band Aid. Love to help but…"

I had been using my Dad's car to travel between London and Birmingham. When in Greece I'd given him some money to help buy it. I didn't have one and when I asked to use it, he couldn't really say no.

I felt bad about it.

I was driving more than 1,000 miles a week.

So I asked Rover - who were based in Birmingham - if they would loan me a car.

They did!

We badged it with the Sport Aid logo to show their support. Given my mileage up and down the M1 and M6 it was a great billboard.

BT had already supplied a few phones for the office and also fitted the car with one of their first hands-free car mobiles. Little did they know that was nothing - compared to what they were going to give later.

It made a massive difference.

But I needed more.

Things were not going as fast as they should have been. The NEC was a big asset but maybe I needed to be in London.

Should I be organising this global event from London?

The travelling time was taking its toll.

I need more people, more resources.

I was getting stressed.

On the way home one night, I called my Mum from my new car phone.

"Hi Mum, its me."

I was doing about 70 mph around that big sweeping bend joining the M6 to the M1.

"Crackly line, where are you?"

"I'm on the M1 – driving."

"Don't be silly, where are you?"

CHAPTER 6
UNICEF

The next morning I woke up early and met Geldof in London. He had just got back from Rome where he'd met an English guy called Simon Dring. Simon had introduced himself to Bob and said he wanted to help.

He worked in television.

Sounded interesting.

Bob gave me his card and I arranged to meet Simon a week later at his sister's house in Barnes. It's where my kids lived and I knew the area quite well.

"I'm an award-winning British foreign correspondent and television producer. I've worked for Reuters, the Daily Telegraph, BBC Television, Radio News and Current Affairs and I've covered major stories and events, including 22 wars and revolutions around the world."

Simon wasn't short of confidence and self-belief and maybe I should have noticed an ego the size of a planet.

But I didn't.

He told me that he had a wide range of experience in many areas of television broadcasting and management. He had long hair and bright blue eyes. He was very personable, softly spoken and a bit rock'n' roll.

Simon had one of those 1980s jackets with the sleeves rolled up.

He poured praise on my plans and it made me feel good.

I liked him.

Simon was incredibly enthusiastic about Sport Aid and felt he could really help. He told me how he got his first media job at the age of 18, working as a proof-reader and feature writer for the Bangkok World newspaper in Thailand. At 19, he was a freelance reporter for the Daily Mail and the New York Times in Laos, before moving to Vietnam, where he covered the war for two years for Reuters as their youngest staff correspondent.

I liked his stories.

He was colourful.

He had lived.

Simon Dring was older than me and that was also a good thing.

I needed some help.

Reassurance.

I missed that big brother figure now Michael was gone.

We talked about my plans for a week-long series of sporting events, culminating in the Race Against Time. I told him about the ice skating, the cricket match, gymnastics, the NEC, everything I had done.

He loved it and it showed in his eyes.

We exchanged contact details and agreed to think about how he could get involved.

I felt pretty good.

My gut told me Simon could be an enormous asset. I had quickly learned that just one passionate volunteer was infinitely better than a hundred pressed men any day.

Simon, it seemed, was prepared to give up his time for nothing.

The next day I was still feeling upbeat when I was summoned to Terry Golding's office in the main building of the NEC.

I walked in and Barry was sat ashen-faced with Terry alongside looking equally uncomfortable.

"What's up?"

Terry pushed a piece of paper under my nose.

It was a telex from the Band Aid Trust.

It wasn't addressed to me.

It didn't even mention me.

It was addressed to Terry Golding.

Band Aid was pulling out.

"What's going on? Do you know about this?"

I didn't.

What the fuck?

It was so embarrassing.

I had heard nothing.

Geldof had said nothing to me.

Not a warning.

Not a mention.

Fucking nothing!

"I don't know what's going on, Terry. I have no idea. Let me speak to them."

I tried Bob but he didn't answer his phone.

I tried Harvey Goldsmith.

Nothing.

In one single instant the Band Aid Trust had made me look like the biggest fucking dick in the world.

How dare they?

This was my project.

Problem was, I had nailed my flag firmly to their mast and it looked like their boat was now heading for dry dock.

The drive home seemed to take forever and my new car phone was getting an early introduction into its work-load for the next few months.

I phoned Bob over and over again in between calls from Barry.

"Have you heard anything"

"No."

Finally, at ten o'clock that evening, Bob answered his phone.

"Bob, its Chris. What the fuck's going on?"

"Sorry man, but we can't do it anymore."

"For fuck's sake Bob, why? You're the one who said Band Aid should be a shining light to inspire others. Well, I'm fucking inspired. I'm trying."

There was an uneasy silence.

I calmed down.

"Bob, I said I would raise money for Band Aid. You said you would get all the money to the people who needed it. The whole world believes you and so do I. That's why I'm doing this. If you pull out now, this project is fucked and you know it."

"We're not sure you can pull it off."

"What?"

"We're not sure you can make it happen."

I took a breath.

"That's OK. I get that."

"We're not sure you can put on all these races."

"OK, so you're nervous. I get it. You have your reputation. But let me prove to you I can do it. Just give me some more time."

I put the phone down and laid awake all night.

I didn't go to Birmingham the next day. I called Barry and told him I had spoken to Bob and everything was OK.

"Will Terry get another telex to confirm?"

"Yeah, sure."

Probably not.

I desperately needed to unload on someone and I called Simon to see if he was free.

I don't know why, I hardly knew him but I felt I could talk to him.

I just blurted it all out.

The telex to the NEC.

The conversation with Bob.

Everything I'd done to date.

We talked for hours.

"Have you ever thought about talking to UNICEF?"

"No, why?"

"I know them. Maybe they can help.

UNICEF is the United Nations Children's Fund. It promotes the rights and wellbeing of every child, in everything it does. Together with partners, it works in about 190 countries and territories, translating its commitment into practical action.

I had heard of them.

UNICEF was funded exclusively by voluntary contributions, and the National Committees collectively raised around one-third of UNICEF's annual income. Serving as the public face and dedicated voice of UNICEF, the National Committees worked to raise funds from the private sector, promote children's rights and secure worldwide visibility for children threatened by poverty, disasters, armed conflict, abuse and exploitation.

UNICEF was also one of the more progressive UN agencies.

It was headed by Jim Grant who was acknowledged as a visionary of his time.

It had Field Offices and National Committees in more than 60 countries.

Could they stage races?

UNICEF headquarters was in New York and it had a UK committee in London, based in Lincoln's Inn Fields.

"Let's go and see them."

Simon arranged a meeting with the UK committee and we went along to their offices the following day.

Lincoln's Inn Fields is the largest public square in London and the UNICEF office was based in a grandiose 17th Century building on the west side.

It was a pretty part of London and not far from Holborn Tube where I met Simon.

When we arrived we were ushered into a dark but rather grand room with beautiful wall cornices and a high ceiling.

Simon and I, dressed in jeans and T-shirts, sat opposite the UNICEF men, dressed smartly in their suits and ties.

They were excited.

This year was to be UNICEF's 40th anniversary and 'something like this could fit in rather nicely', as one of the suited gents pointed out.

Another slice of luck?

One thing was for sure though - the UK committee couldn't make the decision alone. But its influence was considerable, especially given it was here in London and it really wanted to do it.

Only UNICEF headquarters could make the decision I needed.

"We have to go New York."

A few days later, Simon called me to say UNICEF had agreed to pay for a trip for both of us to go to the Big Apple. The UK committee had set up a meeting with Jim Grant and senior UN officials.

Simon and I flew out to New York twice during one week in January, to carve out a deal to save my baby.

In between visits I met with Bob in London to tell him the great news that UNICEF was going to stage more than 60 national races.

"Tell'em to fock off."

It was on the second trip that an excited Jim Grant greeted us with the news that there was to be a UN Special Session on Africa.

Jim Grant was the son of an internationally recognized public health specialist based in Asia. He had worked for UN Relief and Rehabilitation Administration in China after World War II, and then with the US International Co-operation Administration, where he was appointed deputy director in 1958. After working briefly at the US Department of State during the Kennedy administration, he served with the US Agency for International Development during the 1960s.

In 1969, he became the first head of the Overseas Development Council, a private 'think tank' he founded in Washington, DC where he worked until becoming UNICEF's executive director in 1980.

Grant was a visionary who insisted on strategic action and measurable results.

He had led UNICEF in a major campaign to combat what he called a 'Global Silent Emergency,' the deaths of millions of children each year from easily preventable illnesses.

Jim Grant thought outside the box!

"Policymakers are meeting at the UN to discuss the plight of Africa for the very first time."

"Can we have the UN as a stage? Can we use it as the focus for the race?"

"Yes, yes, I'll deliver the UN for you."

Everything had changed.

We talked about my concerns of UN agencies generally. Jim reassured me that **all** of the funds raised for UNICEF would be used for children's programmes in Africa and not one cent would be used elsewhere.

I really liked Jim Grant.

He knew what he was doing and he commanded a massive international resource. He could deliver the UN as a stage, for me to deliver my message from Africa.

Suddenly, I had the support of another organisation with a shit-load to lose.

For the next 24 hours, Jim mobilised his senior staff to help explore the practical and logistical needs of my project.

We worked through the night and next day before heading to the airport to get the British Airways flight home.

It was named 'the red-eye' because you took off at 8pm, flew through the night for just six hours and landed the next day at 7am.

Knackered and with red eyes.

I was to do that trip often, sometimes up to three times a week as Sport Aid built momentum. On this particular occasion, I sat up all night, ignored the movies, the inflight meal and even a strong Bacardi or two.

Instead, I hatched my plan with Simon to deliver the Sport Aid flame from Africa to the United Nations and stage the biggest race the world had ever seen.

This has to work.

CHAPTER 7
100 Days

"Now you've got a focking show!"

For the first time in a while, I agreed with Bob.

It was now a show.

It was a great idea.

An African runner.

A torch of Africa.

A message to the UN.

A petition of blistered feet.

The world does give a shit and it wants something to be done, now!

Importantly for me, Africa could now be seen to be really helping itself.

Band Aid was back on board.

But there was another problem.

A big problem.

Another project was being organised for the same day and it was announced during the Super Bowl XX when more than 100 million Americans were watching.

You are friggin joking me.

Hands Across America was the brainchild of Ken Kragen, who had put together *We Are the World.*

Following the record's success, Kragen trained his sights on a more ambitious task - forming a human chain across the United States of America to raise money for charity. Kragen and his team were billing Hands Across America as 'the largest participatory event in the history of the world.'

It was reported that sponsors including Coca-Cola and Citibank had already kicked in $8.5 million.

By contrast, I had fuck all.

Hands, as it became known, assembled its stars. The event had four celebrity co-chairmen: Bill Cosby, Kenny Rogers, Lily Tomlin and Pete Rose.

Hands Across America had just made its first big splash with an advert featuring its theme song during the Super Bowl TV transmission. The ad drummed up huge publicity but that didn't even begin to compare with what was to follow: a star-studded music video featuring the event's theme song.

Major competition.

It was impossible to compete with Coca Cola's dollars and a home-made apple pie event, so I decided we shouldn't try.

I couldn't change my date because of the UN Special Session on Africa.

That was the only day I could deliver a petition of blistered feet to the policymakers that mattered.

Just get on with it.

Jim Grant and his entourage flew into London and met with Bob. A few days later, on February 14, 1986, we staged a press conference in London and launched Sport Aid to the world.

Bob Geldof, Jim Grant and Seb Coe hosted the press conference. The place was rammed with TV cameras from all over the world.

It was a big story and Bob did what Bob did best.

"We just want people to join our official races or run around their cities or towns. You don't have to run 10km. Just run around your garden. Show that you care."

It was exactly 100 days from that press conference to the Race Against Time and I felt like I had jumped off the biggest bridge in my life, hit the water and still had a long long way to swim.

Sport Aid was now in the media spotlight and me and my baby had just made a big splash.

It was scary.

You're now on the clock!

Hands Across America stole the column inches in the USA and I decided not to compete with that, but I needed at least one race, in New York, to anchor our TV event at the UN. I set off to New York again to meet Fred Lebow from New York Road Runners Club.

NYRR were based at West 57th Street and I took a cab from the UNICEF offices on 1st Avenue.

As soon as I took my seat in Fred's expansive office, my blood turned cold.

I felt sick.

I had left my prized Filofax with all my notes, credit cards, money, addresses, return ticket, everything - my bloody life support pack - in the back of a New York taxi.

Stupid?

Yes.

But before I could say a word, Fred's phone rang.

It was reception.

The taxi driver had found it and returned it.

I couldn't believe my luck and Fred couldn't believe it either. A New York taxi driver returning money. He called the guy up to his office and made him an honorary member of New York Road Runners on the spot.

It was a nice touch.

I liked Fred Lebow.

We discussed the race, the need for a 10 km route starting and finishing at UN plaza.

There was a cost.

It was a US thing.

Or maybe, it was just a Hands Across America thing.

Fred could see Coca Cola paying $8 million for this type of event and just didn't get the fact that we wanted it all for nothing.

They had a home-grown project and were already doing their bit for charity.

"Who's paying for this?"

Back in the UK, UNICEF gave me access to places I could only have dreamed of and introduced me to Chris Patten, who was Minister for Overseas Development at the time. His department was responsible for administering overseas aid. Its goal was to promote sustainable development and eliminate world poverty.

"So, Chris, help us and you help yourself."

It made sense.

I got on well with Chris Patten and he found me an office - 4,000 square feet on Waterloo Road just down from the train station.

I got it for free.

I was never comfortable in front of the cameras. Celebrity was not for me but the press inevitably came knocking on my door.

I remember my first interview.

It was with a young journalist called Alastair Campbell from the Daily Mirror.

He went on to do bigger things later.

He wrote a nice piece and my Dad called me the next day.

"You're in the paper."

"Yes, I know, Dad."

Yes, I know.

As word got out, I started to get calls from various people who just wanted to help. Simon and I started to recruit our team of volunteers. We needed people, many people, and some with specialist knowledge.

I checked London Yellow Pages and found London Road Runners. Their office was in a folly on the edge of Hyde Park and I went to see their main man, Will Chapman.

Will was a runner and as I was also soon to learn, one of the best event organisers I was ever to work with.

"Can you put on a London race for us?"

"Sure."

"In Hyde Park?"

"Sure."

"With thousands of runners?"

"Sure."

Will was a no-nonsense, logistics machine and became a very close friend. At first he started working for me from his folly on the edge of Hyde Park but eventually I sucked him into the mother ship and Will headed up the organisation of all the official UK races from our Waterloo office.

He built a team of about 30 volunteers co-ordinating all the UK events as well as those in the Americas, Europe, Asia, Africa and Australasia.

It was great to have Simon on board full time. He seemed to know his way around television and it was such a fundamental part of the project.

TV was how we would deliver the signal for the world to run.

We sat side by side with our backs to the top end office wall and faced the only entrance, some 50 feet away. Down the right-hand side were windows at ground level looking out on to Waterloo Road. It was the only natural light and the windows were semi-tinted.

The lights stayed on all day and, as the project moved forward, all night as well. On the far wall were clocks, all set to different time zones.

On day one Simon and I sat there alone, looking out over a desolate wasteland of expectancy that was soon to become our kingdom.

When we finished, you couldn't see the floor for volunteers.

Right now, we were just growing.

Will and his team occupied the bottom left quarter of the office. Before them, a chattering telex machine punching out messages to race organisers the world over.

We needed race venues and we needed lots.

My learning curve had been steep and swift and I had realised early on that press and celebrity endorsement were going to be key. The early publicity from the launch had been great but we needed to keep building the momentum.

Nick Cater was a Fleet Street journalist. He had reported from many countries, on stories as diverse as war in Africa, environmental risks in Latin America, disasters in Europe, and the Asian sport of elephant polo.

Nick wanted to help.

He was a pleasant chap and was passionate about the cause. He understood the press and we needed someone like him. He had a big personality, made himself heard and wrote great press releases.

Nick became my press officer and his desk occupied the space between Simon and I and the front wall. As the weeks rolled by, the Press Office grew to more than 70 volunteers churning out press release after press release.

Day by day, Mr Patten's office space filled as I slowly and painstakingly built a team to co-ordinate the biggest mass participation event in history.

The NEC seemed pissed off that I had moved to London but accepted, I think, that they could never have provided the organisational infrastructure I needed. They continued to organise the Birmingham events and we set up a co-ordinator to link both offices.

One day John Anderson arrived in London.

Dr John Anderson was head of Human Resource Planning for UNICEF. He was a large imposing Canadian with a big brain. John wasn't your typical UNICEF man.

He was really useful!

We got on well.

John had been tasked by Jim Grant to evaluate Sport Aid and report back on exactly how much resource UNICEF needed to put behind the project.

He only stayed for a few days before returning with his report to UNICEF HQ in New York.

What I didn't know at the time was that both UNICEF and Band Aid were considering pulling out of the event. They were afraid that it was not going to be the global success I had pitched to them.

I only found out much later that John had been so fired up by the energy, enthusiasm and total commitment of my team of volunteers that he not only advised Jim Grant to proceed, but also to make him Chief of Global Special Events and assign him to London for the remainder of the event.

Jim did exactly that and John based himself in London and New York to help coordinate the UNICEF contribution to our overall organisational needs.

His first task?

Help organise the torch run from Africa to the UN and my mind cast back to that extraordinary day at Live Aid.

Sport can do so much more.

My dream from the beginning of this incredible journey was to make Africa centre stage.

Africa.

Not just the beneficiary but **the** main participant.

Taking the lead.

Demanding change.

Demanding action.

Africa must be seen to be helping itself.

I remembered my pitch to Geldof a few short weeks ago.

"… we'll get an African runner to light a torch from the burning embers of a refugee camp in Africa. Then we'll take him on a journey through the streets of Europe to meet Heads of State and policymakers to demand action. Then we'll fly him to Greece to light the Olympic torch and merge the torch of Africa with the torch of Sport Aid. Then he will meet world leaders before flying to the UN."

I pitched it again, to John.

"OK."

He wasn't fazed at all.

He got it.

This was **the** single most important part of Sport Aid. This was **Africa** taking its message to the doorstep of the UN.

It had to be right.

I found a runner from the Sudan.

His name was Omar Khalifa and he was the Sudanese 1,500m champion. Khalifa had won a gold medal for the 1,500m at the African Games in Cairo and another gold for the 1,500m at the World Grand Prix in Helsinki. He was preparing for the 1988 Olympics at the Italian Institute in Fornia.

He had an amazing face and a statuesque figure. More importantly, he was healthy and represented what all Africans could be, given half a chance.

He was perfect.

We looked over the logistics.

"We need a film crew."

"We need a director."

"We need a support runner."

"We need a doctor…"

"We need a plane!"

I agreed to look after the plane while John put the UNICEF diplomacy wheels in motion to secure us some Heads of State and maybe a King or Queen or two.

Simon would find us the film crew and a director.

Something else to do.

I called British Airways and pitched it again.

Fortunately, British Airways had had a fantastic return from Live Aid for comparatively little input. They flew Phil Collins from Wembley to Philadelphia on the day of Live Aid and Concorde got a huge amount of press and TV coverage during the build-up.

I started a dialogue with their marketing team and after about 10 days of hard negotiation, we thrashed out a deal.

"£100,000 in flight tickets. A Boeing 737 for Omar and Concorde for your team to travel to New York for the final day."

"In return, title status and your logo on everything."

"Done."

Great deal.

Omar was going to New York and he was going to travel first class.

Simon found an aspiring new film director who agreed to film Omar's entire run. We needed footage each day to feed into newsrooms all over the world.

We had been in touch with Visnews and they agreed to help. Visnews was a London-based international news agency. It was owned by NBC News, BBC and Reuters.

Omar's journey was going to help build publicity and momentum and hopefully drive people to sign up for the Race Against Time.

John's task took considerably longer and he set up a team in New York to help create diplomatic bridges with a number of target European countries.

Slowly but surely, Omar's journey started to unfold.

John arranged for him to light the Sport Aid torch from the burning embers of a camp fire in Moweheli Refugee Camp in the Sudan.

"That's where he will start. Then he's going to meet Sadiq al-Mahdi."

Sadiq al-Mahdi was the prime minister of Sudan. He had been prime minister for a period between 1966 and 1967. This was his second term in office and he wanted personally to support Sport Aid. Sadiq al-Mahdi was going to send Omar on his way from Africa to Europe.

The idea was simple yet hugely symbolic.

A message from the poorest people in the world to the richest.

We set up a dialogue with the Greek government and the International Olympic Committee and it was agreed that we **could** light the Olympic torch in Olympia and merge the 'flame of Africa' and the 'flame of Sport.'

Prime minister Andreas Papandreou would greet Omar and officiate at a ceremony at the Parthenon in Athens. It was to be the first time the Olympic torch would be lit outside of the Olympic Games.

A massive statement.

Over the next few days and weeks, diplomatic efforts were stepped up to try to co-ordinate the enormous logistical issues of flight paths, approvals, timings and the diaries of Heads of State.

From Athens, Omar was going to fly to Madrid. He would meet Felipe Gonzalez, Spain's longest-serving democratically elected prime minister, and from there to Rome.

To meet the Pope.

Pope Saint John Paul II was to become one of the most travelled world leaders in history, visiting

129 countries during his pontificate. He upheld the Church's teachings on such matters as artificial contraception and the ordination of women, but also supported the Church's Second Vatican Council and its reforms. He was the head of the Catholic Church and I needed him to acknowledge Omar's journey and cause.

From Rome?

Omar was going to Paris.

John and UNICEF had started a dialogue with Francois Mitterrand, the president of France.

John was hopeful they would pull it off.

The logistics were complicated. We were dealing with the diaries of the world's biggest policymakers as well as flight plans within the world's busiest air space and we had a deadline.

John was pretty upbeat though and he had a short-list of others.

I left him to his plans.

As more and more race cities came on board, Simon and I selected some of the biggest and potentially largest runs to be part of the global TV feed.

The plan was to televise as many big races as possible. We would need a broadcast partner in each city, satellite space to receive each of the feeds and then somewhere to mix them, before sending a finished programme back up to a satellite for broadcast to a worldwide audience.

It would be this feed that would deliver the signal for the world to run.

I was glad Simon was with me.

He seemed to know his stuff.

We got in touch with Brightstar Communications and ended up booking every single inch of satellite space in the sky. This gave us the capacity to include just over 20 live feeds – that was 20 live races from all around the world.

London would be one.

Athens.

My beloved Greece.

Barcelona?

"Yes."

"We need to be in Australia as well."

Australia would have to race in the middle of the night but then someone had to. The Race Against Time had to be truly global and I needed races in Asia, Latin America and of course, most importantly, Africa.

The office had really started to grow and was now a 24/7 operation. At night, we would telex race cities, call press agencies and drive our promotional machine.

We needed more phones and somehow a facility to pay for the calls.

That's when Mr BT turned up.

I never really got to find out who he was or what he did but he turned up one day and said he wanted to help.

"Can we get sponsorship from BT? We need more lines and more phones."

"We don't do sponsorship. It's against BT's constitution."

"Well, how can we get more lines"

"Leave it with me."

And I did.

When we needed them, telephones, mobiles and lines appeared. All arranged by Mr BT.

"I never want to see a bill for these."

"You won't."

And I didn't.

It was early morning one day when I picked up an atlas and turned to the Africa page. I had lain awake all night trying to think of an African city to be included in the TV broadcast.

Nairobi?

It had a TV station and satellite upload links.

Not really representative of famine stricken Africa though.

I looked across the Sahelian belt. Ethiopia, Sudan, Mali, Burkino Faso and then I saw it.

Timbuktu.

That'll be a great vibe.

The Timbuktu Race Against Time and then, below, I saw something even better.

Ouagadougou.

Ouagadougou!

The name screamed out.

Ouagadougou was the capital of Burkina Faso and the administrative, communications, cultural and economic centre of the nation. It was also the country's largest city. It had a population of about one and half million. Apparently, its name was often shortened to Ouaga.

But I wasn't shortening it.

I loved it.

"Guys, I've got it. The African Race Against Time is going to be in Ouagadougou."

When John arrived, I sat down with him and told him that Ouagadougou had to be the African race.

"OK."

UNICEF set up a dialogue with the city's administrative centre and before we knew it, a meeting had been arranged with president Thomas Sankara.

Three years earlier, a close friend and fellow army colleague had led a group that freed him from prison. They overthrew the Ouédraogo regime and formed the National Council of the Revolution (Conseil National de la Révolution) with Sankara as its president.

During the course of his presidency, Sankara had successfully implemented programmes that vastly reduced infant mortality, increased literacy rates and school attendance, and boosted the number of women holding governmental posts. On the environmental front, in the first year of his presidency alone, 10 million trees were planted in an effort to combat desertification.

On the first anniversary of the coup that had brought him to power, he changed the country's name from Upper Volta to Burkina Faso, which means roughly 'Land of Upright People' in Mossi and Dyula, the country's two most widely spoken indigenous languages.

What was even better was, Sankara was a good guy.

So we flew out to meet him.

"Mr President, would your country like to be Africa's official representative in the Sport Aid Race Against Time?"

"Our country would be most honoured. If this gift is bestowed upon us then I will run. I will also issue an edict for all my ministers to run and my entire country to join in."

You listening Bob?

President Sankara had just committed the entire population of Burkina Faso to Sport Aid.

Africa was now going to be centre stage.

A president, his entire cabinet and the population of one of the poorest African countries, was going to show the world it could help itself.

When John got back with the news we were all ecstatic but, as always, good news brought logistical problems.

"How are we going to get Burkina Faso into the global TV feed?"

"They have no TV station."

"No satellite uplink facility."

This was one of the poorest countries in the world.

They had nothing.

Simon had already decided that the TV broadcast needed to be produced in New York. UNTV had the resources and we had just been given access.

"We'll set up the line-production there."

The TV feeds from each race would go to New York via the satellite links we had already booked.

Live Aid, by comparison, was beginning to look like a cakewalk.

But the only way Ouagadougou was going to join our party was if we were able to fly out a complete satellite ground station and crew.

Shit.

That night I didn't sleep – again.

An entire African country had committed to Sport Aid and I wasn't going to let it down.

The next morning, I put a call into a number of TV stations.

"I need an outside broadcast crew with a satellite uplink."

"Where do you need it?"

"Ouagadougou."

You could be excused for thinking the next line was fuck off. But it wasn't.

"Where's that?"

"Africa."

"Fuck off."

It took some explaining but they started to get it. The importance of the African race. The need for president Thomas Sankara, his entire cabinet and the population of Ouagadougou to be seen by the world.

"I'll get back to you."

Over the next few days the sheer volume of what needed to be done took over. We signed up more races and more celebrities.

Claire Davidson was one of our volunteers and she helped with celebrity liaison.

She was brilliant.

Just picked up a phone, found a number and called. Fearless.

"It's Sport Aid, can you help us?"

Celebrities would come into the office or someone from the press team would meet them elsewhere. We'd find a snapper, arrange a press call, get a picture of a celebrity in a Run the World T-shirt and send it to the world's press.

Sometimes it worked.

Sometimes it didn't.

On balance, we got reasonably good coverage.

On this particular day, she stood in front of me with a very tall good-looking person. A man with long dark hair and a very handsome face.

I recognise you.

"Chris, this is Daniel Day-Lewis. He's an actor. He's going to do some promotion for us."

"Thanks Daniel, great to meet you."

I stood up to shake his hand when one of my phones rang.

"Hello."

"Chris, you can have your ground station. The crew said they'll do it for nothing. You just need to get everything there. Sorry, but we just don't have the budget for the air freight or flights."

Amazing.

"Thank you so, so much."

I put the phone down and screamed across the office.

"We need another plane."

Daniel looked startled and I explained as best I could. He was a nice guy and was to support us a great deal. I'd like to think it was Karma rewarding him three years later with an Academy Award for *My Left Foot*.

I was really excited and told Simon and John about our satellite ground station for the African race against time.

"Great news, we got it."

"How we going to get it there. . . ?"

CHAPTER 8
My blind date with 20 million people

The days flew by and soon the nights as well. I was getting knackered like so many of my team but the adrenalin and fear of failure kept us going. Bob would rarely call at the office but on the odd occasion he did, would join Simon and I for a catch-up.

One day, he brought Marsha Hunt.

Marsha was Bob's P.A. She was a no-nonsense, fiery young lady who didn't take shit from anyone. At first, it was like having a mini Geldof around the place and to be honest I didn't like her much. She seemed arrogant and a pain in the arse, as if every request was going to be answered with no or fuck off. After a while, I got to understand little Marsha and even grew to like her. She was fiercely protective of Bob and I liked people who were loyal.

We talked about a music promo for Sport Aid and I think it was Marsha who suggested Tears for Fears. The band had released *Everybody Wants to Rule the World* the year before and the single had made it to No 2 in the UK charts. It went on to win a Brit Award for best British single.

"I'll tell the boys to change the lyrics to 'Run the world.'"

That was Marsha.

She wasn't going to ask. She was going to tell them.

I loved the idea of a music video and just let her get on with it.

Anything you can do Hands Across America.

Marsha knew what she was doing.

Fridays were difficult days for me. I missed my girls like mad. Ellie was now eight and Lydia five. They had moved away from Barnes and lived with their mother in Chichester.

I had to leave the office around four o'clock in the afternoon and head for the A3 before the traffic built up. The journey was always a nightmare. If I left on time, the round trip took about seven hours. Leave late and I'd get home with the girls around midnight and have to put them straight to bed. They would sleep in the car and I would carry on working, thanks to my new mobile phone.

By three o'clock on Sunday, it was time for the return trip. Often I would just head straight back to the office from Chichester.

Occasionally, I'd pick them up and head to my Mum and Dad's house in Trotton. I'd stay there for the weekend. It cut down the travel and gave me some quality time with them.

As we got closer to May, it became more and more impossible to see them.

I missed them like hell and began to doubt why I was doing all this.

First Greece and now this?

My kids were my life and I wasn't there for them.

I'm a terrible father.

By the beginning of May, Sport Aid was consuming my entire life. All day, all night. Every living hour was now being absorbed by my African obsession.

John had been working hard in New York to help finalise Omar's pre-run. He walked into the office with his usual big smile and air of accomplishment. John had just flown in from New York and he had more good news.

"Mitterrand is going to do it."

Mitterrand was the first socialist president of the Fifth Republic, and his government became the first left-wing government in France for 23 years. The Socialists had obtained an absolute parliamentary majority. He was an important world leader and he was now the fourth policymaker confirmed to meet Omar and receive the flame of Africa.

"He's probably also going on to meet Wilfried Martens, prime minister of Belgium. And Wojciech Jaruzelski. That's being set up in Warsaw."

I didn't have a clue who he was talking about and had to check later when I was alone.

Jaruzelski was first secretary of the Polish United Workers' Party and the last leader of the People's Republic of Poland. He was Poland's serving head of state.

We were including Eastern Europe.

We were unifying Europe for Africa.

I looked at John with a blank expression.

"Is that it? What else you been doing?"

I laughed.

John and I had become close friends and I liked to wind him up.

"Fuck off and wait."

I waited two days.

"We've got Helmut Kohl."

My Canadian boy was on fire.

Germany had also joined the Race Against Time.

Simon's pre-run team was also coming together. We had a director, assistant director, camera team, support team, support runner and admin support to travel with the team and to liaise with the British Airways crew who were to carry them on their historic journey.

Do we have a doctor?

What happens if Omar pulls a muscle? Shit.

I picked up the Yellow Pages and looked for a doctor in Harley Street.

I found someone.

"Would you like to give up a week and fly with our team around Europe? We have our own plane."

"When do I start?"

The guy made plans to shut down his practice for the entire week.

I now had a Harley Street doctor on board.

I still needed to find a plane to get our satellite ground station and crew to Ouagadougou. This was really important and had been keeping me awake.

Getting the TV signal from Ouagadougou was crucial.

Nick Cater and I thrashed out a press release and the next day we told the world what we so desperately wanted and needed.

A few days later, a man with a plane turned up.

He offered us a special charter and it was free.

Goodwill started to build. The press office was simply amazing and each day more and more celebrities were backing Sport Aid.

We did a press call with the England football team just before it headed off to Mexico.

Peter Shilton, Glenn Hoddle, Bryan Robson, Ray Wilkins, John Barnes and Peter Beardsley, to name but a few. We had high hopes for them at the time, but no-one could have foreseen that 'hand of God.'

Just before the team left for Mexico, we shot some footage from their training camp. It was to form part of Marsha's promo video. The Tears for Fears boys had said 'yes' and they were on their way to a studio to re-record the lyrics.

News from Birmingham also started to feed into the office.

They had got over their earlier disappointment and were now getting very excited.

The SkateElectric World Ice Spectacular was confirmed. It was going to be on the evening of May 24. Chris and Jayne had done an incredible job and delivered on their promise. John Curry, Robin Cousins, Katerina Witt, Brian Orser, the Protopopovs and more were all taking part.

On May 20, the West Indies were taking on the Rest of the World at Edgbaston. Richie Benaud, Ian Botham, Kapil Dev, David Gower, Ray Illingworth, Clive Lloyd, Viv Richards and many more.

The world's best cricketers were also turning up for Sport Aid.

I was pleased and so was Birmingham.

We shot the Sport Aid video on the athletics track next to Battersea Power Station, a swimming pool in South London and at the Matchroom HQ in Romford, Essex.

Bob and Midge Ure did a funny little cameo role in the park. Frank Bruno, Duncan Goodhew, Tessa

Sanderson, Sharron Davies and Brian Jacks were all in it. We also filmed Alex Higgins, Jimmy White and Kirk Stevens playing snooker.

Barry Hearne arranged it.

Alex Higgins potted one ball while making the cue ball - with the Sport Aid logo drawn on it – spin and then stop, with the logo directly facing the camera.

The mood was amazing.

It started to feel like we really could change the world.

It was brilliant.

We recorded some footage with the great American athlete Carl Lewis and with Peter Ustinov.

Peter was very gracious and did a great piece to camera with our Run the World T-shirt. We would add the England footage to the mix and our post production team headed off to a free edit studio in London to make our pop video.

Will Chapman and the UK race team worked all day and night and we now had 12 official UK races in place.

Even more than I'd planned a year ago.

News continued to pour in from across the world on our (now) four telex machines.

The Ivory Coast was having a dug-out canoe race and in the central African state of Chad, where it would be just too hot to run, they had organized a 10km march. In Abu Dhabi, the capital of the United Arab Emirates, radio promos called people to join their race and remind women taking part to wear long skirts or track suits, in keeping with Islamic dress codes.

Two runners in Nepal had contacted us. They planned to do an uphill run and walk from Kathmandu to Mount Everest base camp in less than five days, to set a new world record for the 160 mile run.

All in the name of Sport Aid.

The Soviet Union had races scheduled in Moscow, Gorky and Leningrad - despite having to deal with the huge Chernobyl disaster - and as many as 10,000 runners were expected in Budapest which, if it happened, would be the biggest race ever staged in Hungary.

Thailand's prime minister had also planned to lead as many people as possible on a marathon walk in Bangkok, and 16 cities were hosting Sport Aid races in India.

Meanwhile, from across the pond, Hands Across America was getting more and more publicity. They needed five and a half million people to pull off their plan of holding hands from coast to coast.

I want more.

The telex machines chattered away.

Press release after press release.

One late night in May, while half-asleep at my desk, I was woken by a call from the office of Mr Javier Perez de Cuellar. He was a Peruvian diplomat and the fifth Secretary General of the United Nations.

The caller was his personal assistant.

"The Secretary General will be in Latin America on May 25. He will start the race from there."

"He fucking won't!"

"I beg your pardon?"

"The Race Against Time starts in New York at the United Nations. If the Secretary General wants to take part he'll have to cancel his plans and get back to New York."

"Unfortunately, that's not possible."

Well, tell him unfortunately to fuck off.

It was hard not to let things go to your head but that night they did a little. I had just indirectly told the head of the UN that unless he got his arse back to New York, he wasn't coming to my party.

There was never any time for reflection or review of what we had done. The boulder had been pushed to the top of the hill and was on its way down. It was gaining momentum and nothing was going to stop it now.

Would anybody be at the bottom to greet it?

Everyone in the office was working towards the common goal of getting as many people around the world to the Race Against Time.

It was as if Sport Aid had flicked a switch within their inner psyche. They seemed to want it as much as me and we all had this inner blind faith that we could actually pull it off.

Simon was also relishing his new found stardom as the producer of the event, a title he had given himself. I had discovered he had a big ego, but I didn't really care. It was channelled in the right direction and he was doing a job I didn't understand. It would have been Simon or someone else, but I was grateful he was giving up his time, like all of us.

For some reason however, he seemed to be pissing off many of our UNICEF friends and I wasn't sure why.

We produced some TV promos and sent these out via Visnews and other agencies. In most cases, the inspirational soundtrack I chose was *Chariots of Fire* by

Vangelis. I loved that movie and the music was incredible. It just seemed so appropriate for what we were doing.

We should have our own music.

I wanted something evocative, inspirational.

A piece of music that could be played while Omar climbed the steps of the UN to light the torch that would start the world running. Something that would inspire the whole world to run.

Vangelis.

Evangelos Odysseas Papathanassiou was not only the composer of *Chariots of Fire*, he was also the man behind the album *Friends of Mr Cairo*. I loved this album and used to play it all the time when I was in Greece. It was released in 1981 and peaked at No. 1 in March 1982.

State of Independence was my favourite.

I decided to call him.

Shall I call you Vangelis?

He agreed to meet.

Vangelis had an amazing flat and studio in London. It was in a beautiful period building with large rooms and ceilings that seemed to go on forever. In one room a TV projector covered an entire wall. Others were festooned with gold and platinum discs. His studio was state of the art with mixing desks, instruments and all the stuff I guessed recording studios should have.

I was in awe.

I pitched my idea again.

"What we are doing is getting a Sudanese runner, Omar Khalifa, to light a torch from the burning embers of a refugee camp fire in Africa. We are then flying him, on our own British Airways plane, throughout Europe to meet heads of state and policy makers to demand action for Africa. He's actually going to your homeland first, Vangelis. We are lighting the Olympic torch in Olympia with your prime minister and merging it with the torch of Sport Aid at the Parthenon. Then, he'll meet the Pope, Helmut Kohl, Mitterrand and others, running through each city. Then on May 25 – on the eve of the very first UN Special Session on Africa - Omar will run down First Avenue, to the United Nations, where he'll light a beacon which will be the signal for the world to run for Africa."

I'm getting good at this.

"Would you please write us an anthem for it?"

"Sure."

And he did.

I visited his studio over the next few weeks as the music came together. Often he would play ideas to Simon and I and it was brilliant to be part of something so creative.

By the end, Vangelis Papathanassiou had produced a stirring, emotional theme; almost a pastiche of *Chariots of Fire*. He played the finished Sport Aid anthem to me and it was incredible. It made the hairs on the back of my neck stand on end.

It was going to do the same to others.

Dr John Anderson was still cooking on gas and confirmed that Omar was now going to Warsaw and Budapest.

"He's also going to Helsinki and Bonn."

"Great news."

But we had a problem with the UK.

Our prime minister, the iron lady, Margaret Thatcher, was not going to be in London at the right time.

She was going to be in Dublin.

"So, let's take Omar to Maggie."

"OK, I'll see what I can do."

"Let's get her in Dublin and maybe Omar can go to the Palace on the penultimate day?

We can try to get the Queen.

Or maybe Prince Charles and Diana, as they were at Live Aid?

"OK."

John was amazing. He just delivered and delivered.

I liked him more and more and, as the days went by we would spend what little downtime we had together.

One night John was happy to stay at my flat and save on a hotel room, so we drove home from Waterloo, via a visitor's tour of London. John phoned his dear friend Naomi in Los Angeles and we gave her an audio version of the London sights, via my new in-car mobile.

We finally ended up in Soho and stopped for a quick Chinese meal with some of my top team members.

I wanted to say thanks by paying for the meal but I was skint. All my credit cards bar one was maxed out. I passed the remaining card to our Chinese waiter along with the bill.

"Let me get this John."

A few minutes later our waiter returned with a big smile on his face and delivered my card, in two pieces.

"You card dead, me cut up. Me get £50."

Fuck.

Everyone pissed themselves laughing and John tossed his platinum American Express on the table.

"Don't worry. I'll get it."

He then turned to the over-excited waiter and insisted he took off the discretionary service charge as he had embarrassed me so much by cutting up my card in front of everyone.

A huge row then ensued and finally the police were called to arbitrate. John made his stand and finally the waiter caved in and we were all allowed to leave.

As we drove home John tried to make me feel better. He also talked about Simon and for some reason, he didn't seem to like him much. It stuck in my mind but I was just too busy and too tired to process it.

I was also wondering how I was going to survive with no money.

Now that we knew where all the official UK races were going to be, I needed a mechanism to register runners.

Bob, Simon and myself were all in agreement that we should have a T-shirt. It would be the 'uniform of the day' and everyone would pay £5 to get one with their entry to the Race Against Time.

A guy called Nick had done all our graphic design for nothing. One particular day he was in the office and we were pouring over designs for the T-shirt.

"I Ran the World."

"Yeah, like it but can we have each word on a separate line? It looks like, 'Iran, the World.'

We played around with design and decided we'd put the words over a graphic of the world.

"Put the Sport Aid logo at the top and the Band Aid, UNICEF and British Airways logos at the bottom.

"On the back?"

"Similar, with The Race Against Time and the date, May 25, 1986."

"That's it."

It was simple. A white T-shirt with a simple design. Just two colours. A red flame on the Sport Aid logo and a red flash under British Airways.

A badge of honour and a souvenir for everyone taking part.

I also needed an entry form. It needed to list all the UK races and give the entrant a choice to pick one race venue.

"That way, we can get an idea of numbers for each race."

It needed to include space for a name and address.

"I'll set up a PO Box."

"… and we must send out sponsorship forms with every T-shirt. I need a sponsorship form."

Nick headed off with his next set of tasks and totally unreasonable deadlines, while I thought about how we could get our entry forms to the general public. I had decided that every single penny raised from donations and sponsorship would go to Africa.

Any costs we had to pay were coming out of the £5.

"Let's make that totally clear in everything we print. Entry forms, donation forms. Everything."

Martin Goldsmith was Harvey Goldsmith's brother. He was a tall imposing guy with a full face and head of hair. He looked like he worked in the music business.

Martin owned his own company, Event Merchandising Limited, which manufactured and distributed T-shirts and rock'n' roll memorabilia at pop and rock concerts. It had specific concessions and distribution rights at some of the UK's most prestigious venues.

Martin become my T-shirt supplier.

The logistics of manufacturing and distributing T-shirts in advance of the Race Against Time - so that people had them on the day - was simply mind blowing.

Omar's run would start one week before and was designed to help build the profile and momentum. The ice skating, rugby, gymnastics, all the events at the NEC, advertising for the big event.

One thing for sure, it was all going to be very last minute. Could we print a number of T-shirts and have them at all the race venues in advance?

If so, how many?

What if nobody turned up?

Who was going to pay for them?

There was no simple answer.

All I could do was put a mechanism in place and pray that people started to register early enough so that we could get T-shirts and sponsorship forms to them in time.

Over the next few days Woolworths and most of the banks and building societies agreed to stock entry forms. By the end of the week all Virgin Megastores had agreed to host registration days. We offered them celebrities in return for providing a chunk of space in their stores.

It was to work well.

Really well!

CHAPTER 9
Sleepless Nights

The New York office had also started to grow.

It was based within the UNICEF HQ building and comprised UNICEF staff and volunteers. I would visit the office every now and then and Simon would go more often. Now that UNTV had provided the resources for our TV programme, New York was going to be the anchor point. We still needed an experienced line-producer for our programme and we decided to try to get Tony Verna.

Verna's broadcast hallmark was an ability to continually come up with advances in the use of cameras, programme content and creative interplay. It was this skill that prompted him to use a trick left over from radio days, in order to outwit the technology of the times and allow for a play on the field to be re-broadcast 'instantly.'

He was the inventor of the action replay.

Verna's varied career including creating, producing and directing Pope John Paul II's billion-viewer television special A Prayer for World Peace and Live Aid.

As president of Caesar's Palace Productions, Verna was involved in all their spectacular entertainment projects.

He was the only man for the job and he was about to add Sport Aid to his CV.

It was a massive coup.

Our TV programme was in good hands.

Back in the UK, I got a call from the British Advertising Industry. It wanted to produce some commercials for us.

Since 1985 there had been much publicity on the real issues affecting Africa. In 1984, the problem was drought and famine. As time went by it was clear it was much more than that. Years of civil war, corruption and foreign debt were as important.

The British Advertising Industry wanted to highlight these issues by producing short commercials, which we could include in our global TV transmission.

It was amazing.

Sport Aid had become a conduit for advocacy and a means of telling the world about the real problems facing the continent. We could now show global policymakers that we understood what was needed.

We demanded action for change.

Of course I said yes and they allocated each major issue to a well-respected director.

'Sallymatu' was the first.

It was an incredible advert focusing on famine and directed by Len Fulford. It ended up winning Silver at the British Television Advertising Awards.

'Give enough' was directed by Peter Webb. This commercial showed that by running and taking part in Sport Aid people could really help. It had an amazing soundtrack and was really positive.

'Give enough and they can win' was its strapline and it also won Silver at the British Television Advertising Awards.

'Blood Money - Bury the Debt not the Dead' was another incredibly powerful commercial. There were more. In excess of £1 million of amazing quality ads produced by the best advertising agencies in the world and made specifically for Sport Aid.

I felt truly honoured.

The more the word got out, the more people got involved.

The phone rang one day and a guy I'd never heard of said he'd been planning a world workout. He came to the office the next day to tell me what he wanted to do.

Cliff Richard, choreographer Arlene Philips and the dance troupe Hot Gossip were involved. They wanted to get people all over the world to do a simultaneous work out for Africa.

I loved Hot Gossip. They were best known for their risqué costumes and sexy dance routines, all designed and choreographed by Arlene. They were like the Pan's People of the 1960s and 1970s.

Those ladies helped me grow up.

"Do it on the same day as us."

"How?"

"I'll give you the stage just before the race starts. More than one billion people will be watching. Warm our runners up."

"Is that enough?"

It was and 'Spare a minute for Africa' became part of Sport Aid as more and more people I'd never met were getting involved.

The French Open tennis tournament was due to start on the outdoor clay courts at Roland Garros on May 26. It was to be the 85th staging of the event and was the first Grand Slam tennis event of 1986.

Ivan Lendl was favourite to win, but everyone was talking about a young German - Boris Becker, who had won Wimbledon the year before.

Ion Țiriac, known as the 'Brasov Bulldozer' was a former professional tennis and ice hockey player and a Romanian businessman.

He was also Becker's manager.

Somehow, I got his home telephone number in the south of France.

The French Open was to start the day after the Race Against Time. Not great timing but I wondered if the players might still do something. Becker seemed like a nice young guy and well, if don't ask, you don't get.

I called Mr Țiriac.

"Who are you?"

I soon got past that tricky introduction and once again, pitched my story on behalf of Africa.

Much to my surprise, he knew who I was and said he would try to do something.

We got a picture of Boris in a Run the World T-shirt and I think that was it. I don't know if Țiriac organised anything else but if he did, Boris got the reward. Two months later he defended his Wimbledon title, beating Lendl 6-4, 6-3, 7-5 in the final.

Karma.

As we got to within two weeks of the big day everything shifted up another gear.

Day and night the office churned out its message. It had become a truly global operation and we were dealing with every country in the world.

The buzz from the office was incredible.

It was my little beehive - its densely packed group of hexagonal, square and prismatic cells all divided by

101

flimsy screens covered in maps, names of organisers and to-do lists.

My little worker bees would shout out every time we secured a new race city and the buzz would intensify and be followed by applause and high-fives.

We all believed that we could and would, change the world.

On May 12 Liverpool won the FA Cup.

It had been a Merseyside derby between Liverpool and Everton at Wembley. The match was played seven days after Liverpool had secured the league title, with Everton finishing as runners-up. At the time, they were the English league's leading club sides. Liverpool won the match 3–1, with two goals from Ian Rush and one from Craig Johnston, after Gary Lineker had put Everton ahead in the first half.

Craig Johnston was an Australian and was going home for a holiday.

We had an idea.

Let's steal the FA Cup!

Let's nick the cup, put it on a plane with Craig and take it to Australia. If we could put the FA Cup alongside the America's Cup, it would be mega publicity.

Australia and the Royal Perth Yacht Club were the current holders of the America's Cup and winning it had been a really big thing down under.

Great publicity here.

Huge publicity there.

We called Craig and he was up for it.

Only problem was, he was leaving in eight hours.

We called the FA and asked if we could 'steal' the FA Cup.

Same old pitch.

"There are millions of African people dying. Different sports are contributing so much and football is doing fuck all … blah blah."

Surprisingly, they said yes. But a security guard had to be with the FA Cup for the entire duration of the trip and we needed to pay for that.

We called a security company and got a guy, for free.

We called Qantas and got a ticket, for free.

We called Qantas again and asked them to delay the departure of their evening flight to Australia.

We put the FA Cup in a fast car to the airport and then called the press.

Everyone in the office tracked the car's progress to Heathrow.

It was tight but we all believed it could make it.

It did and so did the press.

The office went mad.

It was a massive coup and it lifted everyone's spirits even more.

The UK press coverage next day was great and it lasted in Australia for more than a week as Craig took the FA Cup all round Australia.

It was huge and contributed to a massive turnout in Australia, with races in Perth, Adelaide, Melbourne, Sydney, Brisbane, Canberra and Hobart.

Craig Johnston – good egg.

As the Sport Aid week got closer we ramped things up even more.

My sea of volunteers pushed themselves to the brink of exhaustion and the office remained open day and night.

Some of us would just sleep when and where we could - at the foot of our desks or on top of them.

It didn't matter.

I had no real idea of what was happening in the outside world, other than what I could see on the only TV set in the office. It sat on a shelf to the left of me and I would switch it on from time to time to try to catch the news. The internal aerial was crap and to be honest, the picture wasn't very good but it was my only way of gauging the outside public mood.

Simon began to build his TV teams for the international races. In most cases the domestic networks in each country had now agreed to cover their race and take the international feed.

In the UK, we had nothing.

Both ITV and the BBC were being very coy about covering the event and as we got closer and closer, we still didn't have a home broadcaster.

It was just hang on tight and believe time.

The press office received telex after telex from our organising network, which had now grown to more than 85 national organising committees.

News would trickle in of the weird and wacky events that had been planned.

Nottingham and Aquatic Games, a series of water sports including canoe and dragon boat racing.

Ireland was holding an international angling event.

You've got to love the Irish.

Italy was publishing a special postage stamp to commemorate Sport Aid and in England the Royal Mail was producing a special stamp and first day cover.

Tennis was doing something.

I didn't know if it had anything to do with Boris, as it wasn't going to be at the French Open in Roland-Garos.

It was going to be at the Trocadero in Paris.

UNICEF was planning a 10 km human link of school children in Freetown, Sierra Leone. Its own version of Hands Across America.

Hands Across Freetown.

And a number of Ethiopians who had been airlifted out of Africa the year before and now lived in Israel were going to lead the Race Against Time in Tel Aviv.

Hundreds of events had spawned in the UK and more than 1,000 children were going to take part in an event on Capstone Hill in Ilfracombe.

They had planned to spell out the words, Sport Aid.

In Iceland, its president Vigdís Finnbogadóttir announced that she would run alongside Miss Iceland and Miss Scandinavia in the Reykjavik Race Against Time. She hoped their appearance might encourage more men to join up and take part.

And Mickey Mouse was going to lead the Race Against Time though Disneyland in Japan.

Virgin boss Richard Branson was planning to bring Virgin Atlantic Challenger up the Thames for the day. He was going to moor it near the London race route to encourage and support our runners.

The boat smashed the world record for the fastest crossing of the Atlantic just a month later. Branson completed the voyage more than two hours faster than the previous record-holder, the SS United States, which had held the title since 1952. He did it in three days, eight hours and 31 minutes, averaging just under 36 knots.

Our torch relay crew headed out on its specially badged BA Boeing 737.

Bob turned up for that.

The press covered the departure and it was time to ramp up things even more.

Days and nights melded together in what felt like a seamless void of activity and organised chaos as we got closer and closer to my immovable date with destiny.

It was early morning on Thursday May 15, 1986 when Omar lit his torch from the burning embers of the refugee camp fire in El Moweilih, Sudan. Early reports from the torch relay team had said Omar's reception with president Sadiq al-Mahdi had gone well.

It had been covered by numerous UK and international press teams and our film crew had the footage they needed to create a news package for Visnews.

Sport Aid had officially started.

The *Six-O'clock News* had carried a little piece on Omar in the Sudan and that made me feel a little better but I knew I wasn't going to sleep that night.

And I didn't.

The next day we got some coverage in the national papers but not much.

We need more.

The Sport Aid International Sevens kicked off at Cardiff Arms Park. The event was a competition for the Wales Trophy and included top players like Steve Tuynman, Les Cusworth and Frank Boica. Countries taking part included England, Scotland, Wales, Fiji and Australia.

It was to last two days.

We arranged for Bob to travel down by helicopter. It was another reason for the press to be there and we needed all the publicity we could get. Every event was designed to advertise the race on Sunday. It was top sportsmen and women making their contribution to encourage ordinary people to join the Race Against Time.

But there was a problem.

Not many had come to watch.

Bob was interviewed on ITV Cymru and challenged by a young reporter who asked if people were wavering on whether to go along to the Arms Park or not.

Bob's response was typical Geldof.

"Get out and do it even if you don't like rugby. It's like the *Feed the World* record, I don't care if you don't like pop, just buy the bloody thing."

The reporter didn't give up.

"And anybody who's thinking of going shopping that afternoon instead of going to the game?"

Bob paused for just a second.

"Well, if you think it's more important to spend money on food, on the afternoon that everyone is spending money to stop people from dying of starvation, then there's something wrong with your priorities."

The reporter stopped there.

Love him or hate him, Bob was fucking brilliant at what he did.

Omar had reached Greece and the Olympic torch had been lit at Olympia. The Parthenon event went really well and prime minister Andreas

Georgios Papandreou received Omar in a wonderful ceremony.

It was particularly poignant for me.

It was the coming together of the torch of Africa and the torch of sport. It was also happening in the land of my Greek dream.

I wished I could have been there to see it but I couldn't. I was organising the largest simultaneous mass participation demonstration ever mobilised for any cause.

At least, that's what I hoped I was doing.

The week steamrollered on and the pitch in the office shifted up towards its immeasurable crescendo. The noise and energy of my team continued but the Cardiff Arms Park crowd - or lack of it - had left me feeling a little uneasy.

I needed some reassurance and decided to check the PO box to see how many race entry forms had arrived.

There was only one bag.

One bag.

Shit!

That was about 7,000 entries.

We had 12 races in the UK and a huge one in Hyde Park to fill.

7,000 was fuck all.

It was the first time I started to doubt what we were doing and I felt sick.

I was the reason we were all here.

I started all this and suddenly felt a huge sense of responsibility for the outcome.

I was having a massive wobble when Martin Goldsmith came into the office.

I gave him the news that a meagre 7,000 race entries needed processing and he looked as disappointed as I felt.

It didn't help.

I tried to stay upbeat and explained why everything would just build during the week and how the demand for T-shirts would inevitably be last minute.

Martin decided to find a network of European printers who could cope with a late surge.

I also spoke to John Anderson. If we had to take a punt and print T-shirts in advance then only UNICEF could afford to take that risk and give Martin the reassurances he needed.

I left it with him and Martin to sort out.

I had other things to do.

Will and his team were now working all day and night. We had something like 250 cities in more than 80 countries staging official races. He was co-ordinating all of that as well as 12 official UK races, in addition to putting staging plans into action for Hyde Park. Will was the London race director.

His team had already spilled out of their screened enclosure within the office and were now working in walkways and on window sills.

It was crazy.

The weekend was nearly over and Omar and the flame had already passed through Madrid and were now on their way to Rome.

I missed it.

In Rome, the Sport Aid flame was being received by the Pope himself.

UNICEF and British Airways were doing an amazing job and I was so glad I had managed to get them both on board. Meeting so many heads of state, politicians and the Pontiff himself, would have been impossible without them.

The press was following the story and Omar was now picking up TV news and national press in quite a few countries.

The Visnews link was working.

Omar arrived in Paris to meet French president François Maurice Adrien Marie Mitterrand and the International Gymnastics started at the NEC.

Something like 10 nations were taking part in Birmingham and it was a star-studded event with the likes of Sabrina Mar, the USA national all-round champion, Camelia Voinea and Eugenia Golea, both members of the Romanian silver winning team at the World Championships, Hungarian Olympic gymnast Andrea Ladanyi, Iveta Polokova from Chechoslovakia and Anja Wilhelm from the Federal Republic of Germany.

I hoped that the NEC were happy.

They had pulled off some amazing events and more were to follow. It seemed like a million years ago that I had met them for the first time and pretended to be Bob.

I didn't feel so guilty now.

I checked the PO box again.

Two bags only.

Fuck!

We had set up a deal with Virgin Megastores in Oxford Street to sign up runners. Some space had been made available in each store and we were getting celebrities to hand out T-shirts and sign up runners. We publicised it on local press and radio using the same celebrities.

It was to work well.

The cricket at Edgbaston started.

The West Indies, the dominating cricket team of the 1980s, were taking on the Rest of the World with players from England, Australia, India, Zimbabwe, South Africa, New Zealand and Pakistan. It was pretty much the David Gower XI v the Viv Richards XI.

I was told the match was rained off after the West Indies went to bat, starting with a good run rate.

It was a no result but served its purpose to a point.

It helped the publicity keep building and the world's best cricketers had turned out for Sport Aid but it was another dent to my confidence.

Keep believing.

Omar arrived in Germany and met with German chancellor Helmut Josef Michael Kohl and the press carried the story.

Our Tears for Fears record had reached the charts and we had managed to get it on Top of the Pops along with our video.

It was the first time it had been seen by a mass audience and it went down well.

I watched it on the TV in the office.

Omar arrived in Warsaw and the next day we got some really good press.

The vibe was starting to build.

I felt better.

The Ouagadougou crew set off for Burkina Faso. The satellite ground station had already arrived.

Earlier in the week we had recorded some video with Sting. He was a pretty useful runner and we had captured him running part of the London race route.

That video material, along with Bob and Sting, was going on the Wogan Show that night to promote the race.

It coincided with Omar reaching Budapest and by this time, the press were covering the story with more and more interest.

After the show, I left the studio in Shepherds Bush feeling better.

Bob and Sting had been great and had even mentioned the Virgin Megastores.

It was a major turning point.

Finally, the BBC committed to covering the London race and broadcasting our programme.

Thank fuck for that.

The next morning 14 sacks of mail turned up at the PO Box and hundreds of people had descended on Oxford Street.

More than 100,000 entries!

Must call Martin.

Omar reached Budapest as the pre-run team started its penultimate stretch before New York.

I was going to join them for that.

For now, it was in the distant future.

There was still much work to do.

A BBC news crew arrived in the office and wanted me to do an interview for the *Six O'clock News*. It was my opportunity to remind everyone why we were doing what we were doing. The events of the past few days had created a vibe and everyone was looking forward to the fun on the day and having a great time taking part in an important slice of history.

But there was a serious side.

I was asked why was I doing this?

"We are delivering to the doorstep of the UN a petition of blistered feet, saying the people of this world want something to be done, now."

That was it.

I said more but that's the segment they used.

Geldof saw it on the *Six-O'clock News*.

He said he watched it and I was good.

It meant a lot coming from him.

I had pinned down the elusive Margaret Thatcher in Dublin and she agreed to meet Omar at the airport. It was important for me that our prime minister should make time, but we were having to take Omar to Maggie.

It was a big chunk of logistics to make work.

Omar only had time for the airport greeting before he headed off to London.

Airspace waits for no-one.

I heard later that day that Mrs Thatcher had asked after me. Press officer Nick Cater said: "She asked: 'Where is Mr Long?'"

It was crazy and surreal that the Prime Minister knew who I was and I couldn't help feeling quite pleased about it.

It was a nice way to finish the week.

It had been massive and tomorrow was going to be even bigger.

It was midnight and I needed to pack some clothes and get a kip.

I headed off home to grab a few hours' sleep.

CHAPTER 10
The Race Against Time

The next morning, I drove down Lea Bridge Road to the big Lea Bridge roundabout at Lower Clapton. Erected overnight in the middle was a huge scaffolded structure bearing a banner with the words RUN THE WORLD. The letters were massive and I stopped, got out the car and just gazed up at it.

It towered above me and was beautiful.

I couldn't believe it.

The local authority had erected it to advertise the Race Against Time in Victoria Park – our second London venue - and they just did it.

Didn't ask.

Just did it.

Suddenly, it dawned on me that people outside were getting it.

Getting the vibe.

Getting what it was all about.

It was about seven o'clock in the morning when I reached the office and it was heaving. It was at full capacity and I had people working at desks, on desks, on the floor, anywhere we could find room. Our four telex machines chattered away all day and all night. The press office and celebrity liaison were directly in front of my desk and it had grown to more than 80 people. There were more than 130 of us in all and almost everyone was on a phone.

Every one of them a volunteer.

Every one of them in RUN THE WORLD T-shirts.

We were now managing 89 National Organising Committees around the clock. The noise, the vibe and the atmosphere were energising.

I checked the PO box one last time to find more than 15 sacks of mail.

Relief.

A line of people queued at my desk.

Each one with a question.

I'd just answer yes or no and they would peel away to complete their tasks. It was like orchestrating some kind of synchronised dance routine.

I was the puppet master and the line kept coming.

It was about midday when Robert Smith joined it.

Robert was head of the UK Committee for UNICEF. He was a small man with greying hair and a little goatee beard. He wore a perfectly pressed dark blue suit, white shirt and tie and looked completely out of place among our motley crew. Today he had an entourage with him and they swept into the office as if to purposefully add more to the mayhem.

He jumped the queue and made a beeline for my desk.

"You ready?"

"What?"

"You ready? We're going to the Palace now. We're here to pick you up."

Shit, forgot.

It was only yesterday that I'd phoned Mum and Dad to tell them I was going to Buckingham Palace and now I'd forgotten.

Too much on my mind. Too much to do.

"Hi Mum, you OK?"

"Hi Chich, how are you? Do you want to speak to your Dad?"

115

Mum always called me 'Chich' and would always pass me over to Dad as soon as she could. It wasn't as if she had nothing to say. I just think events had moved so fast she didn't know what to say to me anymore.

"No, I want to speak to you. I'm going to Buckingham Palace tomorrow. I'm going to meet Prince Charles and Diana."

"I saw you on the news last night."

"Oh, did you?

"You looked tired."

"Yeah, I know. I've been really busy Mum. I'm going to the Palace tomorrow and then I'm flying out to New York on Concorde."

"Dad's decorating our bedroom."

I smiled. My Mum had an amazing knack of bringing me back to earth.

Don't forget who you are son.

I loved her for it.

"Do you want to speak to your Dad?"

"Oh OK. You take care. I love you."

"Hello."

"Hello Dad."

"Hello Son. Been watching you on the telly."

"Yeah, I know. Mum said. So, are you going to run tomorrow?"

I laughed but knew he would probably try. He was over 70.

"Yep, told everyone down the pub I'm doing it. I'm sponsored."

"Oh, shit Dad, I forgot to send you a T-shirt. I'll send a couple today so you get them tomorrow. Sorry about that, it's been really crazy. You got to have a T-shirt Dad."

I loved my Mum and Dad to bits but they just couldn't get their heads around what was happening to me and to be fair, right now, I was struggling too.

I looked up.

"Well, are you coming?"

"Yes, yes, sorry Robert, I'm coming. But we'll have to go past Virgin Megastore in Oxford Street first. I need to pick up some T-shirts."

The car couldn't get anywhere near Oxford Street. The traffic was a nightmare and it seemed so much busier than normal. It felt strange to be outside. I had been cocooned in my office for the last 100 days and this was my first glimpse of the real world. My fellow passengers kept checking their watches and looked nervous.

"Drop me here."

"What?"

"Drop me here. I'll run up to the store. I've got to get those T-shirts."

Robert looked really stressed at the prospect of me abandoning him and our Royal family for T-shirts and gripped my arm.

"I need T-shirts, Robert. For Charles and Diana. Got to get them."

He released his grip and I jumped out of the car and legged it. As I got closer and closer to Oxford Street the crowds grew bigger and bigger. We were signing up runners at the Virgin Megastore for tomorrow's race and today, Sting was the attraction. He was giving out T-shirts and race forms. Celebrities had helped to build momentum all week.

Shit forgot, got to get T-shirts.

I pushed my way through the crowd and eventually made it to the entrance of the store. The queues were massive and I just couldn't get through. It was mayhem.

"Sting!"

I shouted. Some of my team were working with him and looked up as I screamed like a banshee from the back of the store.

"I need four shirts. Quickly, just chuck them."

"What size?"

"Fuck, I don't know. Anything."

The shirts were hurled at me and it took a few attempts. Eventually, armed with my precious 'I Ran the World' T-shirts, I made off in search of the car with the sweating UNICEF men.

As it finally swept down into the Mall, I noticed huge crowds lining each side of the road.

"Rows of people. Typical. Have we picked a bad day? Is it the changing of the guard or something?"

"No Chris, they're are all here for you."

They're all here for you.

It was like a sledgehammer and suddenly, the vastness of what was happening started to dawn on me. They **were** here for Sport Aid. The crowds at Virgin Megastore. The crowds in Oxford Street. Everywhere.

Maybe, just maybe, I might pull off this blind date I've got with millions of people tomorrow.

As the car reached the gates of Buckingham Palace, the police motorcyclists I hadn't even noticed parted the crowd like Moses in the Red Sea and we swept through the main gate. People stared through the windows trying desperately to catch a glimpse of who was inside. Cameras flashed everywhere.

Is this what it's like to be famous?

118

The next minute we arrived in a courtyard. The car stopped and the UNICEF entourage and I were ushered into a reception room deep in the heart of Buckingham Palace.

Within a few minutes, Charles and Diana appeared. Robert Smith in his finery, tie still firmly in place, took control and greeted their Royal Highnesses, the Prince and Princess of Wales. Prince Charles wore a dark expensive-looking blue pinstripe suit with fashionably wide lapels, chequered shirt and tie. The Princess was dressed in a light grey pleated skirt with a matching bolero style jacket. Underneath was a turquoise blouse matching a handkerchief in her top pocket. Her hair was perfectly coiffed in that typical 1980s Diana style.

I looked down involuntarily as if to prepare for some kind of a bow when I noticed the state of my trainers. I had on a pair of jeans, a tracksuit top and a T-shirt that said RUN THE WORLD. Nothing had been washed for well over a week.

Robert first introduced Charles and then Diana. They both shook my hand and thanked me for what I'd done.

"Chris is the founder and chairman of Sport Aid."

It sounded great.

I was the founder. I was the chairman and he was the next King of England.

Diana was stunning and they both seemed happy together. Prince William was nearly four at the time and Prince Harry about eight months old.

Looking back now, I hope it was a happy time in their marriage.

A memory I'll never forget.

It wasn't the last time I was going to meet Prince Charles but I didn't know that then. I waffled a few minutes and then invited them both to our race in Hyde Park the next day. I gave them both a T-shirt and said if they couldn't make it, to just run around their garden and get their Mum and Dad to sponsor them.

Diana laughed and graciously took both the T-shirts. She got the joke and I liked her very much.

We continued to exchange pleasantries and then went outside to the front of Buckingham Palace for the main event.

Six days ago, Omar Khalifa was the Sudanese 1,500m champion. Now he had become a symbol of what Africa could be, given half a chance. He had lit a torch from the burning embers of a camp fire in the Sudan. He had met the Pope, the president of France, Francois Mitterrand, German chancellor Helmut Kohl, Greek prime minister Papandreou, Sudan president Sadiq al-Mahdi and more. He had flown on a British Airways jet across Europe, carried a torch and become the Sport Aid torch bearer.

His life had changed and so had mine.

Surrounded by children, celebrities and watched by thousands of people, Omar entered the gates of Buckingham Palace. The ceremony began as Charles and Diana were introduced to him and his running companions.

I stood in the background and watched. It was truly moving and the enormity of it all hit me again.

I started all this. I made this happen.

I caught Omar's eye when, all of a sudden, my mobile rang. I carried a phone the size of a brick that sat on top of a battery twice the size of the phone. It hung from my shoulder like a lead weight.

"Hello."

"Chris, it's Will."

Will Chapman was with London Road Runners when I'd met him three months previously and managed to convince him to come and help. He had taken some flack, as did I, when we announced that the London Race Against Time was going to eclipse the London Marathon. The organisers seemed less than pleased and had a pop at our plans to change the world.

"It's preposterous. Dangerous. They'll kill someone."

"Yeah and 18 million African people will die if we don't try."

I liked Will. He knew what he was doing and was a calming influence among the madness of it all. His role today was to prepare Hyde Park for tomorrow's big race and he sounded worried.

"We've got a problem."

"What is it?"

"They won't let us put up the start and finish banners in Hyde Park."

"Fuck. What? Why?"

"Well, apparently, you can't advertise in a Royal Park and the banners have got British Airways on them."

"What? Are they having a laugh…."

"Chris, Chris … I'm in the Royal Bailiff's office and you are on a speaker phone."

A rather gruff and plummy voice came on.

"Mr Long. This is the Royal Bailiff here. I am sorry but you were sent a contract and it did say that you were not allowed to advertise in a Royal Park."

Shit, that's what that thing was. Should have read it.

121

"Seriously? I mean it's British Airways. It's not like it's Cannon or Fuji or Honda. It's fucking British Airways."

I started to lose it a bit as I felt the argument slipping from my grasp.

"I'm sorry, Mr Long, but there is nothing I can do."

"Well, who's your boss?"

Then it came to me.

Royal Park!

I looked across and Charles was stood talking to his private secretary.

"Excuse me sir?"

I shouted something.

"Charles?"

"Charlie?"

"Your Royal Highness?"

Charles turned and looked at me. He walked over.

"Sorry Sir, but we seem to have a problem with one of your gardens…"

I explained the problem and the stupidity of it all. How a banner with British Airways seemed so banal compared to the death of millions of famine victims. I had made this argument a million times in the last year, it being the reason why we were all here at this particular moment in time.

"We really need to be able to break the rules – again, just this once, please."

Prince Charles turned to his private secretary and he, in turn, turned to me.

"His Royal Highness will do what he can."

With that they turned and returned to their formal duties with Omar's reception.

"Did you hear that, Will?"

"What?"

"The fucking banners stay up."

The whole event was the lead item on the *Six O'clock News* that night and the banners stayed up.

When we arrived at Heathrow the crowds were enormous. About 50 of us travelled by private coach to the Concorde terminal at the airport. The production crew for the New York event, TV team, TV crew, logistics team, Omar, the Sport Aid flame - which we carried in a miner's lamp - and the whole pre-run team. Simon and I were meeting Geldof and Vangelis at the airport, along with officials from British Airways, before we all boarded Concorde for New York.

The arrivals concourse at Terminal 4 was heaving and as our coach pulled up outside, the press and paparazzi where about 10-deep.

The arrivals hall was also heaving and Simon and I shoved and pushed our way to a private room where we were meeting Bob.

The door slammed shut behind us.

Silence and then.

"I'm not coming."

"What?"

"I'm not coming."

Simon and I looked at each other.

Did he just say he's not coming?

"The vibe's here."

"Yeah, but the whole fucking point to this thing is over there."

"I'm not coming."

Fuck this. I don't believe it. Fuck, what's happening here?

"Bob, this is where you pass on the responsibility to the policymakers of Africa and the world. This is where you challenge the UN Special Session. This is everything we've worked for. You've got to come."

"Yeah, but Hands Across America. The New York race isn't going to be as big. The vibe's here."

"Fuck that. It doesn't matter. The whole fucking world will be watching and you should be at the UN."

"I'm not coming."

Fuck you.

I left the room and took the door with me.

I was seething when I took my seat on Concorde.

I couldn't believe it.

Now you got a fockin' show!

Why?

Everyone was expecting Bob Geldof.

There was the planned press conference at JFK with Colin Marshall. His arrival at the UN, the entire torch ceremony, everything.

Shit, I'll just have to wing it.

The Rolls Royce/Scecma Olympus 593 engines opened up and the whole plane shuddered before easing its way down the runway. Inside was a simple, fairly short tube with two seats on each side. I sat in one midway down and as it lifted into the sky, I tried to compute what had just happened.

I didn't get it.

His story to the press all week had been he had tonsillitis.

Why didn't he just say sorry guys, I feel shit.

I can't make the flight.

I feel crap.

I'm unwell.

Why come to the airport at all?

The vibe's here.

I must have fallen asleep because when we hit Mach 2, I awoke to see everyone on the plane having a ball.

Omar walked down the aisle of the cramped fuselage holding the miner's lamp with the Sport Aid flame inside. Others laughed and smiled and let their hair down. They had all worked so hard and got nothing for it.

This was a big treat and they all deserved it.

I stretched in my seat and tried to forget everything going around in my head, as it slowly dawned on me that I was on Concorde and flying at twice the speed of sound. I was on my way to New York to meet my destiny and what will be, will be.

An air stewardess made her way past Omar and I grabbed her attention.

"Excuse me, would it be OK if I could see the cockpit?"

"Of course, let me just check with the captain. I'm sure it will be OK – after all, this is your plane."

Your plane.

She returned and I watched her make her way between the rows of leather seats, her hands sliding along the overhead lockers on each side for balance.

She smiled.

"Yes, that's OK, come with me please."

The first thing I noticed was how cramped it was. The cockpit was even more complex than I thought it would be. The captain and his co-pilot sat upfront and before them to the right was another man sitting at a bank of dials, levers and lights. He got up and offered me his seat.

I looked out beyond the distinctive windscreen and noticed at once the curvature of the earth before me.

Above was only blackness.

Cool.

"Take a seat."

"Thanks."

I asked them all what switch did what and what's it like to fly this fast. I must have sounded like an inquisitive, boring school kid but they were gracious with their answers. The captain sounded just as you'd expect a Concorde captain to sound and I imagined him as just as comfortable in a leather helmet, white scarf and Spitfire. It was really noisy and I had to shout.

"So, what time you guys flying back tomorrow?"

"We don't fly 'til the afternoon."

"So, what are you doing at 11 tomorrow morning?"

"Oh, we'll be arriving at JFK to begin our flight prep."

Really?

"Here's an idea. Why don't you guys fly this thing over the UN building at 11 tomorrow – just as the race starts – maybe do a victory roll?"

They laughed.

"Not quite that easy, old boy. You'd need special permissions to do that and I'm afraid I don't have the authority."

"Really. Who does?"

"Well, Colin Marshall might."

Colin Marshall was the chief executive of British Airways and he was on my plane. He was knighted a year later and I'd like to think that what happened next contributed to that. Colin was sat up front by the window and there was a spare seat beside him. I plonked myself down.

"Colin, I have an idea."

"What's that?"

"Just spoke to the guys up front and they're keen to fly this plane over the UN building tomorrow just as the race starts but they need special permission and apparently, you're the man."

He looked at me, as if exasperated.

"You've done a huge amount and this is my way of saying thanks. Just imagine, we have a TV audience of about 1.5 billion people tomorrow and all eyes will be trained on the UN at exactly 11:00 EST. Where do you think all the cameras are going to point if this thing blasts over the UN at 600 feet?"

He just stared at me and I smiled.

"Well, I'll leave that one with you then."

I got up and made my way back to my seat.

It was a long shot but if you don't ask you don't get. *Maybe* . . .

CHAPTER 11
The best day of my life

It had been a very long night and Simon and I stood on the sidewalk outside the UN Headquarters. First Avenue had been shut off from about 61st Street right down to 23rd. This was to form part of the route of the New York run, as well as the final part of Omar's run from Africa.

It was 10 in the morning and the sun was shining and we had about an hour before the start of the Race.

The flags of all the member states fluttered in a light breeze and the sun shone on the huge brass bowl we had erected at the top of the ramp in front of the General Assembly building. The start and finish banners had been put up on 1st Avenue directly in front of UN Plaza. It was a fitting location for us to deliver our message from the people of the world and I was just glad it wasn't pissing down.

Simon sat down on the curb of the unusually empty road and talked to Bob on a mobile phone. Bob was in the BBC outside broadcast truck in London and not in New York where he should have been. We were still having to change things at the last minute.

"So, the Anthem will start and Omar will run up the ramp outside the UN building. Say something like, let's hope the UN pay attention to our millions of runners. Then something like, here's Omar Khalifa, who represents Africa. When he lights the beacon start the race."

But Bob knew what to do.

This was his gig.

This was what he was really good at.

I looked at Simon and walked away.

I don't want to talk to him.

As they talked I wandered away towards the huge Star Vision screen mounted inside the UN grounds.

As I stared at the huge black screen it flickered into life and my mind cast back to the early hours of that morning. At around 3am, we had called all of our TV directors in all the Race Against Time cities around the world to ensure everything was in place and OK to go. When we spoke to the guys in Ouagadougou, it wasn't great news.

"We've got a problem."

"What is it?"

"You didn't tell us its 110 degrees in the shade here. We can't keep the generators running long enough to give us power. They just overheat."

"Guys, you have to find a solution."

"This is the African race!"

"President Sankara has promised his entire cabinet and population will run. We have to have pictures of it."

"What can you do?"

It was probably the worst news I could have heard.

Even worse than Bob saying he wasn't coming.

This was Africa's chance to show the world it was helping itself. I believed President Thomas Sankara would take part and deliver the thousands of African runners he had promised. The world must see them – this was Africa helping itself.

I can't let him down.

"Please, please, please do what you can guys – we **have** to have pictures from our African race."

I left the phone conversation with a heavy heart and wandered back to my hotel room to try to grab a couple of hours sleep before the biggest day in my life.

We have to have Ouagadougou.

The Star Vision screen in front of me flickered again and suddenly, the London feed appeared. There, in front of me, were about 250,000 people in Hyde Park, getting ready to start the Race Against Time.

It took my breath away.

Cliff Richard was leading the crowd in a warm up. The first world workout had its centre stage billing as promised and more than 100,000 people were joining in.

As the camera panned across stage, I could see Diana - Michael's wife - holding her young baby in her arms, both wearing I Ran The World T-shirts and taking part in the fun.

I had sent them VIP passes.

I was so happy they were there.

We were still friends.

The screen flickered again and the Dublin feed appeared.

Then Brisbane, Budapest, Barcelona, Seoul, Rome, Auckland, Athens, Melbourne and Port of Spain.

We were cranking up the system – testing the feeds before the broadcast. Everywhere, thousands had come to tell the world they cared about Africa and wanted something to be done.

My blind date with millions might just work.

But much as I wanted to scream with joy at that moment, I wanted to cry more. There were still no images from Ouagadougou. Just a dark screen with its lonely funny name in the top right-hand corner.

I turned away to tell Simon but he had gone. This was a busy day for him. Tony Verna was line-producing our Sport Aid show and Simon was off to see him. The final part of this 18-month marathon was theirs to complete.

For my part, it was almost over and I walked towards the stage outside the UN to greet the VIPs and officials.

Seb Coe was there.

Seb had supported Sport Aid from that first press conference in London and today he was going to finish his support by running the New York race.

For some strange reason, Harry Belafonte was leading the singing and merriment on the stage. Other guests including Vangelis and Colin Marshall looked on.

Then someone grabbed me.

"Chris?"

"Yes."

"NBC News. Can I have a few words?"

"Sure."

NBC were more interested in why Sport Aid was on the same day as Hands across America and how come the rest of the world was focused on the African famine on the same day America was focused on America. I would love to have told them what I really thought but instead wished 'Hands' the best and explained we just couldn't change our date because of the UN Special Session.

We have to deliver our message today.

I turned away as the huge Star Vision screen cut back to Hyde Park in London. Bob took to the stage to screams and addressed the enormous throng of runners that assembled before him.

"I'd like to say a special hello to everyone in Australia who have been waiting up all night. So, if you can, help keep the Australians awake. We've only got a couple of minutes to wait. Can we say hello to everybody in India, because it's 11 o'clock at night in India? Say hello to India. If we could say hello to everybody in Africa where it is 125 degrees in the heat, say hello Africa."

The crowd went mad.

"If we could say hello and welcome to all the people in America who are joining Hands Across America and Sport Aid today, hello. In Russia, in Japan, in Europe, all across the world, Hyde Park and the rest of England would you please welcome the world to this Sport Aid event and let's hope that tomorrow at the United Nations they pay attention to the blistered feet of 20 million people who will be joining us this afternoon."

Suddenly, as if someone had pressed a switch, the noise cranked up even more.

The Vangelis anthem started and Omar could be seen. Dressed in his pristine white singlet, free of any commercial logos, white shorts and socks and flanked by police motorbike outriders. The most famous man in Africa at that moment was running down 1st Avenue towards the UN.

The Sport Aid torch held aloft.

The flame as brilliant as it was ten days earlier, when lit from the burning embers of a refugee camp fire in the Sudan.

The Star Vision cut back to Bob in London.

"I think we should say a special thanks to Omar Khalifa, the man who came out of the deserts of Sudan and ran with such dignity and such pride and who represents what Africa could be, if it was given half a chance. I'm going to run about 30 yards and then I'm going to fall down dead. Those of you who are watching at home please get ready to leave your front doors right

132

now and join us running around your block. If you're not prepared to do that feel ashamed of yourselves and dig deep in your pockets, and phone up the numbers and bring your money down to the banks and the post offices on Tuesday morning. We need it just as much as we needed it on that fine day last summer. Somebody up there likes us because it's still not raining. I don't have very much else to tell you except that I'm overwhelmed with what's happening here in London today, and what's happening around Britain. It's one thing to ask people to watch a pop concert of stars, it's another thing to ask people to get out and run 10 km through their cities, so thank you very much. You can affect the world you live in."

Omar entered the UN Plaza and slowly with majestic motion, jogged his way to the ramp outside the General Assembly building. The Vangelis anthem still building towards its incredible crescendo.

The Star Vision Screen flickered again and images jumped from city to city. Millions all over the world awaiting the start of the race but Ouagadougou was still dark.

As he climbed the ramp there was a deafening roar and Concorde appeared over the top of the UN building.

It was incredible.

Framed by a clear blue sky as if to sit on the top of the UN tower itself.

The noise was deafening.

Colin Marshall – you fucking beauty.

And then, Omar was standing at the top of the ramp.

He raised both arms in a victorious salute before lowering his torch to the bowl.

It lit.

133

Geldof screamed:

"Change the World."

Thousands of runners in 1st Avenue started their race as images on the huge Star Vision screen cut from city to city.

People started running everywhere.

There were 200,000 runners in London's Hyde Park.

20,000 in Dublin.

30,000 in Athens.

50,000 in Barcelona.

15,000 in Port of Spain.

25,000 in Rome.

10,000 running in the middle of the night in Brisbane and then, miraculously. . .

. . . 25,000 bare-footed black African runners led by president Thomas Sankara and his entire cabinet running down a dusty street in Ouagadougou.

It was too much.

I took off like a greyhound.

I was running the Race Against Time.

By the time I hit 65th Street, Seb was already on his way back, followed by thousands of runners. He looked across at me with a faint look of knowing, before pressing ahead to the finish.

He looked as fresh as he did at the beginning.

I was already wasted.

The last 100 days had taken their toll and even with the vast amount of adrenalin coursing through my veins at that moment, I just couldn't make it any further. I stopped, took a deep breath and turned around. I jumped the barrier and walked with a few stragglers before jogging to the finish with a triumphant burst of speed.

John Anderson was waiting for me.

"That was fast."

I laughed.

"Fastest 10k I've ever run."

Maybe I did a mile.

John had become a true friend during my Sport Aid journey. Head of Global Special Events for UNICEF, he had arrived in my office about two months ago, charged with helping and protecting UNICEF's interests on what was to become a roller coaster of a ride and a complete metamorphosis for UNICEF.

We had another UN guy in London for the last few weeks, Bob Walwer. He was asked later to report on the UNICEF experience with Sport Aid. He wrote 'Managing Sport Aid was like holding a tiger by the tail and if that tiger should ever cross our path again, we should grab it with both hands and hold on tight.'

"Let's go over to Jim's. He's got some important people there to meet you."

We walked down 1st Avenue. The crowds had now congregated in front of the stage and the party was in full swing. Seb, Omar and Grete Waitz were on stage dancing with the Sport Aid flame. Belafonte was singing '*Africa*' and the crowds were joining in.

I looked across to the Star Vision as it continued to show millions running in races all over the world.

My TV feed was reaching over one and half billion people.

They were the ones who really mattered.

Back home a party had also started. Bob, Paula, Fifi, Sting and Trudi had headed off to Tower Bridge to meet Simon Le Bon. He had moored his boat Drum at

St Katherine's Dock and was with his brother Jonathan, Kevin Godley, Duncan Goodhew and more.

Drum had been commissioned by Simon to take part in the 1985/86 Whitbread Round the World Yacht Race.

On August 10, 1985, to assist with crew training and to test the boat's equipment in advance of the Whitbread Race, he had entered the Fastnet Race - a 608 mile round trip from the Isle of Wight to Plymouth.

During the race, the 14-ton keel sheared off the hull due to a design failure, leading to the boat capsizing with six crew members, including him, stuck inside. Thankfully Carat, another yacht competing in the race, witnessed the capsize, raised the alarm and the team were able to scramble to a helicopter.

Simon lived to tell the tale and was now hosting a Sport Aid post-event party in London aboard the very same yacht.

By all accounts it was a great evening and apparently Simon Le Bon even got his arse out for the crowd who had amassed in St Katherine's Dock to see him and his guests.

We arrived at Jim's apartment block just down First Avenue and took a lift to the fifth floor. As I entered, Jim greeted me with a big smile and introduced me to a packed party.

The events of the last year and in particular, the last three months, started to have an effect on me. Instead of relief, exultation, happiness, pride or whatever I should have felt after pulling off the largest mass participation sporting event the world had ever seen, I felt shit.

I went through the motions and did what was required of me but then made my excuses and left. All that back-slapping just didn't feel right.

Tomorrow and the next few days were the important part now.

I wish Bob had come.

Will the UN Special Session listen to the blistered feet of all those people?

We will have to wait and see.

I made my way back down in the lift to the street and walked back to 1st Avenue.

The banners had gone.

The stage had gone and the traffic was back to normal.

Did that really happen or was it a dream?

I made my way back to my hotel on Lexington Avenue and fell asleep - for 36 hours.

CHAPTER 12
Shutting me down

I headed home on what was to be my penultimate British Airways flight for Sport Aid. We had pretty much exhausted the £100,000 worth of flight tickets given to us by BA. The value had only been a guess at the beginning but it had worked out pretty well. Quite a few of the team had stayed on a couple of days and they partied on the journey back across the pond.

I didn't.

It was a strange feeling and although it was all over, something deep down inside told me it wasn't.

I was still really pissed at Bob for not coming.

We should be at the UN today. Going for the jugular.

I headed back to the office in Waterloo as soon as we landed. The press had been given a heads up and there were quite a few reporters waiting for me, including a very young Carole Walker from the BBC.

"What are you going to do if the UN don't listen to your petition of blistered feet?"

"Let's just wait and see."

"Yes, but if they ignore you?"

"Maybe, we'll just have to do it all over again."

I shouldn't have said it but I did.

UNICEF had the responsibility to collect all the funds raised and complete a final audit of the event. I had insisted that all donations, sponsorship and net revenue from commercial income must be split 50/50 between UNICEF and Band Aid. I also insisted that

138

UNICEF produce a statement to show how the money was distributed. Their entire amount had to be spent on projects for children in Africa.

Band Aid's mandate was well known and Bob had always said that every penny would get to the people that needed it in Africa.

I trusted Band Aid like everyone else.

A large part of the post-event work was taking place at UNICEF headquarters in New York but there were still a few of their personnel in the London office. They all seemed in a hurry to close down operations and I wasn't sure why. The office didn't cost anything and all the services were still being provided free of charge.

Marsha was also keen to see things shut down and she was doing it in her own inimitable style.

John Anderson told me a few months later that Bob and Band Aid had instructed UNICEF to shut everything down as quickly as possible.

It pissed me off even more.

This was my project.

The world might think it's yours Bob, but it isn't.

"I'll decide when this fucking office closes."

I arranged a 'thank you' party for the entire London team and everyone who had helped came.

When I say party, I mean more of a gathering.

We had a small tape player for music and some of the team brought booze.

Martin Goldsmith came along and gave a white baseball jacket to everyone. On the front was the Sport Aid logo. On the back it said "I helped organise Sport Aid and all I got was this lousy jacket."

It was a really nice touch.

Martin had done an amazing job.

We sold more than 600,000 'I Ran the World' T-shirts in the UK alone and he produced every one of them. It was the biggest selling T-shirt of all time and was one of several entries we got in the Guinness Book of Records.

Everyone from the London Office was at the party and spirits were high. What everyone had achieved was only just beginning to sink in.

We had huge races all across the UK, in Bolton, Derby, Exeter, Folkestone, Leicester and Gateshead, where Steve Cram and Brendan Foster took part. The race in London's Victoria Park was massive and almost matched Hyde Park. There was a 'toddle aid' in County Durham with 100 children aged between 18 months and five years. Forty galloping grans and grandads took part in an old people's home in Porchester. They were all over 80 years old. In Brighton 70 nuns took part in a sponsored walk around their convent garden.

Weird and wacky.

Jayne and Chris's Ice Spectacular at the NEC on the night before the race had been a sell-out and a guy in hospital got out of his hospital bed and walked around the ward while a nurse carried his drip. The other patients sponsored him.

The news stories just kept coming in and gave everyone an excuse to stay and feel good. What everyone had achieved was nothing short of miraculous. No more so than the TV crew in Ouagadougou. The story unfolded that they had borrowed every single towel from the only hotel in town so they could soak them in cold water to hang on the generators. It was that action alone that enabled us to power the uplink and show Ouagadougou to the world.

The UNICEF men who had arrived a few weeks ago in their suits and ties were now partying in their 'I Ran the World' T-shirts and suit jackets.

Not a good look but nevertheless, a very profound statement.

My UNICEF boys were now rock'n'roll.

Marsha came.

Bob didn't.

The leaving party was pretty emotional. We were happy, but sad it was all over. It was to be the last time we were all together. For many it was probably going to be one of the biggest things they would do in their whole lives.

It was for me.

Everyone in the London office, the New York office and our 89 national organising committees had played a huge part in the success of Sport Aid but no more so than the millions of people who had run on the day.

What they fully achieved had yet to play out.

John Anderson stayed on a few days to complete the UNICEF clear up.

"What are you going to do next?"

"I don't know John. I honestly don't know."

"Come and work for UNICEF."

"What?"

"Why not? You could be a consultant on special events."

Maybe.

One thing was for sure, I was skint and I needed a job. I had survived the last few months on credit cards, help from my family and scraps. Sport Aid had cost me dearly, emotionally and financially.

I needed a job and I needed it fast.

"What about Simon?"

"UNICEF won't employ Simon."

His answer was emphatic and almost angry. I was aware that tension between Simon and UNICEF had got worse but I'd put that down to the day-to-day friction of trying to get things done.

"Why?"

"I'll tell you another time but think about it. You can work with me in New York."

Simon had been pushy and pissed off quite a few people but I was shocked the feelings were that strong. I had been too busy to think about it.

But now I did.

If he had used Sport Aid for self-promotion I didn't really mind.

That was just Simon.

He had an ego the size of a small planet but he'd done an amazing job and we had shared an incredible and hugely intense experience together.

He was now my close friend.

I felt the need to defend him.

"I'll think about it John."

Trinidad was a huge success in Sport Aid with 15,000 runners in Port of Spain. So it didn't come as a huge surprise when I got a call from their Tourist Board to say thanks for all the TV coverage but their kind offer of a free holiday on the beautiful island of Tobago was.

"We'd like to invite you, Bob and Simon to come out for a well-earned holiday."

Where do I pick up the tickets?

I didn't think Bob would want to go so I didn't ask him but Simon and I leapt at the chance. I hadn't seen my kids much over the last three months and here was a great opportunity to spend some quality time with them. We were expected to do a couple of press calls when we got there but that was it.

So, we went.

Tobago is the smaller of the two Caribbean islands comprising the nation of Trinidad and Tobago. It's known for its wide, sandy beaches and biodiverse tropical rainforest. Framed by mountains, the hotel we were staying in offered a great pool for the kids and tons of sunshine.

It was a fabulous place to relax and recharge the batteries. Ellie and Lydia spent all day in the pool or the sea and I just chilled in the evenings with a few cocktails and some early nights.

Simon wanted to talk about what we should do next.

"We should do another one. We can't let the momentum stop."

"I don't think I can do another one mate, I'm knackered."

I didn't know it then but this was to be the start of Simon's long campaign to get me to do another Sport Aid.

After just three months, he still had energy to go but, for me, it was the end of 18 months of the hardest thing I'd ever done and if I never saw another project like it for a long while, I'd be a happy man.

Simon kept raising the subject and I just kept batting it away.

One evening on our lovely little holiday, the phone rang. Some guy with a very plummy voice was on the other end. He was asking for Mr Geldof's telephone number and wondered if we could help him.

"Can I ask what it's about?"

"Of course, but may I be candid?"

"Sure."

I'm calling from Her Majesty's private office. Mr Geldof is going to be awarded an honorary knighthood but, as I am sure you can appreciate, Her Majesty would not want to be embarrassed in any way. We need to know that Mr Geldof will accept the honour before it's formally announced."

Is this a wind up?

I tried to think which one of my mates might be making the call but I didn't know anyone who could speak that posh.

"Oh, I see. Well, why don't you give me your number and we'll phone Bob and get him to call you. How's that?"

The posh speaking gentleman left his number and we called Bob in London.

"Hi Bob."

"Where are you, the line's really crackly?"

"In Tobago – on holiday. You had an invite but I forgot to tell you. Long story, look, you're getting a knighthood, call this number."

We explained the weird events that had just happened. Bob couldn't believe it and sounded genuinely pleased. He shouted to Paula who screamed she was going to be a lady and the Geldof household seemed very happy indeed.

"We'll leave it with you then."

We said our goodbyes to Sir Bob and said we'd be back in London in a few days.

The rest of our trip was great and I was sad to leave the beauty and tranquillity of Tobago.

No more so than when I got back to London.

I arrived at Heathrow on a Sunday with the girls and grabbed a newspaper before herding them on to the tube. I opened it and read the headline.

'Geldof Aid in Debt Crisis.'

What the fuck?

It was a half-page story on me.

Apparently, I owed the guy from the UAE money and hadn't paid it back. It was not a nice story. The suggestion was maybe I couldn't be trusted.

I couldn't believe it.

Geldof gets a knighthood and I get this shit.

I read the article again and could not understand how a national Sunday newspaper could write such crap. The guy from the UAE said he loaned me money and I hadn't paid it back.

They hadn't checked any of their story or even tried to speak to me.

Bastards.

I was fuming.

Over the next few days I took legal advice but was advised to forget it. I got a lawyer to write a letter to the legal office of the newspaper.

I needed them to know they had got it wrong.

I was really pissed off.

Next step would have been to take the newspaper to court but that would cost real money, something I didn't have.

Not even a little.

Sport Aid had left me on empty and staring at a mountain of debt.

I spoke to Bob about it and he said the Band Aid Trust had a whole file of shit from the guy. Apparently, he'd been writing to them for ages, saying I owed him money and demanding it back. I could only guess the guy's wife must have found out about the £3,000 he pissed up a wall and tried to blame it on me.

It must have got out of hand.

Bob said I should just forget it.

"It's tomorrow's fish and chips."

So I did, or tried to. But it really hurt. I couldn't afford to take a national newspaper to court and had to take it on the chin.

I got my own back on Mr Robert Maxwell some five years later.

But that's another story altogether.

Bob had a party at the Hard Rock Café in Piccadilly to celebrate his Knighthood. Everyone from Live Aid was there and the paparazzi lined the entrance blocking off most of the street. Bob arrived last and Sting fake knighted him with a huge silver sword at the door. He got up and walked over to where Simon and I were standing. He gave me a big hug and whispered:

"Thanks."

It meant a lot.

I was one of the first to arrive for the party and probably one of the last to leave. It's not often you get the opportunity to rub shoulders with so many famous bands and musicians.

I made the most of it and got pretty shit-faced.

I didn't know it then but that was to be the last time I would meet or even speak to Sir Bob Geldof.

The trashed office in Waterloo was quite empty and only a few remained. We cleaned it up slowly and some of the team would drift by to say hello. It was as if they couldn't get on with life without Sport Aid.

Leaving the mothership was proving painful.

The pressure was still on to close down the office but at least I now knew who was behind it.

They could fuck off.

It was no skin off their nose if we stayed a couple of extra weeks and I really wanted to produce a video of Sport Aid as a souvenir for all those who took part and to add to the money we had raised. The office didn't cost anything and the video was being done for free.

We should have been turning the screw on the UN special session right now but I couldn't do that. Especially when Band Aid and a pressured UNICEF seemed hell-bent on shutting up shop.

Simon stepped up his campaign to convince me to do another event and I told him UNICEF had asked me to join them.

He wasn't surprised but was quite angry.

"What?"

"Yeah, John mentioned it me. They asked me to go to New York and work for UNICEF on special events."

"They just want to own you. It's their way of owning Sport Aid. You can't let them do that Chris."

I might have to mate.

It was a bit of a conundrum.

Sport Aid was not a company or a legal entity. It was not a registered name or a proprietary mark.

It was just a project.

My project.

Band Aid didn't own it.

UNICEF didn't own it.

Nobody owned it.

Sport Aid, the Race Against Time, Run the World was an event I founded and realised as its chairman and organiser. If anyone owned it, it was me and the 20 million people who took part in it.

The only way UNICEF could continue with Sport Aid was to employ me. The only way Simon could continue with Sport Aid was to convince me to stay with him and do it all over again.

We can't let the momentum stop.

It was the start of a long drawn out tug-of-war with me in the middle. Simon took the moral high ground and denounced UNICEF's intentions. UNICEF questioned Simon's integrity and pursued me to join them.

Maybe that's why UNICEF had been so negative towards Simon?

Maybe it was part of a masterplan?

Press reports confirmed UNICEF's post event audit that about 19.8 million people had actually taken part in the race.

That's a fuck of lot of people who did more than just watch a concert and put their hands in their pockets.

From the outset, I wanted Africa to be centre stage and it had been. I wanted to take passive caring to a demonstrative phase and I had.

Let's change the world.

Band Aid's constituency of compassion was now at a new level and I knew deep down that I couldn't let it stop here but I wasn't going to be pushed into making a decision now, for anyone.

News of the UN special session began to filter in and John was first to tell me that a handful of nations had agreed to cancel all or part of their African debt.

"The benefit to Africa could be as much as $150 million."

"If we did that on the day, just imagine what we might have done if we had lobbied the UN special session."

Instead of pride it made me feel sad.

I still couldn't help wondering why Bob hadn't seized such a huge opportunity.

The vibe's here man.

I so wanted to tell the whole world what they had really achieved but everything was being shut down around me. My press office was gone, UNICEF and Band Aid were gone.

I was just too tired to fight alone.

Bob's book, *'Is that It'*, was out.

Earlier in the year I had a meeting with him while he was pouring over the manuscript for the book with Paul Vallely. Papers were strewn across a desk in a small office somewhere in Soho and it was only then that I discovered he was writing it.

Paul Vallely was a British writer on religion, ethics, Africa and development issues. He coined, in his seminal 1990 book *Bad Samaritans: First World Ethics and Third World Debt*, the expression that campaigners needed to move 'from charity to justice' – a slogan that was taken up by Live 8 later.

Pretty fucking ironic really when Sport Aid had done just that four years before he published it.

Bob's book, unsurprisingly, was a huge success and I think Sport Aid might have helped just a bit.

I was sitting in my empty shell of an office when Robert Smith called me on the telephone.

"You are getting an award."

"What?"

"An award. UNICEF are honouring you for distinguished service in the cause of UNICEF."

"Really?"

"Really."

I was quite taken aback.

I was getting something.

Me.

I never set out to be thanked but, given everything that was happening right now, it felt good to be noticed.

I was to attend a special ceremony at the UN maritime office on the Thames Embankment. A few people were being honoured and I was one of them.

All the UNICEF men came.

Their T-shirts long gone, they were back in their regulation suits and ties.

I still had my Run the World T-shirt and a pair of jeans but at least this time, they were clean.

Some things wouldn't change.

The well-groomed and suited Robert Smith and a bunch of smartly dressed assistants introduced me to the dignitaries and accredited press before sitting us down in a small auditorium.

I sat in the front row.

An official announced my name and gave a little speech on what I had done and why I was getting my award.

I felt quite emotional.

I never courted fame and for the best part of Sport Aid I managed to avoid press attention as much as possible. There were times when I couldn't of course because it wasn't in Sport Aid's best interests. We needed publicity and if I could get it, I did.

But Bob was so much better at it than me and I had been happy for him to be up there in the spotlight taking the glory.

Now it was all over, I felt invisible.

I wanted someone to say 'Well done.'

I needed someone to say we know it was you and today that was happening.

It was my turn to get something.

The Duchess of Kent presented me with a beautiful cut glass bowl inscribed 'For distinguished service in the cause of UNICEF.' She was very kind and gracious with her words. She knew I was the founder and organiser because that's what UNICEF had told her.

It felt really good.

"Where will you put it?"

"I'm going to buy a goldfish."

She smiled.

After the ceremony, I got to speak to her more. She was a wonderfully elegant woman and I found her conversation really engaging. The Duchess had travelled the world for UNICEF and VSO, highlighting specific areas of deprivation. She knew what she was talking about and was really positive about Sport Aid and Run the World.

She thanked me and gave me her private number.

We finished the video or should I say, Simon did. It was a mash up of the live broadcast, music video, ads, some news media coverage and featured Seb Coe. There was music from the Police, the Hollies, Band Aid, U2, Tears for Fears, the Cars and of course, Vangelis.

Simon showed me the first edit.

It included news clips of both of us. The one of me recorded by the BBC the day before the event for the

151

Six O'clock News and another recorded after we got back from Tobago. I looked like two different people.

The before and after shot.

Each clip of a tanned Simon was recorded after the event and carried the title 'Producer' below it.

I didn't get a mention.

I remember the moment well as it was the first time I really started to question Simon's motives. He wasn't the producer of Sport Aid. He was the producer of the TV event and he did an amazing job. But his understanding of his role was getting a tad inflated and it was beginning to piss me off. I put it down to his ego and him just being overzealous with the credits. Looking back now, it actually said more about him but I just didn't see the warning signs.

I liked him.

He had become a very close friend.

In a strange way, he had taken over Michael's role and became that 'big brother' figure in my life.

I told him to put 'Founder and Chairman' under my bits. I didn't really need it but I was beginning to feel every other fucker in the world was taking credit for my project.

When the final edit was complete, he'd added his name alongside mine at the end credits, naming us both as co-producers of the event.

You had to admire his balls. He just did what the fuck he wanted and I soon found myself questioning and defending him all at the same time.

Just after the video was finished, Bob appeared on TV in a milk commercial.

The advertisement showed him running down the Thames Embankment near Battersea Power Station.

He stopped running, took a bottle from a milk float and downed it. The milkman, astonished at who was nicking his milk says "… you're?" and Bob says "… yeah, shattered."

I couldn't believe it. Bob had suddenly been transformed into a jogging icon of health and fitness.

His tonsillitis long gone.

Fuck me, a book promotion, Knighthood and now a fucking income stream.

People were starting to take the piss.

So I took my goldfish bowl and went and joined the UN.

CHAPTER 13
New York

I took up UNICEF'S offer of a job and John started the ball rolling.

It seemed that everyone at UNICEF was pleased and looking forward to me joining them. If it had been their game plan all along, I really didn't care anymore. I told Simon and he was devastated.

I tried to explain my reasons.

"It wasn't really a choice."

"I need a job."

"I'm fucked Simon, I've got to do it. I can't do another year living on fresh air."

He didn't accept my reasons and was never going to give up trying to tear me away.

My new employment meant moving to New York. There was no way I was going to be separated from my kids again and so I negotiated a deal whereby I could work in New York and London. New York would be my duty station and I would work there two weeks in every month. The rest of the month I would be in London and free to see my girls.

John said that I could stay with him and Beth.

Beth was his long-term partner and they were getting married soon. They had a lovely house in New Jersey and John and I could both travel into Penn Station each day, then walk to the UN.

I needed to keep my expenses down.

I had many credit cards to repay.

My official UN title was special consultant for UNICEF. The salary was not huge by UN standards but more than I had ever been paid in my life.

I was really happy and very relieved.

I now had a gold fish bowl, a job and a story to tell my grandchildren.

But then I got something even better.

It was a little blue passport!

As part of my role, I was entitled to a UN passport.

A United Nations laissez-passer is the travel document issued by the UN under the provisions of Article VIII of the 1946 Convention on Privileges and Immunities.

Most officials hold a blue UNLP (up to D-1 level), which is similar in legal status to a service passport.

I had one of those bad boys.

A few countries didn't recognise the UN passport so you were advised to always carry your national passport as well. More importantly, if your plane got hijacked, you didn't show your little blue one.

I loved my passport and especially during my first return trip home.

I had given back my sponsored vehicle to Rover and rented a small car from Avis. I drove it to the UNICEF office in Lincoln's Inn fields one morning. The traffic from Walthamstow was awful. I took a roundabout route through the back streets of Islington and stopped at a junction on Southgate Road to wait for traffic to pass.

As I pulled out, a black BMW came up behind me really fast with headlights flashing and horn on full blast. I quickly indicated and turned left. The car also turned, pulled in behind me and followed just a few feet from my rear bumper. I could almost see the colour of the driver's eyes. He was wearing a black leather jacket and alongside him was another leather jacketed man.

They looked big.

In the back seat was another with long hair, peering with an evil gaze from between the two front seats.

Fuck this!

I hit the accelerator.

I had pissed off my chasers for some reason and I wasn't about to stop and find out why.

They seemed desperate to tell me first hand.

If I was going to be beaten up by three thugs in the back streets of London, I was going to do it with some witnesses around.

There were none.

So I put my foot down.

A chase ensued.

I drove faster and faster as they got closer and closer to my rear bumper. Headlights flashing and horn still sounding, the chase escalated through the back streets of Islington.

We reached a straightish piece of road, with cars parked either side, when the BMW driver decided to try and pull alongside. My knuckles were white from gripping the steering wheel and all I could do was look straight ahead and try not to hit anything. In a split second, I looked across to the front seat passenger of the BMW. It was now right alongside me and I could almost smell the driver.

He was holding something against the window.

I looked again.

Shit.

It was a flying squad badge.

"Fuck, fuck."

I slowed down and pulled over to the side of the road.

The BMW flew past and then stopped in front.

All three of the men jumped out and dragged me from my little car. I was pushed over the bonnet as they started to search me. It was like something out of Miami Vice and I was shitting myself.

"Do you always drive like that?"

"What?"

"Why did you pull out in front of us?"

"I didn't. You came over that bridge so fast I didn't see you."

"Why didn't you stop?"

"You're in an unmarked car. You're in plain clothes. I didn't know who you were. I thought you were going to kick the shit out of me."

Plod number one released his grip a little bit and let me stand up.

He shouted in my face.

"Is this your car?"

"No, it's hired."

His mood changed a little.

"Where do you live?"

I thought about it and then it just came out.

"Edison."

His expression changed and he looked at his mate, confused.

"Where's that?"

"New Jersey. Just outside New York City."

You could see that they were both disappointed with my answers but the best was yet to come.

"Officer?"

"What?"

"I presume you are a law enforcement officer."

"I'm flying squad, mate."

Feeling a little more confident, I looked straight back at him with what I hoped was a menacing look.

"If I were to interfere in your course of duty sir, I could be arrested. Yes?"

"Yes."

He looked uneasy.

At that moment, I revealed my beautiful blue passport from my inside pocket and flashed it right under his nose.

Bending the truth just a little . . .

"Well, I'm a member of the United Nations. I have diplomatic immunity and you are interfering in my course of duty. What's more, you're really beginning to piss me off."

The colour drained from his face.

He looked me up and down again and I could almost hear his brain whirring.

Jeans and T-shirt?

Shitty trainers?

Crappy little rented car?

UN diplomat?

You are fucking kidding me.

He took my passport and just stared at it.

He looked at the photograph and then straight back at me. I thought it was quite a good likeness and showed off my eyes.

I smiled at him with as much sarcasm as a smile can muster.

He stood there motionless, no doubt wishing the ground would swallow him up. Slowly, he moved away and walked over to the abandoned BMW in the middle of the road which was now holding up serious lines of traffic and interested bystanders.

He looked back at me again in total disbelief, before reaching for his car radio.

As he communicated with the forces that be, the enormous frame that had lifted me from my car seat seemed to shrink. His shoulders dropped and he slumped forward shaking his head.

After a couple of minutes, the man, now seemingly half his original size returned holding my passport in a way a Japanese businessman would present a business card - with both hands.

"I'm terribly sorry sir, there has been a mistake."

I swear I noticed a curtsey but maybe that was just wishful thinking.

I snatched my beautiful, gorgeous laissez-passer from his grasp and feeling like the king of the world, I adopted his earlier stance but now with my face just a few inches from his, I whispered.

"Wanker."

With that farewell, I turned and got back into my little rented car. I switched it on, revved the engine as high as I could and departed the scene of the crime leaving as much rubber as a 1.2 litre Ford Corsa could muster.

I loved my little blue passport.

I loved my new job!

The first month in New York was easy. There was no real pressure to do anything and I was working each day with John.

My office was not in the main Secretariat building. It was at 860 UN Plaza. The whole UN complex was located in the Turtle Bay neighbourhood of Manhattan, on spacious grounds overlooking the East River. The term 'Turtle Bay' was used by many as a metonym for the UN headquarters or for the United Nations as a whole. It bordered 1st Avenue on the west, East 42nd Street to the south, East 48th Street on the north and the East River to the east.

UN HQ had been designed by the Brazilian architect Oscar Niemeyer and the whole complex had served as the official headquarters of the United Nations since its completion back in 1952, two years before I was born.

Just inside the complex's perimeter fence stood the line of poles where the flags of all UN member states, plus the UN flag, were flown.

It was a really cool place and I would sometimes just stand outside at lunchtime remembering Omar, Concorde and the best day of my life.

Sport Aid had revolutionised UNICEF's thinking. It took Band Aid's constituency of compassion to another level and had an even greater effect on UNICEF.

Before, the organisation was conservative and measured in its thinking.

Now it was big and bold.

Sport Aid had spawned new opportunities and it was grabbing them.

The First Earth Run was the first of this new era and planned to start within a month.

It was another global event and another torch relay. This time, a torch carried by relay runners who were going to light a flame with native Americans at the UN in a sunrise ceremony.

Great idea.

Fifteen runners from the major geo-political regions of the world were then going to run with the torch in teams of four while, it was hoped, millions of people would take part in ceremonies connected with the coming of the runners. The teams were being led by David Gershon and Gail Straub, long distance runners and founders of the event.

I was to help John in UNICEF's co-ordination of the project.

Another massive spin-off of Sport Aid was the FIFA all-star football match. I think that Mr Havelange and Mr Blatter must have been embarrassed by FIFA's absence in Sport Aid. A dialogue had commenced shortly after and an annual fundraising match was arranged for UNICEF. That event has evolved and continues to this day with Soccer Aid.

Yes, Babby Sharlton, it wasn't a complete waste of time.

I liked New York and I didn't mind the journey in each day. Pennsylvania Station, also known as Penn, was the main intercity railroad in New York City. Serving more than 600,000 commuter rail and Amtrak passengers a day, it was the busiest passenger transportation hub in the Western Hemisphere.

Penn was in the midtown area of Manhattan, close to Herald Square, the Empire State Building, Korea Town, and Macy's department store. Entirely underground, it sat beneath Madison Square Garden, between 7th Avenue and 8th Avenue and between 31st and 34th Streets.

The walk from Penn took about 30 minutes. I always walked faster in New York, as did everyone else. It was a vibrant city and its population always seemed to be on a mission to be somewhere else.

I'd walk towards Korea Town until I got to 5th Avenue. Everyone likes to walk down 5th and I got to do it for two weeks every month. Sometimes I'd take a left at 7th and walk down to Times Square. At 42nd Street

I'd turn right and make my way past Bryant Park Subway with the park and New York public library on the right. It was a straight walk from there down 42nd to Grand Central and then past the iconic Chrysler building. At this point I'd cross Lexington Avenue and my destination could be seen straight ahead.

I got mugged on Lexington Avenue.

It wasn't on the way to or from work but on John's stag night - at about 3 o'clock in the morning. We'd been to Peter Luger's famous steakhouse in Brooklyn.

Afterwards, best man Larry DeBoice and us so-called friends, dumped John in an Asian massage parlour somewhere on the Lower East Side. We were all really drunk and waited a long while before finally giving up and leaving him there. I hailed a cab and made my way back towards 47th and 2nd.

I was staying in Larry's flat in Dag Hammarskjold Park.

The cab dropped me off on Lexington.

A young woman, who only later did I realise was a hooker, walked straight up to me, placing one hand on my crotch and the other hand on my chest. She offered a variety of services by whispering the menu into my ear. Before I could select, negotiate terms or even say no, she was gone – with my wallet.

If that wasn't bad enough, I had no key to Larry's flat and you needed to pay for a hotel in advance in New York City. That night, I slept on a park bench with a homeless chap for company. He was also pretty drunk so we stayed up all night and talked about life.

It was a long night.

Ironically, John had given us all the slip by walking straight out the back door of the massage parlour as soon as he arrived. He was tucked up in bed long before I settled down for the night with my new best friend.

John lived in Edison.

It was a township in Middlesex County, New Jersey, in the New York City metropolitan area. The population was about 85,000 and it was the fifth most populous municipality in New Jersey. Edison has since been ranked the 28th most liveable small city in the United States and second in New Jersey. It was ranked as one of America's 10 Best Places to Grow Up and the rankings focused on low crime, strong schools, green spaces and an abundance of recreational activities.

John's house was in a lovely location and I was able to explore it in Beth's Porsche 911 and on John's motorbike.

John and Beth were pretty comfortable and I was unashamedly enjoying their spoils.

Life was great.

I had a great job.

I lived in a beautiful place and I was suddenly living a life I had only ever dreamed of.

John and I would board the Amtrak train at Metropark. It was only an hour into Penn Station and the journey would take us through Newark Liberty (by the airport), Newark Penn and Secaucus Junction.

I loved the smell from the brakes every time the huge sleek silver beast entered a station. It was a distinctive smell and one I never experienced outside of America.

It was a real train.

Back home I would sometimes get the train from Wood Street Station to London Liverpool Street.

Unlike Amtrak, British Rail had very disappointing rolling stock, with wooden doors on either side, that you would open by sliding down the window to reach the handle on the other side.

During one of my two week stints back home, I caught the early train one morning and took my seat inside a crammed carriage of very sleepy commuters.

The monotony of the journey only added to the demeanour of my fellow travellers and by the time we reached the outskirts of London, the entire carriage was snoring away.

Suddenly, the train braked.

No smell?

A man in his mid-thirties and dressed smartly in a suit and tie woke up in a start.

"Shit."

He jumped up, still in a partial coma and pushed his way towards the exit. Muttering apologies and expletives as he tripped over countless cases and handbags, he slid down the window, reached for the handle and opened the door.

Unfortunately, on this day, the train had not reached his usual destination and he fell out! A woman screamed and the commotion woke the entire carriage. Suddenly the volume increased as everyone was desperate to find out what had just happened.

There were whispers, gasps, cries and even a few giggles.

About six hands reached down to pull the poor man up, who was now sprawled across the tracks below. He slid unceremoniously back onto the floor of the carriage like a beached whale still muttering and chastising himself for being so stupid. At the same time, he tried to stem the blood that was now coursing from a large cut on his forehead.

A woman passed him a tissue.

He took it, got up, dusted himself down, apologised for being so stupid and then pushed himself past the by now all standing commuters to the other side of the carriage where he repeated the entire exercise on the other side.

"For God's sake help him someone before he kills himself."

What British Rail lost to Amtrak in glamour, they made up in droves with entertainment.

News continued to pour in about Sport Aid's achievements and UNICEF were being diligent with the post-event audit process in New York.

It was good to see.

One morning I was sitting in my office when John showed me a clip from CNN Showbiz Today. It had aired on the night of May 26.

"You see this?"

The show was reviewing Hands across America and Sport Aid. Hands footage showed lines of people with interviews from a very young Sean Lennon with mum Yoko, Liza Minnelli, Robert Bell from Kool & The Gang, REO Speedwagon, Kenny Rogers, Ben Vereen and Cicely Tyson.

In the studio via a link was Ken Kragen.

Kragen said between six and seven million people took part in his event but was reluctant to say how much money had been raised. His goal was still $50 million.

Lee Leonard was hosting the show and asked Kragen about Sport Aid. As he spoke the screen cut to clips of our races from around the world.

He asked Kragen if the two events conflicted.

"No, not all. They were completely complementary of each other. Bob Geldof and I were very aware of what we were doing - his was a worldwide event and the other was America's effort to deal with its hunger and homelessness situation. Bob actually flew over here and did PSAs (public service announcements) for us and worked and helped us. And I went out yesterday to support Sport Aid and sent a congratulations wire to him on Saturday for what I knew was going to be a successful event."

Bob flew over here and did PSAs for us.
What?
I couldn't recall anyone mentioning it to me.
To be honest, it really pissed me off.

As the days passed, the US news media picked away at Kragen's post-event stats.

Hands hadn't been the huge success everyone had hoped for. There had been many gaps in the line stretching from coast to coast. It was an enormous challenge to have taken on and I felt the press shouldn't be so hard on them.

Some reports suggested five to six million people had held hands in the human chain for about 15 minutes. Sections of the line had been really successful with six to ten people deep but there were also many breaks.

Kragen had wanted it to be the biggest mass participation event in history but it looked like Sport Aid had beaten him by a factor of more than three.

According to the New York Times, only about $15 million was distributed after deducting operating costs. By contrast, Sport Aid raised $37m on the day with operating costs of just $1.5m and those costs were mainly T-shirts.

We sold more than 600,000 in the UK alone - another world record - and I got a page and a half in the Guinness Book of Records.

John turned his attention to the First Earth Run and I turned mine to what next. I was now on the UNICEF payroll and I thought I should try to understand what the organisation was really all about.

As I did, I became more and more interested in Jim Grant's 'Silent Emergency.'

Band Aid, Live Aid and Sport Aid had all grabbed the world's attention and highlighted the famine in Africa but another worldwide crisis remained largely unknown.

35,000 children were dying every day from preventable causes, including malnutrition.

Someone at UNICEF said 'more press and public attention was being lavished on the world stock markets than on the vast destructive potential of malnutrition.'

Malnutrition wasn't, as I first thought, a simple matter of whether a child can satisfy its appetite. A child who eats enough to satisfy immediate hunger can still be malnourished.

Malnutrition was a Silent Emergency and an invisible one as well.

As I looked into it more, I discovered that three quarters of those children who died from malnutrition-related causes were what nutritionists described as mildly to moderately malnourished. They betrayed no outward signs of problems to any casual observer. Also, child malnutrition wasn't just confined to the developing world. In some industrialised countries, widening income disparities and reductions in social protection were having effects on the nutritional well-being of its children.

Malnutrition had long been recognised as a consequence of poverty but it was now increasingly clear that it was also a cause. In Latin America and East Asia, UNICEF had seen dramatic reductions in child malnutrition but overall the number of malnourished children worldwide was still growing.

It was a major crisis.

Half of South Asia's children were malnourished.

In Africa, one in every three children were underweight and in several countries of the continent, the nutritional status of children was worsening. Illness was frequently a consequence of malnutrition and malnutrition the result of illness.

This was a huge deal.

Malaria was also a major cause of child deaths. In parts of Africa where malaria was common, about one third of child malnutrition was caused by malaria. The disease also had dangerous nutritional consequences for pregnant women. There was no one kind of malnutrition and it took a variety of forms.

I studied all the facts.

Discrimination and violence against women were major causes of malnutrition.

A lack of access to good education and correct information was a cause of malnutrition.

Of the nearly 12 million children under five who died each year in developing countries, mainly from preventable causes, the deaths of over six million, or 55 per cent, were directly or indirectly caused by malnutrition.

More than two million children died from diarrhoeal dehydration as a result of persistent diarrhoea aggravated by malnutrition.

Some 67 million children were estimated to be below the weight they should be for their height and about 183 million children weighed less than they should for their age. More than 29,000 children under the age of five died every day from preventable causes.

That was one every three seconds.

This was not only a Silent Emergency, it was a fucking disgrace.

Around this time Mikhail Gorbachev had proposed a meeting with president Ronald Reagan halfway between Moscow and Washington, DC. The leaders of the world's two superpowers were going to meet at the stark and picturesque Hofdi House in Reykjavik, Iceland.

The expectations for the summit at Reykjavik were low but John and I decided that it would be a good place to highlight the 'Silent Emergency' by way of a kid's torch relay to Hofdi House.

I suggested that we ask Simon to help and John reluctantly agreed.

"You want to help me do it, Simon?"

Of course he did.

We had a month to plan it and put it on.

Compared to Sport Aid it was relatively simple to organise but its potential impact was huge. We both took care to plan the event in detail and once again, UNICEF opened doors we could only knock on.

We staged a torch relay with local children from the airport to Hofdi House. It coincided with the beginning of the Summit and it was well received.

Talks between Reagan and Gorbachev proceeded at breakneck pace. Gorbachev agreed that human rights issues were a legitimate topic of discussion, something no previous Soviet leader had ever agreed to. A proposal to eliminate all new strategic missiles grew into a discussion and for the first time in history, there was a real possibility of eliminating nuclear weapons forever.

Aides to both leaders were shocked by the pace of the discussions. A summit that began with low expectations had blossomed into one of the most dramatic and potentially productive events of all time.

At one point Reagan even described to Gorbachev how they both might return to Reykjavik in 10 years as aged and retired leaders, to personally witness the dismantling of the world's last remaining nuclear warhead.

It was a watershed moment in global history and consumed thousands of column inches across the world's press.

It was a time for optimism and I was proud of our small part in it.

I had missed working with my old friend Simon and after the event, he headed back to London while I went back to my office in New York.

I would always meet Simon as soon as I got back to London. He would quiz me on what was going on and never let up on his relentless effort to prise me away from my new job.

He had bought a car and moved into a really nice flat in Islington. He still didn't have a job as far as I knew so I guessed he must have had some savings from his numerous global exploits.

Must be what got him through Sport Aid.

We'd sometimes meet at a Greek taverna in Bayswater. I think it was called something like Aphrodite and it sat a few blocks behind Queensway tube. It was well known for its celebrity clientele and by all accounts, Spike Milligan and Peter Sellers frequented it.

The owner told one story when Spike marched up and down the pavement outside imitating a Gestapo officer and causing mayhem with the traffic. Peter Sellers and Michael Bentine pissed themselves laughing from a dinner table inside. I didn't know if it was true but I would have loved to have seen it if it was.

Simon's stories ranged from his time as a war correspondent to when he was living with a well-known American actress in Los Angeles. He liked telling his tales and he had hundreds of them. One of his best was when he worked in Tehran reporting on the Iranian Revolution.

Demonstrations against the Shah had started in October 1977, developing into a campaign of civil resistance that included secular and religious elements. The Shah quit Iran leaving his duties to a regency council and an opposition-based prime minister. Ayatollah Khomeini returned to Tehran to be greeted by several million Iranians. The royal reign collapsed shortly after when guerrillas and rebels overwhelmed troops loyal to the Shah in armed street fighting.

Simon was actually there and he told me a story of how he got caught in a street with the Shah's troops at one end and rebels at the other. He hid in a recessed doorway with his cameraman and a few locals. They formed a line with their backs tight up again a wall for cover. There was shooting and one faction scattered. Simon was in the middle of a line of six people, all in the same doorway when the rebels slowly advanced down the street.

Simon and his cameraman pressed themselves back against the wall for cover.

A shot fired and the man on the end of the line dropped dead.

A second shot fired and the man next to Simon dropped dead.

As Simon braced himself to take the third bullet, the soldiers suddenly appeared directly in front of him. The soldiers saw the camera and assumed they were press. They shouted to them to run and they did.

Behind them, Simon heard the remaining shot.

I was transfixed.

It was like listening to my Dad's old war stories when I was a kid.

I loved them and I wanted more.

He told me how he escaped Lebanon in a post plane. He bribed the pilot to fly him to Cyprus, after he had been holed up in the hills overlooking the port in Beirut. Israel and Syria had got involved in the war and were fighting alongside different factions in the Lebanese capital. Simon waxed lyrical on how he hid in the back of the plane, staring through a gap in the postage sacks that covered him. The pilot, struggling with the weight of his newfound cargo, pointed his plane towards a distant drystone wall and opened the throttle. To Simon's utter relief, the plane finally left the ground with only inches to spare but his relief was short lived as he then expected to be shot out of the air.

He wasn't of course and eventually landed safely in Cyprus.

His stories just went on and on and I would find myself repeating them to others.

Simon had become a big influence in my life and his persistent calls to do another Sport Aid were beginning to have their desired effect.

As winter approached, John got more and more involved in the First Earth Run and I used my time alone to think more about the Silent Emergency and how it affected children in every corner of the world.

It was much easier to be free to think and plan when I wasn't constantly trying to find a way to live and pay the bills. My UN salary and low overheads had helped clear much of my debt and for once I could begin to see a light at the end of the tunnel.

New York was my duty station now and like all UN employees, I was entitled to a per diem for the days I spent away from it.

In my case, that was $120 a day.

While the money was much appreciated, I couldn't help thinking it was a bit over the top and exemplified everything that was wrong about the UN.

I was to get $120 a day to live at home.

It made me feel uncomfortable for the first time since joining UNICEF.

It was early 1987 and Simon stepped up another gear in his efforts to prise me away from my new job.

This, combined with nagging doubts over UNICEF and my constant 'what ifs' over Geldof, were making me think seriously about everything.

I spoke to John about Simon.

"Don't listen to him. He has his own agenda."

I knew that but, to be fair, so did UNICEF.

John made a strong case for me to stay. He didn't like Simon and I think his constant character assassination of him only served to push me away even more. Simon and I had been through an incredible experience and I felt intensely loyal to him.

Defending him again.

Simon, as always, made an emotive case for me to leave.

It became a choice between the two of them and looking back now it was a massive 'sliding doors' moment in my life.

Two futures lay ahead of me and I wasn't sure which one I should take.

I had been here before.

ICI or Michael?

Michael or my own project in Greece?

Now, UNICEF or Simon?

Back then, I let my heart rule my head. A huge sense of loyalty and the need to do what I thought was the right thing.

Did I regret it?

Not sure.

Maybe?

Could I have been successful and now living my Greek dream?

You'll never know.

One thing was for sure, if I had taken the investment and pursued a life growing strawberries, Sport Aid and Run the World would not have happened.

Did that make it right?

I poured over my dilemma for days.

UNICEF gave me stability.

It offered me a secure future.

I could remain within my comfort zone with UNICEF and make enough to give my family a very comfortable lifestyle. I could have a lovely house in Edison, like John. Maybe own my own Porsche one day.

But could I still change the world?

Could I enjoy the same freedom of expression within UNICEF?

I had left Greece without a pot to piss in. It had been a tough ride and I didn't want all that again. Looking over my shoulder all the time, living from hand to mouth.

UNICEF had given me security and I liked it.

I was also feeling like a proper father for the first time. Giving my children the things they needed.

Should I stay with UNICEF and take the secure road, or chance it with Simon and try and change the world again?

My heart was with Simon and Sport Aid.

My head was with John and UNICEF.

Fuck, I don't know.

When I got back to London, I talked to Simon about UNICEF's 'Silent Emergency' and he was quick to agree it was a fantastic and worthy cause.

"Let's do that."

"What do you mean?"

"Let's do that. Let's put together our own charitable trust. We can raise money for UNICEF or any other NGOs who are supporting child poverty and malnutrition?"

"Which NGOs?"

"I don't know, Red Cross, Save the Children. There are loads of big charities doing the same work as UNICEF."

I hadn't thought about working with anyone other than UNICEF.

"I don't think I can do another project Simon. I'm really fucked."

"But you have to."

I was short with him.

His pressure had been relentless and I didn't like being pushed into making such a huge decision. The past few years had all taken their toll on me and I felt I needed more time to think.

"Why do I have to? I don't owe you anything Simon."

Then it came out.

The very same fucking speech I had made to Bob Geldof on the night the Band Aid Trust pulled out of Sport Aid.

Simon pulled the guilt card and told me how millions of children would die if I stopped now.

"If you stop now, the whole thing will stop. You don't owe me anything, but you owe it to Sport Aid. Look, I'm inspired. You inspired me but I can't go on with Sport Aid without you."

Fuck.

"But what if I can't do another one?"

176

"You can. I'll do it all. Just be there. Just say you'll do it."

"I can't commit everything like I did before. I have my family. I can't give up my life to another year of this and work night and day for nothing. Even if I wanted to, I just can't."

"Chris, I'll do it. I promise. Just say yes."

Simon and I made an agreement.

I would look after the Children's Focus - another race - but that was it. All his ideas of music, carnival, advocacy was up to him.

"I'll support it but I have not got the stamina to be the main man again."

We agreed to be co-chairmen of a new event.

I told John of my decision and made plans to move back home.

He was gutted that I was leaving UNICEF. We had also become close friends and enjoyed our time together.

"We'll still work together John. I'm doing it for the world's children this time and that will always involve you and UNICEF."

John seemed angry that Simon had finally won the battle and couldn't understand my decision. I put it down to sour grapes but it wasn't.

John knew things about Simon that he thought I knew too.

The problem was, I didn't.

My divorce from UNICEF was very sad and no more so than on the day I relinquished my little blue passport. Gone were the days when I could piss off the

177

Flying Squad and tell customs officials to fuck off and leave my bag alone.

I was to miss it as much as I was to miss my walk to the UN each day. Living in New Jersey and working in the Big Apple was always going to be slightly more appealing than a commute from Snaresbrook to Central London.

I was sad but in a strange way I also felt energised again.

I had been coasting during my time in America. It was the combination of that laziness, a feeling of guilt for being paid so much for doing nothing much and Simon's incessant demands that combined to prise me away.

I still wasn't sure if I had done the right thing but I felt excited again for the first time in a long while.

This was the project planning stage.

The bit I loved best.

A plain canvas and the simple but bold idea to save the world's children.

For the first time since Live Aid, I had that unique feeling of being excited and scared shitless all over again.

Over the next month, I came up with a few ideas.

One was to stage a one kilometre race for children everywhere. We could stage it in every school, in every country of the world, and create national champions. Those champions, a boy and a girl, could go to the UN as ambassadors of **their** country's children. They could take their seats in the UN assembly hall and demand action for the Silent Emergency.

I really like it.

I ran it past Simon and he really liked it too.

"We can take the children to New York and they can start the world running this time."

The logistics were mind boggling and Simon wanted to add even more.

"Let's produce advocacy TV. We can make programmes highlighting the Silent Emergency issues. We can add music and carnival."

"Why music?"

"We have to. The world won't take part in just another Sport Aid. We need music and carnival. Something different to help advertise the event."

"Carnival?"

"Trinidad. They loved Sport Aid. They contacted me and want to do more. They're the land of carnival."

I wasn't convinced.

Music was Band Aid.

We had proved sport was a more powerful call-to-action and I didn't want to go backwards.

I liked the idea of the advocacy conduit. This was a Silent Emergency and if we could use it to tell the world, it wouldn't be silent anymore.

I didn't like the idea of the carnival but Simon was really excited about it.

I didn't have the energy to argue.

CHAPTER 14
Sport Aid '88

UNICEF collected the money during Sport Aid and was responsible for its distribution and audit. If we were now going alone, we needed a squeaky clean, robust method of doing it ourselves.

I suggested to Simon that we formed our own charitable trust.

"We'll need credible, experienced, high profile trustees. We need to be totally transparent and open to public scrutiny."

The world needed to know what we were doing and how we were doing it.

It was an interesting time.

It was like the early days with Birmingham, the NEC, Band Aid and all the event stakeholders. We needed strong partners again and my idea of staging a race for children in every country of the world required one in particular.

The IAAF.

The IAAF is the international governing body for the sport of athletics. It was founded as the International Amateur Athletic Federation on July 17, 1912 by representatives from 17 national athletics federations, at the organisation's first congress in Stockholm.

More recently IAAF president Primo Nebiolo had established the International Athletics Foundation with the 'primary mission to charitably assist the world governing body for track and field athletics - and its affiliated national governing bodies, in perpetuating the development and promotion of athletics worldwide.'

It was perfect.

The man at the top seemed to be on a similar wavelength and if he were a visionary like Jim Grant, he might want to get involved. It would certainly be the resource we needed to help stage the children's races all around the world.

I called the IAAF and arranged a meeting in London.

For once, getting a meeting wasn't difficult. The world didn't know I was the man behind Sport Aid but fortunately, the people at the IAAF did.

The guys in London loved the idea and before I knew it Simon and I were headed off to Monte Carlo to address the Congress of Summer Olympic sports.

The IAAF arranged our flights and hotel and we arrived in Nice airport to find a helicopter waiting for us.

The heli-transfer service runs every half-hour and we had to wait 10 minutes in a bare, anonymous room before being taken in a van to the helicopter landing pad on the runway.

The flight itself was simple safe and quick. It was just me and Simon so there were no issues stowing our small overnight bags. The seven-minute ride was beautiful from start to finish. We flew low and followed the coast the whole time. There's nothing quite like those dramatic views of the Côte d'Azur.

Even though there were only two of us it still took 10 minutes to get our luggage before we were escorted to a jam-packed shuttle van. Luckily it was only a 10 minute ride to our hotel in a vehicle packed with passengers and small children from other helicopters.

Simon and I were booked into the Hermitage Hotel.

As we entered the rotating glass doors we were whisked into a historic foyer dripping with glamour and sophistication.

It was Spring and had been hot and sweaty outside. Inside, the air-conditioning worked effortlessly and discreetly to cool us down.

It was very posh indeed and a marked contrast from the van.

My room was a junior suite and overlooked the sea.

I couldn't count the super yachts . . .

There were too many.

Over the next couple of days we met with members of the Council and Foundation and I presented my idea. One of the IAAF Honorary Members was Hasan Agabani from Sudan. Hasan was very positive, especially given what Sport Aid had already done for the Sudan and Ethiopia.

He had been instrumental in helping find Omar Khalifa and was already a champion of our cause.

Another was Robert Stinson.

Robert was a solicitor by profession and lived his life as a passionate supporter and administrator of athletics both at national and international level. Educated at Cambridge in the early 1950s he had regularly competed in the 220 yard hurdles in the Varsity Match against Oxford University. He was also a member of the world famous Achilles Club whose members belonged to the athletics clubs of both universities.

Robert engaged his passion and administrative skills for the benefit of athletics at international level as a member of the IAAF Juridical Working Group.

Now he was the IAAF Honorary Treasurer.

Robert lived in England. He was a true gentleman and I was delighted when he agreed to be our first Trustee.

With Robert and Hasan's support, we headed off to Rome to meet the head honcho.

Primo Nebiolo was a long jumper and active athlete in his younger days. He later studied law and political science and became a businessman in the construction industry. He became president of the International University Sports Federation, whose remit included the Universiade. He was president of the Italian Athletics Federation and we met him at their headquarters in Rome.

We stayed a few days and conducted numerous meetings with Primo and his team. As I learned more and more, it became obvious that we needed the IAAF.

Fortunately, they seemed to need us as well.

The 2nd World Athletics Championships were being held in the Stadio Olimpico in Rome between August 28 and September 6.

This was to be Nebiolo's home championships.

It was a big deal.

If we could launch our event there, it would be amazing.

Simon and I stayed in a little pension just off the Colosseum. He knew it well and had stayed there before. He also had friends who worked for the UN in Rome and one evening we all met for dinner in a little restaurant just off the Piazza Fontana di Trevi.

One of the guests was Princess Margareta of Romania.

She worked for the International Fund for Agricultural Development where she handled relations with non-governmental organizations and assisted in raising funds for IFAD programs.

She was a laugh and we all got on really well.

I remember telling jokes into the early hours of the morning. She was really funny and I loved the fact that I was sharing my best and worst jokes with a real-life Princess.

We exchanged numbers but never kept in touch.

Too busy.

Meetings continued and finished successfully after a couple of days.

We had the IAAF World Championships as our launch pad.

We had a global school's network to help organise the Sport Aid 1000 and we had the IAAF as a committed partner.

What did we have to give in return?

I agreed to work with Hasan Agabani to fund a children's athletic project in the Sudan.

That was it.

We were on our way again.

When we got back to England I contacted Band Aid to tell them we were doing another Sport Aid.

"We're not getting involved."

"You can't use our name."

"You can't use the logo."

To be fair, I hadn't asked them to be involved.

Neither did I want to use my Sport Aid logo. For me, that represented something special.

Something I did.

My project.

This project was different and would involve Simon from the beginning. It was to include his idea of carnival and music and advocacy. It needed its own identity and Band Aid had just made my job of convincing him much easier.

"We need a new identity. A new logo for Sport Aid '88."

I showed him the message from Band Aid and he agreed.

"So, its Sport Aid '88 and the Sport Aid '88 Trust."

We turned our attention to who would be our other Trustees.

Simon wanted to be co-chairman.

I knew he'd struggled with me being both founder and chairman of Sport Aid. He desperately wanted top or at least equal billing.

It looked like the project was now going ahead and I needed to sit him down and tell him exactly how it was going to happen.

"I'm doing this with you, Simon, because I believe it's the right thing to do but I'm fucked. I haven't got the resources to do another event like last time and I can't commit every waking hour of my life for another year. I've done my time. I'll commit to do the Sport Aid 1000 and the Race Against Time again but that's it. The rest is up to you."

"I'll do it all."

We talked about beneficiaries and Simon still seemed keen to involve others rather than UNICEF alone. We needed both children's and international

185

charities, given the reach of Sport Aid '88 was more than just Africa.

"The Red Cross."

"Save the Children."

"OK, let's talk to them.

I set up a dialogue with the British Red Cross which quickly advanced to meetings in Geneva. The International Committee of the Red Cross (ICRC) is part of the International Red Cross and Red Crescent Movement along with the International Federation of Red Cross and Red Crescent Societies (IFRC) and 190 National Societies. It is the oldest and most honoured organisation within the Movement and one of the most widely recognized organisations in the world, having won three Nobel Peace Prizes in 1917, 1944 and 1963.

They seemed keen to be involved and offered an even bigger global infrastructure than UNICEF.

Save the Children was an international non-governmental organisation that promoted children's rights, provided relief and helped support youngsters in developing countries. It was established in the United Kingdom in 1919 in order to improve the lives of young people through better education, health care and economic opportunities, as well as providing emergency aid in natural disasters, war and other conflicts.

In addition to the UK organisation there were about 29 other national Save the Children organisations which were members of the Save the Children Alliance, a global network of non-profit organisations supporting local partners and Save the Children International in more than 120 countries around the world.

Save the Children were also keen but then, why wouldn't they be? We were riding quite high off the back of our previous success.

In the end, we opted for UNICEF - my choice - and the Red Cross.

We had got to know them both very well.

We needed legal help to put together the Trust and we also needed a good accountant.

One of Band Aid's trustees was John Kennedy. John was a British entertainment lawyer and his profile had risen substantially since Band Aid and Live aid.

Maybe there's another one out there.

I found Clintons.

Clintons was a law firm, based in Covent Garden in Central London. It was also a market leader in the entertainment and creative industries. Its senior partner was John Cohen.

I called him and arranged a meeting.

John was such a lovely guy. He knew what he was talking about and was keen from the outset to give us free advice on how best to set up the charitable trust. We explained our plans and he loved the concept.

"You should also set up a company limited by guarantee. That way you can put on the event and protect the Trust funds."

It was profoundly important advice that stood me in good stead for the year that lay ahead.

John was on board and now we were four.

Babby Sharlton!

He had to be a trustee.

Bobby had been there that day in the Peloponnese although neither he nor I had known it then. A true gentleman who would bring kudos and weight to our Sport Aid '88 Trust.

I called Bobby and he said yes.

Next, an accountant.

One of the biggest accountancy companies in the world was Price Waterhouse. Samuel Lowell Price, an accountant, founded the practice in London in 1849. In 1865 Price went into partnership with William Hopkins Holyland and Edwin Waterhouse. Holyland left shortly afterwards to work alone and the firm was known from 1874 as Price, Waterhouse & Co. The comma was then dropped from the name.

They had a senior partner called Robert Brooke and he was based in their office near Tower Bridge in London.

I called him.

He was very enthusiastic and said yes.

Finally, John Burke-Gaffney of the British Red Cross and Robert Smith of UNICEF.

We had our Trustees.

John Cohen helped put together the company and the Trust Deed. All of the costs were absorbed by his firm, Clintons.

He was an absolute star.

We poured over the Trust Deed for a few days but finally it was agreed and signed on June 8, 1987.

'(a) to alleviate extremes of poverty, disease and malnutrition among children. (b) to provide educational and physical educational facilities for children deprived of or with limited access to such facilities. (c) to provide recreational facilities with the object of improving the conditions of life for such children who by reason of

188

their poverty or social and economic circumstances have need of such facilities.'

Eighty percent will go overseas.

Twenty percent will be spent in the UK.

We found an office in Battersea.

It was above a gymnasium on St John's Hill and comprised just one room with a vaulted ceiling. We rescued some of the staging components from the London Race Against Time which included a huge black and white photograph of two beautiful African children. The picture was about six foot square and we put it up on the wall behind our two desks.

And that's how it all started.

Sport Aid '88.

I found a new flat in Snaresbrook, East London. It wasn't anything special, just a two-bedroom box with a small kitchen and lounge but it got me away from Harrow Road.

Sometimes the smell of traffic fumes there reminded me too much of my old office in Athens. I would have liked to have been nearer my new HQ but there was no way I could afford the rent in Central London.

I bought a second-hand car from a 'Del Boy' dealer just around the corner from my new flat. I didn't know when I bought it, but it quickly turned out to be a money-pit. I took it back to Del Boy to complain but soon realised if I pushed it with him, I would end up the same way as the car – broken. I bit my tongue and spent £2,000 of my precious UNICEF savings fixing it.

Expensive mistake.

Life quickly settled into a new routine. I would drive or train into Battersea each day and spend a couple of hours in the gym. Simon and I negotiated a deal with the management of the club and knowing who we were, they helped us out with the membership fee.

It was an OK time for a while.

There were no real time pressures.

No deadlines.

Just another global event to create and make happen. *Somehow.*

The Sport Aid 1000 was taking shape in my head and we designed a new logo and strapline.

When Geldof started the Race Against Time he shouted 'Change the World.' It seemed the perfect link between the two events and a poignant signature statement for our new project - to help change the world for children everywhere.

Simon worked on his idea for music, carnival and advocacy and before long a plan started to emerge.

The logistics of organising a 1 kilometre race for children in every country and sovereign territory of the world were simply mind-boggling. Sport Aid had been complicated enough but this new challenge took everything to an even more stratospheric level.

The national federations of the IAAF would help, but kids did their track and field sports in the summer. This meant I couldn't do them all at the same time. The only way was to schedule events by country and season.

It was also going to take about a six-week round trip to get children from countries like Vanuatu and other Pacific Islands to the UN and back.

It was complicated.

I spent much of my time with the IAAF poring over logistics and it soon became apparent that the Sport Aid

1000 was going to take a year to stage. There were more than 180 countries in every time zone and climate and I needed all of them to be involved.

This was going to be about all of the world's children.

I had an idea.

We could put on the UK Sport Aid 1000 first. The winners of that race could go to the IAAF World Championships in Rome and launch a year of Sport Aid '88. It would show the UK taking a lead again which, let's face it, it was. I could ask Tessa Sanderson and maybe Linford Christie to join us at the Stadio Olimpico.

They had both become great ambassadors.

It would be a great launch pad.

I'd then have a year to organise all the other Sport Aid 1000 races to find a boy and girl to represent each country. I could fly them to the UN in New York one year later and stage another Race Against Time in support of all of the world's children.

It made sense.

I ran it by Simon and he loved it.

"We can put on a concert to celebrate the launch of a year of sport and carnival."

I felt like saying 'why', but didn't.

It was now mid-March 1987 and the World Championships were in September. We had less than six months to pull it together and that was just to get us to the start line.

After that, it was going to be another year of pain.

We were going to need real manpower to organise this project and it quickly became obvious that volunteers were going to be difficult to find. Sure, we could probably use them for the last month or two but this project was going to take a whole year.

We had TV and radio advocacy to produce.

We had more than 180 countries to co-ordinate.

We had another Race Against Time to stage.

We needed money.

Sport Aid had been funded out of commercial income and sponsorship. Every single penny donated had gone to Africa but we had made it clear that only the proceeds from T-shirts would go to the cause. That way I was able to use some of that money to support staging costs of the event.

Not everyone did it for free.

I had sold more than 600,000 T-shirts grossing £3 million, of which £1 million was used for staging costs. UNICEF had fronted some of that money as it was needed. T-shirt income was all back-ended though and we couldn't wait a year for it this time.

We needed an advance on the funding.

When Simon and I approached this with UNICEF and the Red Cross they both became more hesitant.

UNICEF was showing much reluctance and I didn't understand why.

Was it the prospect of sharing with another organisation?

Had I put their noses out of joint by leaving them?

Was it something to do with Simon?

Something wasn't quite right but I didn't have the time to find out.

I put it down to sour grapes and we went ahead and put together a group of target beneficiaries who all had the same objectives.

Robert Smith and John Burk-Gaffney resigned from the Sport Aid '88 Trust. Neither relished the prospect of funding.

Robert Brooke was well connected and helped to set up a meeting with the manager of Midland Bank in Regents Street, London.

Simon and I went along dressed in our customary jeans and now 'Change the world' T-shirts to meet a number of high powered, suited bankers.

We pitched our project, our rationale for funding, our heritage, our experience of Sport Aid and asked for help.

"We need to fund this thing for a year."

"What security can you offer."

"None."

A few days later we got a call from the bank manager.

We'd got our facility.

They were backing us.

I launched UK Sport Aid 1000 and it took place in schools all across the country throughout June and July. In most cases, it was a simple bolt-on to existing sports days. National Schools Athletics Associations helped co-ordinate regional knockouts and we ended up with the final to decide our UK winners at Crystal Palace.

It was a great evening and I went along with Simon and a few members of our team to watch. The crowd was told of the importance of the 1000 metre race and our kids were cheered and applauded during each of the boys' and girls' races.

Melanie Pickersgill won the girls' race, and James Murphy, a taller leggy young athlete, the boys'.

These two youngsters were now our national ambassadors.

It was a proud moment.

I contacted Downing Street feeling optimistic that our country's premier would be willing to meet our Sport Aid 1000 boy and girl. After all, the kids were going to launch Sport Aid '88 at the World Athletics Championships.

It was the least our Prime Minister could do.

To be fair, I was only expecting a quick handshake and photo call and was pretty surprised to be told we were to be given a guided tour of 10 Downing Street by the Iron Lady herself.

Young James and Melanie had beaten 753,000 children in the UK to win their respective 1000 metre races and they now sat alongside me, proudly dressed in their Change the World T-shirts and tracksuit bottoms.

The kids were really excited as we turned off Trafalgar Square into Whitehall. The car turned right into Downing Street, as the police and security parted the crowds and opened the big iron gates to allow us entry.

The front door to 10 Downing Street has got to be the most famous feature of the building. Large, shiny and bearing the number 10 in large brass plates, it's probably the most photographed door in the world.

It's made of Georgian oak.

We were ushered inside and the big black door closed behind us.

"Please wait."

A few minutes later, the lady herself made her grand entrance. Dressed in a black and red houndstooth jacket and black skirt, pearls and distinctive hairstyle, she held out a hand to greet us.

"Good morning, Chris."

"Good morning, Prime Minister."

We shook hands.

It felt strangely pleasant to hear the Prime Minister call me by my first name. It made me think she knew who I was and I wondered if I was really worthy of such an honour. I might not have agreed with her politics, but this was the UK Prime Minister and you couldn't help admiring her for reaching the top job in the land.

She introduced herself to James and Melanie who looked back at her like two little rabbits caught in headlights.

"Let me show you around."

Beyond the door, black and white marble tiles lined the entrance hall with a guard's chair designed by Chippendale in one corner.

"Policemen used to sit in that to watch the street outside."

This is surreal.

"You can see scratches on the right arm of the chair where their pistols rubbed against the leather."

The kids were transfixed by our tour guide.

Many famous feet had trodden this entrance hall, from world leaders to sporting heroes. This was also where the PM's staff and ministers came each day to make their way to work along the myriad corridors and staircases which seemed to snake around the building.

It was like a Tardis.

With a beautiful wrought iron balustrade and mahogany handrail, a triple stone staircase rose from where we stood to the third floor. We took to the stairs and gazed at the wall full of engravings and photographs of past Prime Ministers. I couldn't help noticing that there were two of Winston Churchill.

The largest State Room was the Pillared Room. According to the Prime Minister it took its name from the twin Ionic pilasters with straight pediments at one end. A portrait of William Pitt was hung over the fire place – her choice.

A Persian carpet covered almost the entire floor. It wasn't the real one apparently. It was a copy of the 16th Century original kept in the Victoria and Albert Museum.

It was sparsely furnished with a few chairs and sofas around the walls. The State Room was used to receive guests en route to the State Dining Room.

Before long, we were all engrossed in our tour. Mindless of the fact our guide was the UK Prime Minister and this was the middle of her working day.

Amazing.

Between the Pillared Room and the State Dining room was a smaller Dining Room. It had a flat unadorned ceiling, simple mouldings and deep window seats and was quite intimate and comfortable. Furnished with a mahogany table, Prime Ministers apparently used the room when dining with family or when entertaining special guests on more personal state occasions.

Today, it was being used again.

"Would you like tea?"

"Thank you, Prime Minister."

"Children?"

They couldn't answer. Their voices long gone.

"I think they would love a cup of tea, Prime Minister."

With that, she left us seated and disappeared. Shortly after she returned with a short, smartly dressed man holding a silver tea tray and tea service.

We sat around the table.

The Prime Minister poured four cups of tea.

While I tried to get my head around the moment, wishing desperately I'd brought a camera, the Prime Minister stood up and announced we were missing something.

"Oh, I know what you would like."

She disappeared again, returning a few minutes later with a tin of Peak Frean biscuits.

She sat down and opened the lid.

"Help yourselves."

We did.

She then shut the lid carefully and placed the tin on the table.

"You always have to seal them otherwise they go orf."

Now I'd seen it all.

My mum and the Prime Minister had something in common.

"Finished?"

We had and the tour continued.

Number 10 is filled with fine paintings, sculptures, busts and furniture. Only a few are permanent features. Most are on loan. About half belong to the Government Art Collection. The remainder are from private collections and from public galleries such as the National Portrait Gallery, the Tate Gallery, the Victoria and Albert Museum and the National Gallery.

Changes are made when a new Prime Minister takes office and redecorates. These refurbishments reflect both individual taste as well as making a political statement.

When Margaret Thatcher arrived in 1979 she insisted that the artwork had to be British and that it celebrated British achievers.

She was proud of the fact.

I was unaware that she was a former chemist and took pleasure in devoting the Small Dining Room to a collection of portraits of British scientists such as Joseph Priestley and Humphry Davy.

It was bizarre.

I was falling in love with Margaret Thatcher.

She gave up at least an hour of her time. She was gracious with the children, complimentary to me and she liked biscuits.

As we neared the end of our tour we congregated outside No 10 for a photo call and, as I had done for our future King and Queen, I had brought a T-shirt for our Prime Minister.

I gave it to Melanie, suggested she give it to Mrs Thatcher and ask for a fiver.

She did.

The PM scrambled in her bag and produced a crisp note.

It was a nice touch.

She thanked Melanie and James and very carefully folded up the shirt so as not to display the graphic.

My hope from the outset was to get the big money shot of Maggie in a Change the World T-shirt. It would have made a great front page.

Now, I didn't mind.

She was excused.

She had made two of my children of the world feel really important and given me a memory I would never forget.

As we gathered for the final photo call, a seasoned hack shouted from across the street.

"Can you get down on your marks with the children, Prime Minister - as if to start a race."

She glared back with a look that could kill.

My tea party with the Iron Lady was over.

She was back on duty.

CHAPTER 15
The Launch

On August 29, the second IAAF World Championships started in the ancient city of Rome. It had been four years since the inaugural event held in Helsinki. In terms of participation, there weren't too many differences. Helsinki brought in 1,572 athletes from 153 member federations while Rome was playing host to 1,451 athletes from 159.

What did differ greatly was the number of spectators.

Over half a million were coming to Rome.

A large increase in the television audience was also expected. The first event received approximately 1.3 billion viewers while Mr Nebiolo's event was expecting two billion.

All these people would see Melanie and James run into the stadium and round the track to start our year of sport for children – Sport Aid '88.

That was the plan.

That was the agreement.

Primo Nebiolo had given his blessing.

As the games opened the hype began to build towards one of the most anticipated duels in athletics history. The USA's Carl Lewis and Canada's Ben Johnson would sprint for gold in the men's 100 metres. On the day, Johnson powered past Lewis, taking both the gold medal and the world record, breaking Lewis's 9.93 with a time of 9.83.

The second IAAF World Championships were a huge success and adulation flooded over Nebiolo.

So much so, he changed his mind about our plans.

Now, not wanting anything to detract from him and the successful 'Primo' World Championships, he reneged on the agreement for us to launch our event from the Stadium on the final day.

On September 6, 1987, he shut us out of the Olympic Stadium.

We weren't told until the very last minute and were forced to create an outside event.

Fortunately, Ron Pickering was in Rome commentating for the BBC. He had already agreed to help us light the Sport Aid '88 flame in the stadium.

Understanding our dilemma, he joined Melanie and James along with Tessa Sanderson, Linford Christie and our TV crew to enable us to get us some kind of live feed back to London to rescue our launch event.

We filmed it outside the stadium.

I couldn't fucking believe it.

The man had delivered the best World Championships in history and decided unilaterally he wasn't going to let anyone steal his thunder.

Not even two young kids who represented the UK and were setting out their challenge to all the world's children.

Back in London, Simon's music concert at the QPR stadium in London went as planned.

Floella Benjamin and Gary Davies were our party hosts with Janice Long and Simon Bates from Radio 1 and Carolyn Marshall and Jake Abraham from the BBC show *'It's Wicked'*.

The line-up of bands at the Loftus Road Stadium included Curiosity Killed the Cat, ABC, Wet Wet Wet, Pepsi and Shirlie, Erasure, Labi Siffre, Then Jericho, Princess and Paul King. Many other stars including John Craven were there to give support to our cause.

I had always doubted the need for music in the project and now that the important part had been fucked up, I questioned it even more.

The launch of Sport Aid '88 had become just a concert.

I had ended up with a music event to launch a year of sport.

It really pissed me off.

The IAAF officials were hugely embarrassed and in particular, my new Trustee, Robert Stinson. He tried to apologise and explain Nebiolo's actions, but found it impossible.

There was no explanation.

I felt like telling them all to fuck off but, unfortunately, the whole project had been launched and we were now totally committed.

I needed all the national federations.

I needed their links to all the schools' athletic associations.

Without that infrastructure it would take forever to create a new network.

I just didn't have the time.

I bit my lip and carried on.

With the launch out of the way, Simon turned his attention to his programming. His plan was to produce advocacy videos and radio programming to demonstrate the Silent Emergency and help promote Sport Aid '88 and the next Race Against Time.

Many developing countries could not afford to buy quality TV programmes and so the idea was to give it away for free.

We started a dialogue with the express parcel delivery service DHL. The company was based in the United States, but had grown significantly. With a global network in more than 180 countries and territories across the globe, DHL offered solutions for an almost infinite number of logistical needs.

DHL could deliver our programming to TV networks all over the world.

It had a London office and I contacted them.

Simon and I went along to pitch our plan.

"Sport Aid '88 is a year-long programme of carnival and sport for children everywhere. Fifteen million children will die this year from diseases we can immunise against. We want to tell the world that. We want to change that. We're producing free TV advocacy programming and we need your help to deliver it to TV networks all across the world."

It worked.

They loved it and agreed to support us by providing free distribution of all our TV and radio programming.

DHL was our first official sponsor.

Simon set about his tasks and I worked with the IAAF to schedule and plan the national Sport Aid 1000 races. He organised a tie-in with our own radio Sport Aid and John Craven's *Newsround*.

Newsround was a BBC children's news programme which had run continuously since April 1972. It was one of the world's first television news magazines aimed specifically at children. Initially commissioned as a short series by the BBC Children's Department, which held editorial control, its facilities were provided by BBC News.

The programme was aimed at six to 12-year-olds.

We launched a Sport Aid Roving Reporters competition on Newsround and invited children to submit a one minute audio tape on how they would help change the world.

It was a massive success and we set up a judging panel with John Craven to review all the tape submissions and decide the finalists.

Thanks to the BBC we were offered a film crew to travel with a boy and girl finalist to each continent of the world to report on a specific children's issue. The finalists' reports were going to be aired on *Newsround*.

The competition lasted a couple of months before the kids took off on their global assignments.

I'll never forget the face of our winner - a young girl.

She went to Africa and Burkina Faso and interviewed president Thomas Sankara. At the end of her report she looked directly at the camera and said:

"Before I went to Africa I thought people were only dying. Now I know they're alive as well."

It still makes the hair on the back of my neck stand up.

What makes it even more powerful was she was the last person to interview Sankara. The very next month he and 12 other officials were killed by an armed group in a coup d'état organised by his former colleague Blaise Compare.

It was a sad time and I couldn't forget the image of the great man leading his entire cabinet and 25,000 bare-footed Africans down the dusty street of Ouagadougou.

I tried to put the Nebiolo fuck up behind me but it had taken its toll on my enthusiasm. I felt depressed and needed something to light that spark again.

I didn't want the music element or the advocacy to overshadow the run. For me, the Race Against Time was still the most important part but I needed to freshen it up somehow.

Do something different.

I had a meeting with the fulfilment house that had processed all my Sport Aid entries and despatched T-shirts to runners all over the UK.

I needed them again and we talked about how best to improve the process.

They gave me a tour of the factory and showed off their new machinery for processing bank letters.

"We work for most of the major UK banks. This piece of equipment reads data from a computer and then prints relevant text on to individual letters."

Customers' data had been keyed in and the printing machine was reading that and printing personalised letters. It put on a name and address, the surname again after the salutation, then it typed other specific data into the body of the letter. Numbers and account names were all different

Every A4 letter was different.

I had an idea.

"Can you print a race number?"

"What do you mean?"

"Could you print a number in a big font that would be sequential. Say, from one to 20 million?"

"Sure."

"Could you also print a name and other specific information on other parts of the paper?"

"We can print whatever you want. It's just down to what information you capture."

It was my Sport Aid '88 eureka moment and suddenly I was energised again.

Nebiolo became a distant memory as I had a fresh idea for a new Race Against Time.

I got back to the office and started to scribble out some designs.

A large race number taking up most of the space on an A4 page but with a perforated strip down one side. On that strip, details of the race venue, a map and how to get there.

It was brilliant.

I could devise a race number that would start at one and finish wherever it finished.

We could have a runner in Hyde Park with number 100 running next to someone with number 20,000,000. Or we could have a runner in Beijing with race number 10,000,000 while the runner with 10,000,001 was in Sydney.

What's more, the runner's race number would be specific to the race they had registered for. All the details could be printed on it and could be torn off and kept separate.

It would be a truly global race number.

Like a petition, giving everyone a sense of the scale and enormity of what we were trying to achieve.

Maybe I could give Omar number one?

Over the next few days I worked solidly on my global race numbers checking with the fulfilment house to ensure they could do everything I wanted.

The paper needed to be water-resistant and stronger than conventional A4 paper.

I explored samples and found a solution.

It could all work but data capture was going to be the important element. As long as we recorded all the relevant information, I could produce the best sequential race numbers ever seen.

I needed computers.

ICL had helped on Sport Aid and I contacted them again.

International Computers Limited (ICL) was formed in 1968 as a part of the Industrial Expansion Act of the Wilson Labour Government. ICL had been an initiative of Tony Benn, the Minister of Technology, to create a British computer industry to compete with major world manufacturers like IBM. ICL represented the last step in a series of mergers that had taken place in the industry since the late 1950s. ICL was concentrated in the United Kingdom, with its corporate headquarters in the London borough of Putney.

I went to see them.

They liked the idea a great deal and agreed to support it.

We were going to need computers as we grew and ICL was now going to supply them. They would help me with the data capture for our new race numbers and provide all the equipment needed.

ICL became our second global sponsor.

We had raised a little money from the launch and the Trustees had allocated the funds to specific projects.

Some were in the UK and one in particular was a British sub-aqua snorkel training scheme for physically handicapped children in inner city areas throughout Yorkshire and Humberside.

The president of the British Sub-Aqua Club (BSAC) was my old mucker Prince Charles and he agreed to come along and receive my cheque.

It was good to see him again and he seemed very appreciative of our contribution. He told me he was very impressed with Sport Aid and was delighted I was doing another project.

I just loved the fact he called me Chris.

Simon's programming was starting to take shape and the first Sport Aid '88 Global Report was nearly ready to air. His idea was to produce a report from every continent highlighting sport, music and children's issues from each.

The first was Latin America.

He had finished the opening and closing credits and they looked pretty good.

He had children of different ethnicities taking part in an arts and crafts group painting our logo in different shapes and colours. The resulting artwork comprised a spinning globe around which a sash with the legend Sport Aid '88 would be wrapped.

It was our logo and it looked OK.

We had a young presenter called Sunie Fletcher and she began by introducing Brazil and the story of football.

It showed kids from the slums of Brazil playing the game and it explained how football was perceived as a way out of poverty for most children. It showed the passage to superstardom and demonstrated how few children ever made it.

"Thirty million children live in poverty and seven million are abandoned to live on the streets. Of a population of 130 million, 90 million do not have enough to eat."

It was an incredible statement and it was true.

The programme moved on to show Trinidad's carnival.

Simon's love.

Young Trinidadians playing and singing in Change the World T-shirts, then more images of carnival and a child singing at a disabled school.

The Global Report explained what Sport Aid '88 was all about and focused on Rio's street children: kids occupying half-finished buildings and a car park.

It introduced the Brazilian Red Cross and the great work they were doing there and it culminated with an image of a little girl standing alone in a wasteland.

"This is Christina . . . there are 36,000,000 others like her in Brazil today."

It was good.

I told Simon I liked it and I really did.

The programme looked professional and it got a point across. He had produced it with the help of numerous people and organisations and had done an amazing job of getting them all to come on board.

Visnews, Sony Broadcast, Sony (UK), Ampex, Samuelson Film Services, Samuelson Lighting Ltd, Telefex, B. Vinten, Mag Masters Sound Studios, Molinare, Cliktraks, Eel Pie Studios, Trinidad Tourist Board, Dominica Tourist Board, Brazil Red Cross, B.W.I.A., Varig Airlines, Walpax Transport and the Hotel Gloria in Brazil.

I was grateful to them all and just hoped people would watch it.

While in Rio the film crew ran into Ronnie Biggs.

Ronald Arthur 'Ronnie' Biggs was an English criminal, known for his role in the Great Train Robbery of 1963, for his escape from prison in 1965, for living as a fugitive for 36 years and for his various publicity stunts while in exile in Brazil.

He signed a Sport Aid T-shirt for me and it said 'Keep on running Chris', signed Ronnie Biggs.

I still have it.

Simon got us a deal with the BBC kids' programme, *It's Wicked*, which aired live on Saturday mornings.

Looking back, the show was a diabolical attempt by the BBC to get 'hip' after seven years of Mark Curry. It failed to get a second series but that didn't matter. It gave us a prime-time slot to promote Sport Aid '88 and our Silent Emergency.

It was made on location around the country, the first four being in Liverpool, Arundel, London and Newcastle-upon-Tyne. The presenters were Jake Abraham and Carolyne Marshall. Each week they would arrive in a red 1960s Ford Mustang on to a set resembling a drive-in diner. Other regulars on the show were Cheryl Baker, David English, Nick Sanders and the omnipresent Paul King of 'King' fame.

After a couple of shows it was decided that Paul King and a kid of our choice would head up a weekly live Sport Aid '88 slot.

Given our project was about kids and the world's children taking the lead, it was important we had a child who could get the Sport Aid '88 message across.

I don't know why Simon chose Martin Goldsmith's son to be our representative but he did. Paul Goldsmith was a good-looking articulate boy and just happened to be the nephew of the great Harvey Goldsmith.

I liked young Paul and thought he would actually make a good double-header with Paul King. Because of his father, he was well versed in Sport Aid and could at least talk about it without too much scripting.

After a few dry runs, young Paul and older Paul made their debut live on Saturday morning television. Simon and his rapidly expanding production crew travelled up north to be on set.

I watched it from home.

Little Paul and Big Paul were playing their respective parts and things were going quite well when all of a sudden Little Paul forgot his lines. He hesitated for a second, looked flustered and then said it.

"Shit."

Our young Sport Aid '88 ambassador said 'shit' on live television.

Children's live television.

Shit.

I called Simon on his mobile.

Unsurprisingly, he didn't answer. I guessed he had his hands full at that time.

Later it emerged that we actually got some good publicity out of it and Little Paul was now fully recovered from his error and subsequent meltdown.

I couldn't help thinking his uncle would feel very proud.

It was kind of funny.

I met up with Little Paul about 15 years later when he wasn't quite so little anymore.

He thanked me for that opportunity and in particular his 'shit' moment on live television. Apparently, his street cred went through the roof at school and he was hailed a hero. It held him in good stead for the remainder of his school days and I imagine he had many girlfriends.

Can't remember what happened to Big Paul.

The Saturday TV spots continued and we enlisted the services of Jake Abraham and Carolyn Marshall to shoot a music video to promote the Sport Aid 1000.

We chose a comprehensive school in south east London and took our crew along to meet a few others who had offered to help.

Erasure had agreed to re-record *It Doesn't Have to Be*, which they released in February 1987. It had been issued as a single six weeks before the release of the duo's second album, *The Circus*. Following their No 2 UK placing of *Sometimes, It Doesn't Have to B*e became Erasure's second Top 20 hit in the UK.

It was a great song and the lyrics worked well for our message.

They changed the middle lyrics, pertinent to apartheid, to 'you can affect the world you live in – change the world.'

It became the chorus.

Tessa Sanderson, Anneka Rice, Glenn Hoddle and a few others also turned up to be in the video.

Glenn Hoddle was leaving Tottenham to pursue a career overseas. I sat in the OB truck with him and stared out at the playing fields where we were filming.

We talked.

He was excited at the prospect of playing European level football. English clubs had been banned after

Heysel. He had just joined AS Monaco and was about to head off to his new life overseas.

There was a football in the truck.

"Fancy a kick about, Glenn?"

"OK."

I stepped down from the truck and placed a couple of jumpers on the ground as goalposts.

I went in goal.

It was a surreal moment.

I thought back to when I was a kid and did the very same thing in my back garden but with my friend Trevor from down the lane.

Glenn Hoddle was better.

Sorry Trevor.

Time ticked by and our team started to outgrow the Battersea office. I called Chris Patten and asked for our old office back.

Fortunately, it was still available and we moved in, along with some of the old team. It was strange being back on such familiar territory with a familiar project but I kept reminding myself this one was different.

This one wasn't all my baby.

The Sport Aid '88 Trust would meet every month and we would consider projects to support. We started to raise money from our early exploits and preferred to spend it quickly on those that were most needed.

All the trustees made an effort to attend. Even Bobby Charlton who was a busy man and had to come down from Manchester each time.

I loved Babby Sharlton.

CHAPTER 16
Déjà Vu

Back in the old office Simon and I sat in exactly the same place and divided up the office as before. In front was the press office and Nick Cater had returned to take up his old chair. To my left now was all of Simon's crew. His TV and radio production team occupied most of the space.

ICL started to install a new computer system for us. There was a work station on each desk connected to a central hub which would record all activities on tape.

The network gave us something new.

It was called email.

Email enabled us to send messages to each other without having to get up. It was revolutionary but, ironically, the novelty only served to reduce our performance capacity temporarily while everyone in the office sent funny, rude and irrelevant messages to each other.

We'd got mail.

As the year ticked by the team continued to grow.

Happily for me, Will Chapman and his crew came back for another go. Will assumed his same position both in terms of office space and responsibilities.

Many of the race organisers from Sport Aid had signed up to be part of the new Sport Aid '88. They'd got so much from the first one that they simply couldn't resist being involved again.

The USA however remained largely untouched.

Given Hands Across America, I had only one race in the whole of the USA in 1986 and that was in New York. Fred Lebow had agreed to do that again but I needed more.

The USA was a big place.

CARE USA had expressed an interest in being involved and was a global leader within a worldwide movement dedicated to ending poverty. It was known pretty much everywhere for its 'unshakeable commitment to the dignity of people.' CARE's programmes in the developing world addressed a broad range of topics, including emergency response, food security, water and sanitation, economic development, climate change, agriculture, education and health. CARE also advocated at a local, national, and international level for policy change and the rights of poor people. Within each of these areas, it focused particularly on empowering and meeting the needs of women and girls and promoting gender equality. CARE USA was happy to distribute funds to projects supporting children only and in return, assist with the US Race Against Time.

I asked Will to pick out the major cities and set up meetings with the key race organisers in each.

He did and we got on a plane and went to see them.

We flew into Boston first and ran a 10 km route along the edge of the Charles River before meeting up with the Boston race director.

We were there one day and then flew to Philadelphia, where we ran another 10 km and had another meeting.

Then it was another plane to San Francisco. A longer flight which enabled us both to catch up on some sleep.

We arrived in the evening for the next day's Bay to Breakers run.

This was an annual footrace in San Francisco, normally on the third Sunday of May. The phrase 'Bay to Breakers' reflects the fact that the race starts at the northeast end of the downtown area, adjacent to San Francisco Bay and runs west through the city to finish at the Great Highway, where breakers crash on to Ocean Beach. The complete course is 7.46 miles (12.01 km).

Bay to Breakers is well known for the many participants who wear fancy dress. In 1986, it was officially the world's largest annual footrace with 110,000 participants.

Another 100,000 plus runners joined Will and I at the start the next morning.

It was a beautiful day.

The sun shone down as you would expect on a Californian May Day and the trees were in full bloom.

It was an amazing sight.

We both walked and jogged for about half an hour before we even got to the start.

The San Francisco Fire Department were fielding about eight runners and they were all dressed in full uniform. Each had on his fireman's helmet with engine number. It looked like a race number and I remember thinking it was more striking than mine.

More impressively, they carried a yoke between them. Slung below was a 56-gallon keg of beer. Feeding pipes snaked their way along the yoke arms from the keg to feed the mouths of its thirsty carriers.

Will and I joined them and finished the race a bit worse for wear.

Best run I ever did.

From San Francisco, it was off to Atlanta where we did another 10 km and met with another race organiser. In every case the reaction was positive, albeit seed capital was needed in most places.

US race organisers didn't do it for nothing.

That evening, Will and I had dinner with an old chum of his. He had been living in the US for several years and was a doctor.

Not just any doctor.

He was THE doctor who was called out to Mr Elvis Presley when he died.

He explained how he found Elvis. Trousers round his ankles, slumped forward on a toilet seat. The guy was really interesting and I liked him even though he had single-handedly destroyed my image of the King.

We shared a few more stories before heading off to bed. Will and I had one more run to do the next day and it was in Miami.

We caught the early morning flight from Hartsfield-Jackson airport and settled back in our seats to catch up on some more sleep. I couldn't help noticing a strange vibration every time the plane increased speed. After a short while the pilot sensed the problem and kept speeding up and slowing down to increase and then isolate the vibration. Finally, the news came. We were heading back to Atlanta.

Something had come loose.

We finally got to Miami after boarding another plane a few hours later but we missed our Miami run. So we just met with the race organiser there and managed to convince him to stage a Race Against Time.

It was a good trip and set the basis for the USA runs.

CARE USA came on board and agreed to manage and seed all the races where necessary in return for some of the donations.

A deal was done and we launched their participation from their New York offices.

Madonna and Mike Tyson agreed to be at the press conference and CARE USA was very happy indeed.

On the day of the press conference Tyson was late showing up.

Madonna called him on her mobile phone and told him to hurry up.

Not bad for a little lady.

Tyson was about to take on Michael Spinks to become the undisputed world heavyweight boxing champion.

Back in the UK we were stepping up a gear.

Simon's global reports were in full swing and we started Radio Sport Aid to produce advocacy and Public Service Announcements (PSAs) for the event. Radio was becoming a forgotten means of communication yet in much of the developing world, it was the only medium for advocacy and PSAs.

We needed to maximise this so Virgin Radio's John Revell joined us.

John - better known as Johnny Boy - went on to start Ginger Productions with Chris Evans a few later years but for now, he was our man at Radio Sport Aid.

I liked John and he helped produce some great radio programming for our cause.

As the momentum intensified we created events and opportunities to help build the profile of Sport Aid '88 and the forthcoming Race Against Time. Many of the

Sport Aid 1000 races had happened and many more were starting around the world as the season shifted. Spring and Summer had returned to the northern hemisphere and it was time for Europe, North America and parts of Asia to begin.

Almost simultaneously, some bright spark in the office came up with the idea of putting a banner on the front of Battersea Power Station. It overlooked the Thames Embankment and a lot of traffic passed there every day.

It wasn't a bad idea so I called John Broome.

Leisure entrepreneur John Broome had ambitious plans to create an indoor attraction at Battersea Power Station, featuring dozens of white-knuckle rollercoaster rides, a huge ice rink, a waterfall and a vast oceanarium big enough to be explored by mini-submarines. Other planned features included six themed floors of cinemas, cultural experiences and restaurants each representing one of the earth's continents. There was to be a Tivoli gardens style pleasure park by the river, a conference venue and an upmarket shopping mall. There would even be balloon rides inside the cavernous atrium. One of the most ambitious ideas was for a direct bullet train rail link to Victoria Station with passengers whisked to the attraction in three and a half minutes.

John Broome owned Battersea Power Station, he had big plans and he liked publicity.

"Sure, let's do it."

We planned to hang a 'Change the World' banner across the two big chimneys overlooking the Thames but it emerged it would act like a giant sail and probably send the entire power station down the river on a windy day!

Instead we created two massive Sport Aid '88 logos, each with a telephone number and hung them under each chimney. Between the huge structures we strung a 'Change the World' banner.

It went into the history books at the time as one of the biggest banners in the world.

A load of us went to Battersea on the day and the press lined up on the Embankment to record the momentous occasion. We had enlisted the help of rock climbers, mountaineers and steeplejacks to erect the enormous advertisements. As the central banner unfurled a huge crowd clapped and cheered. John Broome had flown in on his helicopter and was keen to get in front of as many cameras as possible.

I don't think he knew too much about Sport Aid '88 up to that point and he quickly started to quiz Simon and I as the cameras flashed.

"… and after the Race Against Time we're putting on the First World Carnival in locations all around the world."

"Really? Where are you doing the UK event?"

"Probably Hyde Park."

"Why don't you do it at Alton Towers?"

Before we knew it, Simon and I were being bundled into his helicopter and flown off to Alton Towers. Along the way, John Broome pitched its virtues as a first world carnival venue.

"You can stage your concert right in front of the house and the lake."

It actually sounded great and I liked the connection between the children of the world and a theme park.

Mr Broome seemed very keen.

We landed by the house at Alton Towers about an hour later and John took us on a personal guided tour of the park. Close behind were his bodyguards watching every step. As the day passed the weather changed. Instead of heading back to London by helicopter, we got a ride by car. It took hours and we both sat in the back twiddling our fingers, watching the clock and listening to the radio.

That was when the *Chicken Song* came on.

The *Chicken Song* was a novelty number from the British satirical comedy television programme *Spitting Image*. I found out afterwards that the lyrics were written by Rob Grant and Doug Naylor and the music by Philip Pope, who also produced the song. It was a parody of summer holiday disco songs such as *Agadoo* and *Do the Conga*, which were in vogue during the mid-1980s.

We arrived back in London quite late and I couldn't stop humming that fucking tune.

Annoying as it was, it gave the production team of Granada TV's *The Funny Side* an idea a few weeks later.

They called us.

"Let's do a parody of football songs for Sport Aid '88?"

Football songs, like *Blue is the Colour* were absolute shit and they thought it would be very funny if they could capture that in a similarly amusing way and raise some more money for Sport Aid '88.

I agreed and they called Rob Grant, Doug Naylor and Phil Pope to ask if they would write us a song.

They did.

It was called *The Worst Song Ever* and it was brilliant.

We asked a bunch of football managers to sing it and within a week or so most of the first division managers met at Olympic Studios in London to record it and shoot a video.

The Boss Squad was made up of Dave Bassett, Billy Bingham, Jack Charlton, Brian Clough, Alex Ferguson, Bobby Gould, George Graham, Bobby Robson, John Sillett, Jim Smith, Graham Taylor, Terry Venables and Lawrie McMenemy.

In support were the England football team, Ian St John and Jimmy Greaves from TV's *St and Greavsie* and their colleagues from ITV and BBC sport including John Motson.

The video was hilarious.

Cloughie appeared alongside his *Spitting Image* puppet. They all played electric guitars, Subbuteo and even Cheryl Baker got in on the act.

The record with *The Worst Song Ever* on the A side and the *Sick as a Parrot Remix* on the B side was finally released. Lawrie McMenemy went on TV to launch it. It was a great success, helping to raise more money and publicity for the Race Against Time.

Our relationship with the Red Cross continued to build. Simon and I were invited to Beijing to meet with the Chinese Red Cross to see how best China could get involved.

We flew out courtesy of British Airways again and stayed in a central hotel near Tiananmen Square. The city square in the centre of Beijing was named after the Tiananmen Gate of Heavenly Peace, located to its north and separating it from the Forbidden City. The square contained the Monument to the People's Heroes, the National Museum of China, the Mausoleum of Mao Zedong and the Great Hall of the People.

We were greeted by the Chinese Red Cross at their offices in Beijing and invited to meet some very important dignitaries at a reception in the Great Hall.

The Great Hall of the People is the state building located at the western edge of the Square in Beijing. It was used for legislative and ceremonial activities by the People's Republic of China (PRC) government and the ruling Communist Party of China.

The Great Hall functioned as the meeting place for the Chinese Parliament and the National People's Congress. The latter convened every year along with the national session of the Chinese People's Political Consultative Conference. It was also the meeting place of the National Congress of the Communist Party of China.

We arrived at the main gate where the national emblem of the PRC hangs and were ushered into what I think was the State Guest Hall.

We both wore our jeans, a Change the World T-shirt and trainers and looked really colourful against the matching grey uniforms of our hosts.

To this day I still do not know who they were. I was meeting many important people around this time and my ability to recall all of them was becoming as grey as my current host's attire.

For all I know it was Deng Xiaoping with his small entourage who sat in the grand state chairs positioned so exactly in front of us.

I was invited to take an empty one.

I was then told that the important man would speak on behalf of the People's Republic of China and only when he'd finished, could I reply.

I had no idea we were doing this and couldn't understand a word he was saying. A small diminutive translator tried desperately to keep up with proceedings and I got every other word.

When he finished, the floor was mine.

I turned towards the man who could have been the paramount leader of China and thanked him for his hospitality. I also thanked him for the participation of all of China in Sport Aid '88 and looked forward to his country taking a lead on September 11.

I finished and there was just silence.

Tough crowd.

The important man then nodded and he and his entourage stood.

We shook hands and with that he was gone.

The Red Cross men were gushing with pride as we were all quickly ushered back outside on to the square.

I think that went well – whoever he was.

Back in London, the office was growing again as we marched towards our date with destiny for a second time.

Things were going really well when all of a sudden, shit happened.

The UK was hit by a postal strike.

It was the country's first national strike in 17 years and no one saw it coming. It began after Royal Mail postal workers walked out in protest over bonuses being paid to recruit new workers in London and the South East. As a result, postal deliveries throughout the United Kingdom were disrupted.

The mechanism for registering people for the Race Against Time relied entirely on post. The public sent in race applications by mail. We fulfilled them and sent their race number and sponsorship forms back the same way.

We discussed the strike at the Trustees meeting and agreed we couldn't do anything about it. We weren't going to change the mind of hundreds of postal workers. It seemed they had a genuine grievance. All we could do was hope it would soon be over and we agreed to try to find other options in case it wasn't.

It was a really worrying time and I hoped it would be over very soon.

The Tears for Fears record had worked really well for Sport Aid in 1986 but there was no Marsha Hunt around this time to organise it for me.

I really needed another pop video and now was the time to get it out there. One record I really loved was the one that kicked off Live Aid.

Rockin' all over the World.

I remember humming *running all over the world* for days after Live Aid and in a way, it was funny I hadn't done that first time round.

The power of Marsha.

I couldn't get it out of my head and I hoped others couldn't either.

We gave the band a call.

Status Quo was and still is an English rock band playing a brand of boogie rock. The group originated in The Spectres, founded by schoolboys Francis Rossi and Alan Lancaster in 1962. After a number of line-up changes, including the introduction of Rick Parfitt in 1967, the band became The Status Quo and then Status Quo in 1969.

They had more chart hits in the UK than any other rock band. These included *Pictures of Matchstick Men* in 1968, *Whatever You Want* in 1979, *In the Army Now* in 1986 and of course, *Rockin' all over the World*.

The boys were right up for it.

They came to the office which gave the team a great lift.

Rick Parfitt, Francis Rossi, in fact all of them were very gracious with their support of Sport Aid '88 and their contribution made an amazing difference.

They agreed to go back into the studio and re-record the lyrics.

We shot a great pop video to support it and released it as a single.

The boys appeared on TV to launch the song. We had a great set design with a huge Sport Aid '88 logo behind them and they wore our Change the World T-shirts.

I had planned a big race in Belfast and the Lord Mayor had offered us a double decker bus in his parade to help promote it. All we had to do was put on some banners and fill it with a few celebrities.

I headed off to Belfast the night before. It was my first time in the city and I went out for dinner with some of the race organisers.

I was on my main course when the bomb went off.

It was three buildings down from the restaurant and it shook violently. I couldn't help notice how everyone just carried on as usual.

It was just another day in Belfast.

I didn't mention it when I joined up with Jermaine Jackson the next day.

Jermaine was the fourth child of the Jackson family. I met his sister La Toya a few years later and Michael at the UN for Mickey Mouse's 60th birthday.

For now though, he was the only member of the Jackson Five I had ever met and I was ever so slightly star struck.

I grew up with the Jackson Five.

I confess I spent most of my time on the Mayor's bus talking to Jermaine and didn't notice when we left the route to avoid a low bridge. Jermaine and I were sitting upstairs when the first rock flew past his ear and crashed into the seat in front. I looked behind and a bunch of kids was running after the bus hurling stones, bricks and anything else they could get their hands on. In a bizarre way, I was glad it had something to do with Northern Ireland's troubles.

For a second I'd thought, 'Shit, these kids sure hate the Jackson Five!'

The onslaught continued for a few minutes. We made our escape unscathed down the stairs to cover. Noticing our dilemma, the driver had already put his foot down and we soon re-joined the safety of the parade further up.

It was an experience.

As soon as the parade finished, I was escorted by police motorcyclist back to the airport. It had been a strange day but at least I finished it feeling important.

As we got closer and closer the vibe in the office seemed to increase exponentially. We were filling all the space again and more. News of the Sport Aid 1000s was coming in from all over the world and we were close to knowing the final numbers - 110 countries had already taken part and were sending 220 children to the United Nations via us in London.

Kids from Vanuatu and other Pacific islands had already set off.

It was a long way away.

By September 5 the Post Office industrial action had spread with a quarter of the country's postal workers now on strike. By the following week, it had spread throughout the British mainland. No mail was being delivered and, in order to ease the backlog of post, bosses at Royal Mail placed an embargo on the delivery of overseas mail.

We hadn't received even one bag of mail and I was quietly shitting myself.

If this went on we could have a real problem. I continued to explore other ways to register people for the race.

Banks, building societies and Woolworths all agreed to stock registration forms. We also got them printed in regional papers, but this didn't really help. We needed to get race numbers, T-shirts and sponsorship forms to people before the race.

I arranged for entry and sponsorship forms to be placed in the banks and building societies.

Our only real option was to pray that the strike would end soon. Hopefully, people would still register in spite of it.

It was a message we tried to get out by hell and high water.

Simon and I did a lot of press around this time to try to get our message across. TV, radio and kids' shows where we could.

The Children's Channel - also known as TCC - was on air almost exclusively to cable households owing to the low proliferation of domestic satellite dishes in the UK and Europe at the time. Originally operated by Starstream who were backed by British Telecom, DC Thomson, Thames Television and Thorn EMI, they had a programme called *Roustabout* and it aired in the UK, Ireland, Benelux nations and Scandinavia.

We went on it along with the Oliver Twins.

The Oliver Twins were two British brothers, Philip and Andrew, known for their work as video game developers.

They started developing professional computer games while still at school and contributed their first type-in game to a magazine in 1983. They worked with the publishers Codemasters for a number of years following their first collaboration *Super Robin Hood*. Most notably, they created the *Dizzy* series of games and many of Codemasters' popular *Simulator* Series.

At one point during the 1980s it was reported that seven percent of all UK games sales were attributable to the Oliver Twins.

Shortly after the show they gave me a call.

"Can we develop a game for Sport Aid '88?"

"You bet you can."

The game came out a few months later, made for the Commodore 64/ZX Spectrum and Amstrad CPC video games. It was called *The Race Against Time for Sport Aid '88 by the Oliver Twins*.

The background music was a modified version of Peter Gabriel's *Games without Frontiers*.

It was quite brilliant and all proceeds came to us.

Sport Aid '88 was now pushing the edge of the technological envelope.

One week before the Race Against Time the office was buzzing and not just because we were a little busy.

Omar Khalifa was coming in.

Today we were printing Omar's race number which I had reserved for him.

We had developed a mobile race registration vehicle. It was a just an ordinary van, but it had an integrated

ICL computer, screens and printer built into it. The van looked great with Sport Aid '88 branding and we took it around schools and local UK events to sign up runners and promote the Race against Time.

Today it was at our office in Waterloo so that we could register and print race number 1.

It was great to welcome Omar's beautiful smile back into the office and we hugged it out like two long lost brothers.

The press had been invited and there was a good turnout.

Omar stood next to the portable registration computer as we tapped in his details.

This time he wasn't running.

Instead Omar Khalifa was going to light the cauldron outside the UN to start the world running on behalf of the children of the world.

I hit a button and his number printed out.

Number 1.

Everyone applauded and the press got their pictures.

I hit the button again and my number printed out.

Number 2.

It was my lucky number and I'd saved it from the start.

Everyone clapped.

Shit, I AM a number 2.

CHAPTER 17
Sport Aid '88 and The First World Carnival

It was the penultimate day and it was going to be a long one.

The children of the world had now arrived and were staying with chaperones in hotels all across London.

Today we were leaving for New York and tomorrow they would take their seats within the United Nations General Assembly hall.

Big day.

I was nervous, but excited.

I would see John again and it had been a while. UNICEF were hosting the children at the UN and my dear friend John Anderson had been instrumental in organising that part of it, again.

Simon and I headed out of the office to Hyde Park.

Will Chapman and his team had already set up the park for the Race Against Time. They had built a stage for the First World Carnival.

No problems this time with the Bailiff and no need to call Charles.

Simon's carnival was to immediately follow the race and London was just one of the venues.

The staging had been completed and it was where we met all the children for the first time.

We sat on the edge of the stage and looked out at these young people.

Our young ambassadors.

The children of the world.

For the first time, I felt a real sense of pride for Sport Aid '88.

All of these children had taken part and won their national races.

They all knew what Sport Aid '88 was about.

They all understood what the Silent Emergency was.

They knew why they were here.

I stood on the stage and looked across a sea of faces that represented almost every country in the world.

"Tomorrow you will represent the children of the world at the United Nations in New York. Do not underestimate what you have achieved and never underestimate your ability to affect the world in which you live."

It was liberating.

Empowering.

A profound moment for them and for me.

I handed over to Simon to discuss logistics and headed back to the office.

As in 1986, the race would start at 11 am Eastern Standard Time tomorrow and there was a lot to rehearse.

And a plane to catch.

The postal strike was still on and now in its tenth day. Press reports indicated that an agreement might be reached next week but that was too late for us.

Not one bag of mail had arrived.

I'd asked senior officials at the Royal Mail if we could at least look in the nearby sorting office to see what was waiting for us but they refused.

I was getting really worried and could only pray that the strike would end soon.

We had a Boeing 747 to take everyone to New York.

It was scheduled to depart Gatwick at 3pm and there was still much work to do.

The hype had built like last time although the buzz in the UK wasn't the same.

I had expected that and while a little disappointed, I felt buoyed by what was going on overseas in places like China and Malaysia.

I finished my last press and radio commitments and headed to the airport only to discover we had another big problem.

Our eager passengers massed in a noisy queue, trying to check in while just one of our team stood behind a desk holding hundreds of passports.

Someone thought taking control of all the passports was a good idea. We were now having to reunite them with each of their respective owners.

It was bedlam.

"Why the fuck did you take all their passports?"

Not sure why I said it because it didn't help.

Our scheduled take off time quickly passed and only a quarter of our passengers had checked in.

It was time to take over.

We sorted the passports by name into alphabetical order and then dealt with each passenger on a first come, first served basis.

Slowly, the queue got smaller until eventually, like a captain on a sinking ship, I was the last to leave that frenzied check-in desk to find my boarding gate.

My passengers were accounted for and our flight finally took off. . .

Three hours late.

I made a quick call to warn the guys in New York and made my way to an empty seat.

I noticed every head rest cover had a Sport Aid '88 logo printed on it.

I had absolutely no idea who'd organised it but it looked fantastic.

We might get a lot wrong but we also get a lot right.

It cheered me up.

I sat back in my seat and started to think about what might happen next. The delay was going to be a big problem. We had been scheduled to arrive in New York about 5 in the afternoon. Now it would be about 8 in the evening.

The children needed to get to their hotels quickly and rest. Tomorrow started early with a full rehearsal before the main event.

At 11 o'clock.

I woke up as the plane thumped the runway at JFK. The kids and accompanying adults all clapped and seemed to be having fun.

I stretched in my seat and looked at my watch.

It was gone midnight.

Shit, that's about seven thirty here.

Need to move fast.

Fortunately, John Anderson was there and our New York team were prepared.

They had arranged a clearance lane through immigration and a fleet of iconic yellow school buses to escort the children and carers to a variety of hotels pre-booked across Manhattan.

The plane slowly emptied and our very tired passengers were shepherded to their respective vehicles.

It seemed to take an age.

I was looking forward to my bed when John called.

"We have a bus load with no hotel."

"What?"

Shit.

It didn't matter how at this moment so I didn't ask. It was more about getting these kids to bed and it was now gone 10.30pm.

They had to be up in the morning at 7am.

I headed over to John and by the time I got there he had found a couple of hotels with rooms but they were expensive.

I tried to explain my dilemma but the people on the reception desk didn't give a shit. The rooms were $200 a night and I needed twenty.

I checked in the kids and carers but had to pay up front. I handed over my American Express card and held my breath while the hotelier sought approval for $8,000.

It was the longest three minutes of my life and I couldn't bear the consequence of another cut up card incident.

Please god.

It went through and my children were all going to bed. That's all that mattered right then.

I headed back to my hotel and passed out for the night.

I awoke early after a few hours' restless sleep and made my way to the UN. Simon, the production crew and all the kids had just arrived and he was rehearsing them on the ramp outside the UN building with Omar.

I took them inside to take their seats inside the UN assembly hall.

Countries are seated alphabetically in the General Assembly according to the English translations of their names. The country which occupies the front-most left position is determined annually by the Secretary-General via a ballot draw. The remaining countries follow alphabetically after it.

The children were evidently good at the alphabet. They found their seats and sat down.

It was a hugely symbolic moment.

The children of the world were taking control and demanding action for all children suffering from poverty and malnutrition. They represented all the world's young people and our TV cameras were there to broadcast the moment to the world.

The Secretary General and other UN officials addressed them in the Assembly hall and then they filed outside to line the ramp for the arrival of Omar Khalifa.

Today, he was passing the torch of Africa to the children of the world.

This was their turn.

The familiar sound of the Vangelis anthem started and it still sent a chill up my spine.

Omar could be seen running down 1st Avenue - as he had in 1986 - flanked by police motorcycles.

He entered the UN concourse and made his way towards the ramp outside the General Assembly building.

He was dressed in his Change the World T-shirt and blue shorts. Gone was the pure white of 1986. He was more colourful, promoting hope and positivity and he wore his race number with pride.

Number One.

He jogged past a huge blue Sport Aid '88 logo draped in front of the ramp and then slowly past all the children. The UN flags bearing each of the national colours fluttered in the light breeze of an incredible September morning.

The weather had been kind again.

It was a nice sunny day in the Big Apple.

Omar reached the top of the ramp as the Vangelis anthem reached its incredible climax. He lifted both arms skywards as if greeting the gods. One arm held the Sport Aid torch aloft, burning brightly in the morning sunshine.

There was a huge roar from the crowd and the hairs on the back of my neck stood on end as the world seemed to stop for a split second.

He lowered the torch and the cauldron beside him instantly burst into flames.

The huge Star Vision screen cut to the start of races all around the world.

First London and in Hyde Park more than 50,000 runners began their race.

It made me feel better.

Barcelona, Kuala Lumpur, Havana, Dubai, Nuku'Alofa, Bejing, Warsaw, Berlin, Karachi and Reykjavik.

More than 30 million people had signed up for a unique race number and it looked like they had all turned up.

The world was running again.

I looked down at my race number.

Number 2.

I didn't run and instead looked at the masses as they took off down 1st Avenue again.

Many more this time.

It gave me a sense of enormous relief and for a moment, a feeling of vindication for taking the journey a second time.

I could have stayed at the UN and taken the easy path but I hadn't. I chanced it with Simon and for now, I was glad.

Our TV programmes, our radio programmes, our advocacy had reached billions and the Silent Emergency wasn't so silent anymore.

I took my place alongside the Secretary General of the United Nations and the children of the world while Labi Siffre sang from the stage inside the UN Plaza.

I wanted Labi Siffre and asked Simon to get him.

His songs resonated with me and two in particular were perfect for the occasion - *Listen to the Voices* and *So Strong*.

I stood back watched and listened.

Feeling emotional I fought back a few tears as I could finally relax for the last time.

My part was over now.

Simon's First World Carnival was next.

I looked over to the huge Star Vision screen.

The TV programme opened with a spinning globe, transforming itself into our logo and then to a 'Run the World' banner.

This was being broadcast to an even bigger global audience than in 1986.

Images of African children appeared against a backdrop of Battersea Power Station, where we had unfurled the world's biggest banner. The gigantic banner with the words 'Change the World' had been one of the best things we did in London to help promote the event. It was massive advertising in the literal sense and it translated across TV, radio and press.

The TV screen cut to images of young people of all nationalities and then two small children using a water pump bearing my Sport Aid logo. It was a clean water pump UNICEF had installed in Africa from money the world had raised in 1986.

The screen then cut to an old Korean man running the first Race Against Time, struggling to complete his race and deliver his personal petition to the world's leaders. The screen then faded into the Sport Aid '88 music video. It was a pretty good introduction and I loved a section that showed my unique race numbers increasing by millions.

Each one of them belonging to someone running at this exact moment in time.

A young runner in London told me a few days later that they ran with the number 1,000,000 next to someone with the number 21,000,000.

They had held hands knowing that exactly 20 million people ran between them.

It was incredible.

There was no Concorde, or Ouagadougou, but there were children from every corner of the globe and I had helped bring them here. The Sport Aid 1000 had worked and now it seemed, so had the second Race Against Time.

The carnival wasn't my baby and I still couldn't get my head round why we were doing it but that was the deal I had made with Simon.

This was his gig.

Last's night nonsense had taken it out of me and I was feeling pretty fucked and emotional.

As the song played out, the Star Vision screen cut between runners and the children of the world who now stood at the steps of the UN demanding action for their future.

This bit **was** my baby and I took another second to feel proud of what I had done.

As the formalities closed in New York, the First World Carnival took over.

Simon's First World Carnival comprised Sheffield, London, Trinidad and Dubai.

The Sheffield concert was in Hillsborough Park and the sun was shining there. The stage was festooned with vibrant, coloured cloth banners that fluttered in the light breeze. At the back was a huge Sport Aid '88 logo printed on the same material. It billowed up like a massive sail caught in the wind.

Simon had developed graphics for his First World Carnival and this theme carried through all the different venues.

It looked pretty good.

Big Country opened the Sheffield show with *King of Emotion*. A crowd of some 20,000 danced in front of the stage in the bright afternoon sunshine. The band was at the height of its popularity, its sound infused with Scottish folk and martial music styles.

The crowd loved them.

The programme cut to Trinidad, where carnival was already in full swing in the pouring rain. Crowds in amazing costumes partied to the sound of steel drums, waiting for the global line-up of celebrities including Five Star, Aswad, David Rudder, Billy Ocean and Eddie Grant.

In Sheffield, Climie Fisher came on with Simon Climie wearing a Change the World T-shirt and black leather jacket with the sleeves rolled up.

Very 1980s.

The guys finished their set with *Love Changes* and the huge crowd sang along to every word.

In keeping with Simon's theme, Orchestre Jazire and the Four Brothers then played a carnival set from the London Hyde Park stage.

London's returning runners joined the carnival atmosphere in the park and a huge crowd danced in front of the stage.

Five Star played an energetic rendition of *There's a Brand New World*, all dressed in sparkly silver jump suits.

Back in Sheffield and Hillsborough Park, the Proclaimers started a set with *500 Miles*. Their performance was full of energy and if the growing crowd of runners were tired from their run, they didn't show it.

They must have marched another mile as they clapped to the beat with their hands raised above their heads. It was a moving sea of emotion and happiness. The band finished with *A letter from America*.

Next, came Heaven 17 with *We Don't Need This Fascist Groove Thang* and *Train of Love in Motion*, followed by Helen Watson with *When you love me I get Lazy*.

The crowd went mad when the Hollies took to the stage with *He Ain't Heavy*.

That song was in the post-event Sport Aid video and I loved its significance. The video sound track cut to images of people helping each other during their races. I still see those images in my head every time the song is played.

The song resonated with me.

It was impossible not to get lost in the moment.

The Hollies only sang the one song but for me they stole the show.

Then came Mica Paris with *Breathe Life into Me*, the Primitives with *Way Behind Me*. Tracy Tracy, aka Tracy Louise Cattell, looked stunning all in black with her customary 1980s leather jacket.

Womack and Womack followed with an energetic rendition of *Love Wars*. Cecil took to the runway in front of the crowd and nearly disappeared. Our security staff shadowed his every step and at times it looked like Womack, Womack and whoaaa.

It was a great performance.

They ramped up their finale with *Celebrate the World* and two young kids with tambourines sang along. Cecil took off his shirt and went mad.

As did the crowd.

The First World Carnival was getting lively.

The TV feed cut to Dubai where a young Steven Dante was on the First World Carnival stage. Dante was a British soul singer and songwriter who had several singles released in the 1980s. He had agreed to perform in Dubai for Simon.

That was pretty revolutionary, as was a mass run and a pop concert in the Middle East for the very first time.

Back in a dusky Sheffield, the band Squeeze went on stage with *Is that Love*, *Annie get your Gun* and *Hourglass*.

And then . . .

The First World Carnival cut to three Russian cosmonauts in the Soviet Space Station Mira over the Pacific Ocean. The feed was being transmitted to us live via Moscow so that the spacemen could send their best wishes to Sport Aid '88 and the children of the world.

Finally, back in Sheffield (now in the dark), Eddie Grant started his set with *Electric Avenue* and *Gimme Hope Jo'Anna*. He commanded the crowd and got them all singing 'gimme hope.' Stage lights lit up the massive crowd bouncing in the darkness of the night.

Simon's show was coming to a close.

Fireworks thundered into the Sheffield sky as Eddie closed the First World Carnival and the end of Sport Aid '88.

Somehow, I couldn't help remembering Bob's criteria when he chose his line-up for Band Aid and Live Aid.

The best in the world to raise as much money as possible.

These guys had been great and I thanked them all from the bottom of my heart but would they have got a call from Sir Bob?

The First World Carnival had been a nice way to say thanks but did it raise any money?

Any more awareness?

Add anything to the Race Against Time?

I still wasn't sure.

CHAPTER 18
The worst days of my life

I would have slept another 36 hours given half a chance, but the children of the world needed to get back home, and I was discovering more logistical fuck ups.

Unfortunately, it had not been well explained to the guardians of the world's children that a re-entry visa into London would be required. Given they'd all entered the UK before departing to New York, their 'single' entry visas had now been used.

I now faced the prospect of trying to get a jumbo jet full of kids and minders into the UK with outdated visas.

Fuck.

Fortunately, I knew a man who knew a man.

My press office had recruited a guy called Alec Howe. He worked alongside Nick Cater and had been a great asset to the press office.

No more so than today.

You see, Alec had a dad called Geoffrey and he happened to be the UK Foreign Secretary.

After the General Election in 1983 my tea-drinking companion Margaret Thatcher reluctantly appointed dear old Geoffrey as foreign secretary.

He then set off on a tour of Warsaw Pact countries, interviewing communist leaders and sounding out opponents. The trip opened the way to further discussions with Mikhail Gorbachev, who I bumped into in Iceland and who believed that he and Thatcher shared 'extraordinary chemistry.'

Howe was also closely involved in negotiations leading to the 1984 Sino-British Joint Declaration on the future of Hong Kong where my other big helper Chris Patten finally ended up as governor.

Small world.

I called Alec and explained my dilemma.

I set the scene of the potential carnage at Heathrow if all our young ambassadors were not allowed entry into the UK, especially after everything they had done for the Silent Emergency that kills 15 million children every year.

"I'll leave it with you, mate. We'll be arriving in about 10 hours."

I couldn't think of anything else to do and so crossed my fingers, put my faith in politics and headed to the airport.

Alec must have been a good son and Dad must have listened.

On arrival at Heathrow a planeload of kids was whisked through the airport with emergency visas.

It's not what you know.

The postal strike finally ended on September 13 and it soon became obvious that its impact had been huge.

The number of runners in Hyde Park alone was 50,000 and should have been more than enough to cover our costs.

It was the second largest race London had ever seen and that bit was good news.

There had been other big races across the UK but the postal strike, during the most important phase of our project had rendered the entry mechanism completely useless.

The numbers of participants across the world had also been huge.

Early reports suggested more people had taken part in China than did in the whole world in 1986. Not understanding the concept of sponsored runs, the Chinese had set up a nationwide network of doctors who received patients on the day for a small donation.

Police riding camels supervised the race near Cairo where about 8,000 men, women and children ran a course past the 4,500-year-old Sphinx and the Pyramids.

In Bahrain, about 600 people coursed mainly through desert, starting an hour earlier in 100-degree fahrenheit temperatures to finish before nightfall.

Sudan organized a run alongside the flood-swollen Nile River in Khartoum, but Bangladesh, also devastated by floods, had to postpone its Race against Time.

In the United States, official races took place in 15 major cities.

All 58 residents of Pitcairn Island in the South Pacific also took part.

The entire population apparently.

At dusk, a dozen free-fall army parachutists heralded the start of the race in Oman by descending into Muscat's Sultan Qaboos Stadium.

Malaysian Prime Minister Dr Mahathir Mohamed lit a flame in a Kuala Lumpur field, to begin a relay race by government ministers. Malaysia had seen a massive response and new countries had also seized the opportunity of our second event and turned out in their millions.

In Harare, Zimbabwe, the Pope sent off dozens of young runners with words of advice during a rally at Glamis Stadium.

"Continue always to live in the love of God and to love one another from the heart. Then the race against time shall be for our world not only a race against hunger and disease but also a race for goodness and right, a race of love that gives us all new hope and joy."

But none of that seemed to matter right now.

Overseas income was collected locally.

Only UK entry fees covered our costs.

Just three sacks of mail arrived after the strike and following processing, the inevitable was finally confirmed.

We had a big problem.

I called an emergency meeting of the Trustees and explained exactly where we stood. Everyone was shocked and desperately disappointed.

The national postal strike had decimated our commercial income. It had lasted from August 31 to September 13 and had ripped the fucking heart out of our project.

The Trustees all agreed it wasn't the fault of the company or the Trust but if the company could no longer pay its debts, we were obliged as directors to put Sport for Sport Aid Limited into liquidation.

This would be huge fucking news.

I suggested to the Trustees that I contact Chris Patten as a last resort.

"Sport Aid has done much to help prop up his foreign aid budget. Surely a high-profile failure wouldn't be in the government's best interest?"

I said it and hoped it might be true.

They all agreed and I called his office.

A meeting was arranged in Whitehall the next morning.

Chris was very sympathetic to our problem.

The national postal strike had been well publicised and he immediately grasped how it had such a profound effect on the mechanism for signing up runners.

He seemed genuinely sorry for us.

"How much do you need?"

We were hurrying accounts and a final audit but thought £250,000 would be enough.

He asked that we leave it with him and I exited the meeting feeling a tiny bit more positive.

He hadn't said no.

Simon seemed relieved also but, as the next few days rolled by, his mood changed and so did mine.

To utter despair.

Invoices for goods and services that I'd never heard of started to come in from Trinidad, production companies, TV, carnival costs and more.

Within just a few days the creditors doubled.

Three days earlier I had made an impassioned plea to a government minister for £250,000 and now we needed more and I couldn't say why.

I sensed his frustration and could feel it myself.

We must have looked like a couple of prize wankers and for my part, I felt like one too.

And it got worse.

Within a few more days, the size of the hole got even bigger. There was no way Chris Patten was going to find that much and he confirmed it during our final meeting. We had fucked up big time and our credibility was on the floor.

I felt sick.

Back in the office Simon and I were alone for the first time.

The mothership was eerily quiet and unusually empty. It was the first time I'd seen it like that since we moved in together more than two years ago.

I looked across at him as he sat in the desk he had occupied during our entire Sport Aid journey.

"What the fuck happened?"

He didn't look at me, or maybe couldn't.

I stared at him, lost for words.

I felt empty.

Let down.

I didn't say anything.

Couldn't say anything.

I just got up and walked out.

That day I lost everything: my confidence, my best friend and what was to be a large part of the rest of my life.

I called a meeting of the Trustees and reported Chris Patten's decision to them.

I didn't spare them the details.

It was a difficult meeting and I couldn't bring myself to say what I really felt.

It wouldn't have helped or changed anything.

We had already collected more than £1 million in donations in the UK and that was safely banked in the Sport Aid '88 Trust account. Almost US$10 million had been collected overseas and both figures were still climbing.

But that didn't help either.

The Trustees agreed that we needed to exercise our duty as directors of Sport for Sport Aid Limited. The company could not pay its debts and must now be put into liquidation.

When the press got hold of the story it became front page news.

The creditors meeting was a high-profile media circus. The trustees all attended but it was me who had to stand up and explain.

It was an unpleasant angry affair.

It felt like blame was being heaped my way and I felt like screaming. I was still owed money for the New York hotels. I was never going to see that again.

I should be sitting with you lot.

It was the worst fucking day of my life.

I just wanted to crawl away somewhere and die.

The press picked over the bones of the Sport Aid '88 carcass for the next few weeks. The worst story printed suggested that Sport Aid '88 would be the demise of charity fundraising for ever.

It was hard to take.

American Express cancelled my credit card and I had debts again, no job and now it seemed not much prospect of getting one.

If I could have taken that road trip to Sounion right then, I probably wouldn't have hit the brakes.

I felt empty and very alone.

It was a dark period of my life and the days and weeks following the collapse of Sport Aid '88 were extremely difficult.

I kept reminding myself that the event was, for most of the 131 countries that took part, extremely successful. We had reached millions of people and brought them together to take action against hunger, poverty and disease.

We had made the Silent Emergency a little less silent.

The involvement of millions of young people had empowered them to help affect the world in which they lived. From the richest countries in the world, to the poorest, the Sport Aid 1000 and Race against Time had reached almost all of them.

I had raised more than $47 million dollars since I started four years ago but this was not how it was supposed to end.

I felt responsible for everything that had happened and the overwhelming feeling was a sense of failure and grief for my beloved Sport Aid.

"Big people with big ideas will always be shot down by small people with no idea. Never stop thinking big."

That message arrived by email one day and it helped a little bit.

Someone out there got it.

Slowly and painstakingly, I continued to clear up the mess. As the weeks rolled by a friend put me in touch about a job at the British America's Cup Challenge.

Businessman Peter de Savary who had reached the Louis Vuitton Cup Challenger final five years earlier, wanted to take part in the America's Cup with a new futuristic monohull yacht.

His hydrofoil-stabilized *Blue Arrow* had just been launched and they needed a fresh pair of eyes to help the marketing campaign.

It was a lifeline.

I got the job.

Keeping my head down, I got on with balancing time between Sport Aid '88 and my new tasks.

But then all of a sudden, a new problem came along.

A big problem.

Some of the creditors of the company were now seeking payment from our Trust donations.

"No fucking way."

I would die before anyone got their hands on that.

"That's for children's projects. No way is anyone getting their hands on that."

The Trustees agreed to put forward a defence of each action and what started that day was a long protracted process through the UK courts.

I couldn't say anything in fear that it may start a potential avalanche of claims. There was no other choice than to protect the funds at all cost, keep quiet, keep a low profile and just try to get on with my life.

The claim disputes went on for a long time and then it seemed, as quickly as he arrived in my life, Simon disappeared.

I didn't know where to find him. He left his flat in Islington and just vanished. It wasn't until a later Trustees meeting that John told me.

"He's resigned."

"What?"

"He sent me a letter saying he's resigned. He's gone overseas."

What?

I couldn't believe it.

No explanation, no goodbye, nothing.

Simon had fucked off into the sunset and was nowhere to be seen.

It hurt.

It really really hurt.

It wasn't until many years later I discovered he had been in Bangladesh. I read an article in the Telegraph newspaper.

'Simon Dring, 56, leaves Bangladesh after the government closed the country's only independent television station, which he set up in Dhaka two and a half years ago.'

So that's where he went.

I continued to meet my Trustees regularly and became solo chairman in Simon's absence.

We decided to put the funds in a high interest-bearing account. They had to go somewhere we could get to quickly if needed.

The Trust still had a few claims ongoing, though the possibility existed that further claims could be made by any party before 1994.

One by one, Clintons dealt with each action.

Winning a case was such a rewarding feeling.

We had protected the funds and were one step closer to allocating money to much needed causes.

I loved those moments.

They made me feel a little better.

Partly vindicated.

I so desperately wanted to spend the donations as originally planned.

After all, it had been a Race against Time for a reason.

CHAPTER 19
Life after Sport Aid

It was so painful getting over Sport Aid '88 and to be honest, I don't think I ever did.

I always felt responsible for what happened, although I could never have seen any of it coming.

Hindsight is a wonderful thing.

Looking back, I think it made me ill.

The massive highs and gut-wrenching lows had taken me on a roller-coaster ride of emotion that not only destroyed my self-esteem, but also shattered my confidence.

Getting over all of it was difficult and those 10 years post Sport Aid were pretty shit if I'm honest.

I kept in touch with John and Beth Anderson and we would meet up every time he came to London. After I managed to clear my credit card debts and hold down a job for a while, I flew out to see them.

They had moved to Denver in Colorado and now lived in a beautiful house just outside Boulder.

I cleared immigration and John was waiting for me in the arrivals lounge. I couldn't miss that large frame and bearded smile waiting at the gate. I missed my mate and often wondered what life would have been like if it had not been for that crossroads moment.

"Hi Chris, this way."

John's smile was beaming brighter that day and when we exited the terminal building, I found out why.

Parked on the concourse was a gleaming 1992 red Ferrari 512 TR.

It was John's.

"Like it?"

"Fuck off."

We got in and headed out of the airport on to E64th to the City centre. The epic exhaust sound rattled out behind me. It was brutally loud and John laughed as he fluttered the throttle. It was his new toy and I was pleased to see him looking so content and happy.

"Let's eat."

He explained he was now partner and owner of a really excellent restaurant down town.

"I'll buy you dinner."

He liked dining with me because it gave him an opportunity to retell the story of my credit card being cut up by a Chinese waiter.

The attention the car got was immense. At every traffic light, windows would roll down on adjacent vehicles and some petrol-head or young lady would engage in a bit of banter about our little red car.

As we got closer to the restaurant, I would gaze at my reflection in a shop or office window. I was sitting on the right and it looked like I was driving.

We got to the restaurant and had an amazing meal. The head chef was eager to please but then my dining partner was paying his wages. When we finished, John said I needed cheering up and we headed to a pole-dancing-bar, for a beer and a leer.

Word got around the bar about the two guys who had just pulled up in a Ferrari and I have to say we got a lot of attention. Fortunately for me, John had some ten dollar bills.

By about 10 o'clock I was pretty knackered. It was four in the morning GMT and way past my bedtime. We spent our last ten bucks and headed for the car park.

We had only driven about five miles when I said those fatal words.

"So, how fast does this thing go?"

I glanced at the speedo and it read 70 mph when we left the road. There was a lot of loose pea gravel and the noise from the tyres only served to further raise my expectations of doom.

There was a massive bang, darkness and then silence.

I remember waking up upside down hanging from the seat harness. It was pitch black and all I could hear was the cracking noise from the flat 12-cylinder, 4.9 litre engine as it cooled down just a few feet from my head.

Fuck me, these things blow up in the movies.

It took a few minutes to get my bearings. I undid the latch on the two seatbelts and dropped onto the roof below me.

It was covered in glass.

The windscreen had shattered.

John didn't move. I called out to him.

"John? John? You OK?"

Nothing.

I was getting really scared and tried desperately to open my door. Fumbling with the lock and fighting tiredness and jetlag, I scared myself more.

The door didn't move.

I tried turning sideways to kick out the window. I put my back up against John and kicked with all my might.

The window didn't move and John groaned.

"For fuck's sake, just open the door."

"You all right?"

"No, please don't do that again. It really hurts."

"Sorry mate, can you move?"

"No."

"Are you bleeding?"

"Yeah, yes, I think so."

Fuck.

"Can you get out?"

"No."

The door opening mechanism was on top of the arm rest but I was upside down. I took a second to reorientate myself and tried again. My hand searching underneath.

Click.

The door opened and I pushed with all my might, carving a furrow in the sodden wet ground we had landed on.

I got out and stood up.

It was pitch black and only the moonlight cast a few shadows. As my eyes adjusted I could make out the outline of the car. I felt my way round to John's side and tried to open the door.

It didn't move.

All I could see was John's large bulk wedged around the steering wheel. The roof had been flattened on his head and the damage had jammed the door shut.

"I can't get you out."

"Just go and get help."

I looked up and could make out a high bank up to the road.

That must be where we came from.

"Hang on mate, I'll be back."

I carefully climbed up on to what seemed like the gritted road we had just launched ourselves from. I tripped on something that felt like a cable and kicked it away.

A car headlight in the distance lit up the road and I looked down at the cable. It was a high-tension power cable. We had hit the pole holding it up and it now lay between the road and the embankment we had rolled down.

Shit, could have got a shock from that.

I looked up as the car's lights got closer and stood in the middle of the road with my arms waving in the air.

It drove towards me and then straight past.

What the fuck?

I stood in darkness again as I watched it drive on for at least another 100 metres before it stopped. It then turned around and drove back. As it pulled up beside me I could see the Boulder Police sign on the side with the strapline 'Service and safety.'

"We've had an accident. Please help. My friend, he's still in there."

I pointed in the direction of the Ferrari.

The driver repositioned his vehicle and its headlights bathed my dear friend in light.

The car was a complete right-off and John was still inside, squashed to within an inch of his life.

I think I passed out.

I woke up on a trauma stretcher inside an ambulance. A paramedic greeted me with a hello and asked my name.

"Where's my friend?"

"He's OK, they're cutting him out now."

A fire tender was also on the scene, along with another ambulance. They were trying to take the roof off with the jaws-of-life.

Finally, after what seemed like hours later, he was alongside me in the ambulance as we were blue-lighted to Boulder Community Hospital.

"You, all right?"

"Not sure."

"They cut the roof off?"

"No, couldn't. I told them to cut my seat belt and I climbed out your side."

Fuck, why didn't I think of that?

It had been a long time since we left the bar and while I'd had only a couple of beers, they were now pressing heavily on my bladder. When we arrived at the hospital, a trauma team took over and a male nurse and doctor stood over me asking lots of questions.

"What's your name?"

"Chris Long."

"Where you from, Chris?"

"England."

"Are you in pain?"

"Yes."

"Where's the pain Chris?"

"My bladder. I really need to go for a pee."

"Oh, well you'll have to wait till we x-ray you."

They made me wait and the pain was unbearable. They told me John had a cut head, fractured rib, fractured pelvis, double C7 fracture and a spiral peel of his right ear but, right then, I thought he was the lucky one.

A police officer stuck a breathalyser in my mouth and asked me to blow hard.

I nearly pissed myself.

Surely, you can't think I was driving.

A nurse finally brought me a pee bottle and I filled it to the brim and then another and another.

"Good god, you did need to go, didn't you?"

With my bladder fully relieved I could now focus more objectively on John's problems.

He wasn't in a good way.

I found a pay-phone in the corner of the main hospital and called Beth. She was beside herself with worry. She had called the restaurant and been told we left hours ago. She was understandably scared and sounded angry.

I felt it was all my fault.

Eventually, the hospital released me and Beth drove me home.

I was OK except for a very sore neck and I couldn't move my head for days. John remained in hospital for a few days and I stayed to check on him.

Slowly, he got better - much to the relief of us all, and especially Ferrari Denver.

They were the first to send him a get-well card.

John and I had survived another big life experience together. It seemed to bring us closer still. I was sitting by his bed when he looked across at me. His head was swathed in bandages.

"You know Simon was paid during Sport Aid?"

"What?"

"Simon carved a deal with UNICEF on that first trip to New York."

"Fuck off."

"Seriously, he was on UNICEF's payroll."

"You never told me that."

"I'm sure I did."

He hadn't and I wasn't quite sure why he was telling me now.

I looked back at John covered in drips and bandages and couldn't help thinking how different life would have been if I had stayed at the UN with him.

The crash had shaken me up a lot.

I got news from John that he had to go to court. The police had charged him with reckless driving and being unable to produce insurance. They had wanted either one of us to have had too much to drink, but we hadn't.

Finally, they dropped all charges, but John still had to pay $600 for the pole that had flattened his Ferrari.

His news about Simon was a revelation but I didn't care anymore.

It didn't surprise me.

In a strange way, it helped me start to get better. I had not truly understood just how depressed I had become. It was only coming so close to meeting my maker that I began to understand what was really important to me.

Back in London I got an opportunity to do what I loved most.

Work on a new charity project.

I had been approached by Youth Clubs UK. They wanted to do some fundraising and raise their profile.

Make their image a little more cool.

I was still getting requests to help various charities but I had been hesitant to get involved. It had been a confidence thing and to be honest I was scared of putting myself in the firing line again.

Youth Clubs UK was a bit different though.

It resonated with me.

I grew up in a tiny little village in Sussex which had a youth club. It had been my salvation as a kid. From the age of about 11 to 15 I pretty much lived there.

So, I came up with an idea to help them.

Satellite television was in its infancy then.

British Satellite Broadcasting had just won a 15-year franchise over four rival bids to operate the Direct Broadcasting by Satellite System.

It had a licence to operate three channels.

At the time, BSB believed 400,000 homes could be equipped during its first year. The Cable Authority welcomed the service, believing it would encourage more users, especially with a dedicated movie channel.

Around the time of the licence award, Amstrad withdrew its backing as it believed it was not possible to sell a satellite dish for £250.

Australian businessman Alan Bond joined the consortium along with others including Reed International, Chargeurs, Next plc and London Merchant Securitie.

Rival tycoon Rupert Murdoch, having failed to gain regulatory approval for his own satellite service and failing to become part of the BSB consortium, announced that his pan-European television station Skyl would be relaunched as a four channel UK-based service called Sky Television using the Astra system.

The stage was set for a dramatic confrontation.

Satellite TV was here to stay and the market was extremely competitive.

Not many households had satellite TV at the time, but those that did had MTV.

MTV Europe was a pan-European 24-hour entertainment cable and digital television network. Initially, the channel served all regions within Europe.

It was one of the very few channels that targeted the entire continent. MTV Europe had started under a co-operative agreement between Viacom and BT, but Viacom had taken over full ownership.

MTV revolutionized the music industry.

Slogans such as 'I want my MTV' had become embedded in the public conscience alongside video jockeys (veejays).

MTV was cool.

So, this was my idea . . .

Put a satellite dish, box and TV into every youth club in the country and get MTV to broadcast a 12-hour dance marathon for kids to have fun and raise sponsorship.

Simple.

So that's what I did.

I pitched the idea to MTV Europe

They loved it.

To be fair, they really didn't have to do much. They were already on air so they just had to brand and stylise a programme for me. In return they got another million or so kids watching their channel.

Kids - bang on their demographic.

The 12-hour dance party was anchored from the Hammersmith Palais in London. I put together TV feeds from other youth clubs to create a pan-European feel. Kylie Minogue, Jason Donavan and various top bands came along to the London venue and it was broadcast all across Europe.

BSB provided free dishes and Radio Rentals supplied the TVs.

The Satellite Jukebox - as I called it - was a big success and it ended up including youth clubs all across Europe. They got to keep their free dish and had a special event to help them raise money.

The Sun newspaper promoted it and that's when I met Piers Morgan. I did a deal with him to promote the Satellite Jukebox in return for tickets to the Hammersmith Palais event.

The Satellite Jukebox helped repair my confidence a bit.

Unfortunately, it didn't last long.

The Satellite Jukebox had been my contribution to a company set up with the late great Bobby Moore and the same guy who had employed me at the Blue Arrow America's Cup team, John Mitchell. John and Bobby had played professionally together at Fulham Football Club and had remained good friends.

I liked Bobby a lot. He was a true gentleman in much the same way as the great Bobby Charlton and I felt very privileged to have known them both. I was lucky to be invited to Bobby's 50th birthday party to witness George Graham and Terry Venables doing Karaoke together into the early hours of the morning. The very next day the two of them led their teams out on to the hallowed turf of Wembley for the FA Cup semi-final between Tottenham and Arsenal. Spurs won 3-1 and went on to beat Nottingham Forest 4-0 in the final a month later.

John Mitchell was a bright guy and we all became friends as well as business partners.

John discovered the World Yachting Grand Prix while he was working on the America's Cup team. He believed it had an enormous future and had invested a lot of time and money in securing the rights for the UK from its Australian owners.

Yachting didn't really float my boat.

I thought it was really boring but John convinced me otherwise and cited the Australian America's Cup win as an example. He thought the Grand Prix format could generate massive interest among the general public, much the same way as the America's Cup did.

One weekend we both flew down to Perth, Australia, to meet the World Yachting Grand Prix owners. On arrival, we were whisked off to Freemantle to board Australia II (KA 6). This was the Australian 12-metre-class racing yacht that won the 1983 America's Cup for the Royal Perth Yacht Club.

It was **the** yacht that won **the** America's cup that I had put alongside **the** FA Cup that I 'stole' for Sport Aid.

It seemed like fate.

We were treated like stars during the trip and the experience was amazing. I started to believe John might actually have something.

UK coastal cities were invited to bid to host the inaugural UK Grand Prix and the city of Glasgow won.

As the first race day got nearer and nearer, the working relationship with the Scottish Development Agency started to break down and the event got some bad press.

The consortium behind the World Yachting Grand Prix was also having difficulties and when the day of the event finally arrived we had just three boats and only two of them were actually finished.

The event was a complete fucking disaster.

Having promised Inverkip Marina as the best venue in the UK, the Scottish Development Agency seemed hugely embarrassed by the event and the miserable turnout. Only a few hundred people came following a lot of negative press in Scotland.

And it got worse.

A few weeks after the event I was jumped on by a BBC film crew in London.

Scared the shit out of me.

A reporter for the BBC programme 'On-the-line' had written to the Sport Aid '88 Trust asking why funds of the Trust had not yet been distributed. He was trying to establish if creditors of the company were pursuing the Trust for payment. It was to be the subject of a programme being aired in a few weeks and he had submitted a questionnaire.

My trustees considered each question in detail and it had been agreed that Simon should prepare a written response.

It was also agreed that we make the point that our intention was for 100% of the funds go to meet the objectives of the Trust and it was this that the trustees were trying to achieve. Therefore, until all claims were dealt with, it would not only be sub judice to comment on any specific claim, but moreover not in the best interests of the Sport Aid '88 Trust to do so.

I guess the reporter either ignored it or didn't get it because an interrogation commenced on the pavement of a busy London street.

They asked me questions about Sport Aid '88 and the World Yachting Grand Prix.

I answered as best I could and suggested it might have been more proper to consider our formal written response.

A few weeks later the programme aired.

The subject matter?

The demise of Sport Aid '88 and the World Yachting Grand Prix.

The implication seemed clear.

Thirty minutes of what felt like a complete unmitigated character assassination.

It was horrible and I wanted to crawl away and die.

One step forward and two steps back.

What the fuck did I do? Kill someone in a previous life?

My confidence took another massive hit and to be honest, never really recovered. I called John Cohen the day after and he tried to make me feel better.

"Shall I sue, John?

"Just forget it Chris. It was horrible, really horrible, but try to forget it."

The Sport Aid '88 Trust was still in court with companies allegedly contracted by it and my hands were tied.

I couldn't defend myself even if I'd wanted to.

I couldn't tell anyone why they had got it so wrong.

My mood darkened and I became even more depressed.

Waiting for a train one day, I considered ending it all. I watched as a fast train passed through the station and wondered if I could time my jump just right to avoid any pain. Fortunately, I overthought the whole process and convinced myself that I couldn't and it would hurt. I also concluded that I shouldn't do it – for the sake of the driver and my children.

I didn't want my kids to think their father had just given up.

The months continued to tick by and I picked up some work here and there, but my passion to change the world dried up.

I lost weight, became irritable and felt a total sense of helplessness and hopelessness.

I was just too scared to stick my head above the parapet for fear of it being kicked again.

I still got the odd call to help some charity or other but even they got fewer and fewer.

By chance, I had met a couple of guys who were keen to support the Jordan Formula One Team. Eddie Jordan had just started out in the sport and the Irish loved him.

They had an idea to somehow embrace the Irish passion for sport and translate it into sponsorship for the Jordan team.

They asked for my help and although I was still feeling a bit vulnerable I went along with them to meet Eddie at Silverstone.

I liked Eddie.

Having suffered a number of major accidents, he'd retired from racing to set up his team in 1980, finding young drivers and giving them a chance at success.

Having given Senna his first ever Formula 3 drive in 1982 (which was later repeated with Damon Hill in 1985 - both becoming world champions), he signed Martin Brundle to lead the team for the British Championship in 1983.

Jordan then moved up to Formula 3000 for the years 1988/89/90, winning races with Donnelly, Herbert and Irvine and taking the championship in the 1989 season with Jean Alesi.

Inspired by the success of his junior drivers, Eddie established Jordan Grand Prix in 1990 and entered Formula One.

It was still early days at Jordan Grand Prix and Eddie had hired Italian veteran Andrea de Cesaris and Belgian Bertrand Gachot to race his first cars, powered by Ford.

The Jordan team had completed a great debut year finishing fifth in the Constructors' Championship, with de Cesaris finishing ninth in the Drivers' Championship.

The Jordan cars had been green with sponsorship from 7-Up and this served to heighten its Irish heritage.

The team was also very rock'n' roll and it was this Celtic sense of fun that the boys were trying to harness.

I came up with an idea for a 'Racing for Ireland' Supporters Club in which big Irish corporates and regular supporters could get involved.

Eddie liked the idea and 'Racing for Ireland' got its logo on the side of the car, just below the cockpit.

The following year I helped them try and sell it.

We staged a big corporate dinner in Dublin and Eddie and I went on the Kenny Live Show to promote the club.

I liked Eddie more each time I met him and on one occasion he said I should join Jordan Grand Prix and help sell sponsorship.

I should have.

To be honest, it was only my confidence that stopped me from saying yes at the time.

Outwardly, I looked OK.

I could still sell sand to Arabs but deep inside I was still wrestling with myself big time.

I set up the Jordan Grand Prix Supporters' Club and ran it on behalf of the team.

I enjoyed my time working with them.

It was exciting and a lot happened.

Bertrand Gachot was replaced by Michael Schumacher, for whom the Jordan team received $150,000 from Mercedes. They were keen to give the young German sports car star experience of Grand Prix racing.

He wasn't there long before being signed by Benetton-Ford. Eddie applied for an injunction in the UK courts to prevent him driving for Benetton but lost the case. It was a mad time and I enjoyed going to a lot of F1 races.

The supporters' club worked well but the team evolved and finally Eddie sold it.

Life continued to tick by but nothing really stirred my imagination. I needed something to force me to take another chance.

To change the world.

To reboot my soul once again.

Around the middle of 1994 I attended a meeting of the Sport Aid '88 Trustees at Clintons offices in Covent Garden. All the Trustees were there including Bobby Charlton.

It was a very special occasion.

It had just been announced my Babby Sharlton was to become Sir Babby Sharlton.

We were all absolutely delighted for him.

The 15th FIFA World Cup was being held in America, for only the third time in history.

England had failed to qualify.

Two World Cups had taken place since the day I went to Mexico with Bobby and it seemed that our national team had declined a lot in between.

The Trustees couldn't help but ask Bobby why.

He was gracious as always with his answer. An explanation he must have given a thousand times before and it got me thinking.

Kids don't just kick a ball against a wall or play in the street like I did or when Bobby was young.

They don't hone their skills, their touch, their ball control like we did back then. Now they just wanted to emulate their heroes by wearing replica kits and playing on full size pitches.

"They prefer to play football on video games."

Our kids are not learning the basic skills they need to become great players.

Was this why we weren't going to the World Cup?

Should our kids be learning skills again?

Learning the basics?

Learning how to kick with both feet?

I loved football.

I got scouted when I was 15 by Stan Cullis and was asked to Arsenal for a trial. Unfortunately, my Dad couldn't afford the petrol, so I didn't go. I spent hours on my own just kicking a ball against our shed wall.

I had this idea to produce a massive rebound wall, covered in player graphics, that kids could use for skills practice. Full-size photographs of their heroes playing football with them and targets and games to hone their skills.

I ran it past Bobby and then someone at the Premier League.

The Premier League agreed to trial the idea and suggested I build one of my rebound walls at Aston Villa's training ground.

"It's in the middle of the country, so everyone can see it."

Around this time, outdoor advertising was big business. A national advertising campaign involving 1,000 boards of 96 sheets could command more than £250,000 revenue.

For just one week!

One of the biggest outdoor advertising agencies in the country was Maiden Outdoor.

I went to see them.

"If I can get planning permission to build a 96-sheet advertising hoarding for you, will you pay for it?"

"Yes"

"When you change the poster on the front, will you change a poster on the back as well?"

"Yes."

That was it.

I would build huge rebound walls, in parks and recreational areas, with changeable graphics of life-size professional players. All paid for by Maiden Outdoor and its advertisers.

I built my first wall at Aston Villa and trialled it for over a year. It was great, looked good and even the pro players liked it.

There was a problem though.

Maiden wanted to be by roadsides, near to traffic, and I didn't. Eventually I scaled back the walls and produced a smaller one for schools.

Glenn Hoddle, who was then England manager, supported it. We did a press conference together at Bisham Abbey to launch the idea.

I never asked Glenn if he remembered me.

I thought it better not to remind him of Sport Aid '88.

My confidence was still fragile, six years on.

I eventually got 1,000 rebound walls into schools and put on a national event with the English Schools Football Association.

They weren't as good as the big ones and eventually I lost interest.

I remember December 14, 2000 as if it were yesterday.

All claims against the Trust had been concluded favourably and a six year period since had caused any further claims to be statute barred.

My Trustees had been magnificent.

The final cheque was drawn, signed and sent off to its long waiting beneficiary. Cessation accounts were complete and the Trustees could finally put the carcass to rest.

I was invited by the Save the Children Fund to meet Princess Anne at a special function in London. She was very gracious and thankful of the money Sport Aid '88 had raised for her charity.

I liked her.

It was a nice way to finish.

It had been more than 16 years since the day I stood in front of the TV at Martin's flat and gazed in awe at Michael Buerk's report.

The years had taken their toll but I now stood triumphant, in the knowledge that every single penny raised had finally got to its destination.

My Trustees all shook hands and vowed to keep in touch.

Somehow, I knew we probably wouldn't.

It had been a tough ride and we were all a lot older.

I met John Cohen from time to time and we had lunch together a few years later.

I haven't seen him since.

Robert Brooke went off on a Whitbread Round the World yacht race and Sir Bobby's life has been well documented since.

The lovely Robert Stinson passed away in 2015. The world is a sadder place without him and the IAAF much less rich.

Fuck knows what happened to Simon.

It was the end of an era and it hadn't come too soon for most of us.

CHAPTER 20
New Beginnings

I hadn't been living life for long after Sport Aid when, driving through Luton one day, I passed a shop called Deep Dive.

It grabbed my attention.

I stopped the car, parked and strolled over to take a look.

Surely not.

Ever since I was about five years old I'd always wanted to be a diver. The underwater world had fascinated me. I loved Jacques Cousteau programmes as well as nature programmes involving the oceans, while my favourite James Bond was Thunderball, which was mostly shot underwater.

I also had a scary love of sharks.

As I walked closer to the shop I could see all manner of dive equipment hanging in the window. Masks, tanks, buoyancy jackets, everything a little frogman could want.

Why? This is nowhere near the sea?

A little bell rang as I walked in and a follically-challenged young man greeted me with a warm 'Good morning.'

"Is this a scuba diving shop?"

He looked at me as if I were mad.

Er, yeah, what else could it be?

"Yes, recreational and technical diving. We supply equipment, fill tanks and run courses."

"From here?"

It just seemed so incongruous that a scuba diving shop should be in a busy town centre miles from the sea. I explained that I'd always wanted to be a diver, how life had passed me by and that I'd never got the chance to do it.

I rattled on about my very first job interview as a research assistant at the Royal Naval Physiological Laboratory in Gosport, Hampshire. I could even remember the advert in the paper.

To work on 'breathing limitations in diving.'

I even remembered the interview.

I said I'd played football and was utterly confused when my prospective employers asked: "What type?" I looked blankly at the panel of experts while stuttering for an answer.

What the hell do they mean?

"Rugby or Soccer?"

"Oh, soccer."

I felt a right dickhead which made me even more nervous. Then, when asked what the Doppler effect was, I answered something like 'a train gets noisy as it gets closer and a bit quieter when it goes away.'

Not my finest hour and unsurprisingly, I didn't get the job.

It brought it all back and I talked to the young shop assistant for ages about my life-long fascination with being underwater while I explored his veritable treasure trove of a dive shop.

This was to be the beginning of my delayed love affair with our oceans.

That Christmas I opened my presents to discover a PADI open water dive course.

My wonderful partner Tracey had been listening and had not only bought the course for me but also one for herself.

I was so excited and after a few confined dives in a Luton swimming pool, we headed off to the island of Filetheyo in the Maldives to experience open water diving for the first time.

Just before we were about to leave, my Mum died.

Mum had been suffering from dementia for a few years and lived in a home near my sister in Kent. I'd visit her whenever I could but, near the end of her life, she wasn't sure who I was anymore.

She thought I was her brother, Arthur.

"How you get here, Arthur?"

"By car Mum."

"You can't drive, you don't have a licence."

I did have a licence but my uncle didn't.

It was sad to see her deteriorate so much towards the end and in a way, it was a blessed relief when she finally passed.

My Dad had died a few years before and as so often happens, Mum just faded away after that.

We delayed our trip for a few weeks to arrange and attend her funeral before finally heading off to Filetheyo.

I loved my Mum and the timing of her death only served to heighten what came next.

I'll never forget my first dive.

So many things went through my head.

The reef.

Millions of fish.

The colours.

My Mum.

The life I'd had.

The life I didn't have.

The trials, the tribulations, the rewards.

That dive was everything I dreamed of, and more.

After the dive Trace and I sat on a beautiful jetty watching the sunset.

We drank a toast to my mum.

It was really emotional but I had this strange feeling that I was about to start a new chapter.

Sport Aid was over and I was getting my life back together.

During the trip, we made some new friends. Bob McCusker - a Scot from Worthing and a BSAC diver - and Angela, his partner. Angela was also learning to dive and was on the same course as us. We all got on well and shared dinners, alcohol and our new dive experiences.

We are still friends to this day.

A couple of years after Filetheyo, we all went on another dive trip to Mexico.

We had been diving on Chinchorro Banks all day and were relaxing under a huge blanket of stars on the Yucatan peninsula. I loved stargazing at the best of times, but here there was zero light pollution and the sky was immense.

As we knocked back the best margaritas ever, I had another epiphany.

While I'd been fucking around growing tomatoes and then trying to get the world to run, about 20 million people had taken up recreational scuba diving.

Every single one kept a log book.

If, like me, they recorded everything they saw then surely that data could be really useful?

Bob and I concluded that it must.

The assumption was mainly fuelled by tequila at the time, so I decided to check it out for sure when I got home.

I called someone at the United Nations Environment Programme (UNEP).

UNEP is a UN agency and co-ordinates its environmental activities, assisting developing countries in implementing environmentally-sound policies and practices.

It seemed a good place to start.

They told me to get in touch with the World Conservation Monitoring Centre (WCMC) and so I started to make travel plans again. WCMC sounded exotic and distant and I expected to find them based in Hawaii or Fiji or somewhere like that.

I found them in Cambridge.

I took a trip to their offices and met with senior marine biologists. I presented my idea of 'citizen science', collecting data from divers' logs and giving our oceans a health check.

"Would the data be useful?"

"Very. If we could get divers to act like twitchers (another name for birdwatchers), the data could be really valuable."

It was an amazing response and for the first time in a very, very long time, I started to get a little excited again. It seemed that life had gone around in a great big circle, that my destiny was diving from the start and my incorrect answer to my first interviewer's question just threw me off at a tangent for 30 odd years!

Our oceans were the lungs of our planet and they were very unhealthy.

I knew that much.

Fish stocks were harvested well beyond their sustainable limits and climate change threatened rising sea levels, increased salinity and the loss of the beautiful coral reefs I had just been so privileged to see.

Citizen Science.

Could 20 million people become scientists, collect data and give our oceans the health check they needed?

Maybe.

Over the next year, I worked closely with UNEP and about 30 marine biologists around the world. We considered every inch of coastal water and broke it down into specific eco regions. Each biologist selected marine indicator species for each eco region.

When tallied, the species would tell us a considerable amount about each region and overall, the changing state of the world's oceans.

I designed a website - earthdive.com - to provide an online platform for divers to share their logbooks and indicator species.

My dear friends Bob and Angela became involved and a great guy called Matt Lovell helped build the website for nothing. UNEP-WCMC became a partner and the website was launched.

We made a great team and I went on BBC News to tell the world about it.

I was so fucking nervous that day.

Anxious to lift up my head again.

But I did.

It had taken a long time but I was ready again.

I still wanted to change the world.

I believed I could and I would die trying.

Let'em kick me if they wanted.

UNEP executive director Klaus Toepfer said something supportive:

"The conservation of marine biodiversity is a vital issue of our age. By collecting valuable scientific data, Earthdive's citizen scientists will actually take part in a massive global effort to monitor and help conserve life on this planet."

I was on my way again and very soon, Earthdive attracted citizen scientists in more than 100 countries.

As my confidence came back I looked at other ways in which I could enhance and improve the programme.

It soon became apparent that divers weren't all like me and needed encouragement to share their dive logs.

Earthdive needed a lot of publicity for it to really work. It needed to make its citizen scientists important in much the same way Sport Aid made its 20 million runners the stars of the show.

We needed to take control of our world again.

We didn't need scientists to do our work. We could collect data for them and take our findings to the policymakers of the world to demand action for our oceans.

I needed to get that message out.

I needed to tell the world that our oceans were the largest sink for anthropogenic carbon in the world and that we needed to protect them.

Bigger and more important than any rain forest.

I needed to tell them that an estimated 12.7 million tonnes of plastic – everything from plastic bottles and bags to microbeads – ended up in our oceans each year.

A truck load of rubbish every minute!

I needed to tell them that yes, sharks do kill a few people each year by accident but we kill 100 million of them each year, by design.

281

I needed to tell people everywhere that we were fucking things up big time and needed to change.

That's when my soul rebooted again and I dreamed up Earthdive Explorer.

Earthdive Explorer would be an ocean-going research ship. My plan was to sail it on a global voyage of historic importance. Originally, it was to leave San Francisco on the 50th Anniversary of the United Nations and its departure was to form a major part of the UN celebrations.

The team aboard would consist of men and women of various nationalities, ages and backgrounds. All would be divers, marine scientists or filmmakers. Together, they would form the ocean-based element of the Earthdive project. Fully equipped with satellite communication technology, scuba and film recording equipment, Earthdive Explorer was designed to link to the world via television, radio and the unique land-based operation and website.

The ship was to travel from ocean to ocean, recording data, mobilising support, lobbying policymakers, diving with celebrities, meeting heads of state and creating extensive TV footage.

One year later, it was to return to the United Nations in New York to deliver specific recommendations for the preservation of our oceans, along with an international petition demanding action.

The TV programming included video news releases, news-feeds, long-run series, mini-series, blue-chip specials, documentaries, UN special event(s) and a special documentary of the voyage.

I set up an amazing collaboration with National Geographic and Granada TV.

Earthdive Explorer was to engage a whole new generation of global television viewers and empower them to make a difference to the world in which they lived.

Fantastic animals and underwater locations always hold an audience's attention. But if we could add inspiring human stories about ordinary people who set out on a voyage to change the world - then I believed a huge global audience would be captivated and my citizen scientists would be inspired.

The Earthdive Explorer series would be visually stunning. On-board technology allowing filming as never before. All crew gear, down to the covers on dive tanks, designed specifically for the project. The TV series could be directed, shot and edited using the most innovative and imaginative techniques to be found across mainstream documentary and drama.

As well as two natural history and documentary crews, a specialist crew would film the lives and work of the crew's scientists, biologists, divers and filmmakers.

The Earthdive Explorer series was designed to be family television that offered something for everybody. ROVs exploring shipwrecks or searching the ocean depths for mythical giant squid. Viewers experiencing the adrenaline rush of being buzzed by sharks as they 'climbed' down an underwater mountain, wondering at the breath-taking beauty of an ocean at night.

Watching celebrities nervously diving with great white sharks. An audience of citizen scientists helping to make decisions that affect the world they live in.

Its similarities with the best parts of Sport Aid were no accident.

For over a year I worked with Granada Television and an amazing guy, underwater cameraman Jeff Goodman, to develop major strands for the programme schedule. At the same time, I explored sponsorship.

Earthdive Explorer was going to be expensive but the combined reach of the National Geographic and ITV programme made the return on investment really doable for a blue-chip brand.

I started a dialogue with a few potential sponsors and very soon I was travelling the world again to seek support for another project.

Once again, using money I didn't have.

Where I could, I'd combine my US trips with seeing John.

I'd sometimes stay with him and commute into Washington DC to meet National Geographic. They also had an operation in London and I was able to develop the main concept with them here.

Seeking and chasing down sponsorship took a long time but finally a serious dialogue started with British Petroleum (BP).

They seemed very interested.

Before long, I was working with their designated advertising and promotion agencies and we got closer and closer to the finer details of a partnership.

Weeks turned into months and before long a whole year had passed. ITV, Nat Geo, the agencies, me, we all committed a huge amount of time and resource and inched closer and closer to a final agreement.

Then something really terrible happened.

The Deepwater Horizon oil spill, also referred to as the BP oil spill was an industrial disaster. It began on

April 20, 2010, in the Gulf of Mexico on the BP-operated Macondo Prospect.

Killing 11 people, it was the biggest marine oil spill in the history of the petroleum industry, estimated to be between eight and 31 per cent larger in volume than the previous record held by the Ixtoc I oil spill.

The US Government estimated the total discharge at 4.9 million barrels. It took nearly five months and several failed efforts before the well was finally sealed on September 19, 2010.

A massive response ensued to protect beaches, wetlands and estuaries utilising skimmer ships, floating booms, controlled burns and 1.84 million gallons of oil dispersant. Due to spill and adverse effects from the clean-up activities, extensive damage to marine and wildlife habitats was reported.

In Louisiana, 2,222 tonnes of oily material was removed from the beaches, more than double the amount collected in 2012. Oil clean-up crews worked four days a week on 55 miles of Louisiana shoreline.

Oil continued to be found as far from the Macondo site as the waters off the Florida Panhandle and Tampa Bay, where scientists said the oil and dispersant mixture was embedded in the sand.

It was reported that dolphins and other marine life continued to die in record numbers with infant dolphins dying at six times the normal rate.

It was a disaster in so many ways and was the death knell of the BP Earthdive Explorer.

A lot of physical and emotional energy in addition to money went into that project and I was forced to take a big step backwards and lick my wounds for a while.

Had it been 30 years ago, I would have battled on, single-mindedly, and might have found another sponsor.

I was nearly 60 and things were different.

I maintained a web-presence for Earthdive, a portal for news and information for the diving and marine conservation communities which I continue to run today.

I marvel at the Blue Planet and Blue Planet II programmes. The BBC series has given me much comfort that the concept of Earthdive Explorer was right and proper.

It highlighted the issue of ocean plastic throughout, with breathtaking, heartbreaking and brutally honest images of its impacts.

The footage of a sperm whale attempting to eat a discarded plastic bucket and a mother pilot whale carrying her dead calf for days outraged people.

It is images like this that galvanize public opinion and help effect change.

The footage was not typical of Blue Planet in that Sir David Attenborough and his production team tended to steer clear of conservation issues in the past, preferring instead to celebrate the natural world.

Blue Planet II was different.

It pinpointed these issues - head on.

Couple this with elements of Earthdive Explorer and so much could be achieved for ocean conservation and the future of our planet.

Maybe one day. . .

CHAPTER 21
Is that it?

It was 2014 when Band Aid 30 was announced.

A gentle reminder that 30 years of my life had passed by in a flash.

A new line up for the record *Do they know it's Christmas* was announced by Sir Bob Geldof on November 10. He said that he took the step after the United Nations had contacted him, saying help was urgently needed to prevent the 2014 Ebola crisis in western Africa spreading throughout the world.

It really surprised me.

This time to raise money to support the fight against Ebola, the track was re-tweaked with lyrics to reflect the virus epidemic with all the proceeds going towards what Bob described as 'a particularly pernicious illness because it renders humans untouchable and that is sickening.'

Bob still had a way with words and the pulling power to get the world's press on board.

His last 30 years had been well documented.

Some parts of his life I would not have wished on anyone but, overall, he was still Sir Bob and Saint Bob - the man who saved Africa - and his profile continued to command attention.

The revised song was recorded by some of the biggest-selling British and Irish pop acts of the time, including One Direction, Sam Smith, Ed Sheeran, Emeli Sandé, Ellie Goulding and Rita Ora. Bastille and

Guy Garvey of Mercury prize-winning Elbow also came on board, along with Chris Martin and Bono.

The official music video for Band Aid 30 was first shown on the results show of the X Factor on November 16, 2014 with Geldof suggesting that the song and video may not be the finished version.

"We'll have a rough edit on the X Factor and we'll have a rough edit of the film."

The video was introduced by Bob, who described his new recording as a 'bit of pop history.' He said the video - which began with shots of Ebola victims - was 'harrowing and not meant for an entertainment show but was something the X Factor audience should see.'

The song was made available for digital download, just 11 days short of the 30th anniversary of the release of the one that changed my life. The physical version of the song was released three weeks later and featured cover artwork by Tracey Emin. The download cost 99p and the CD single retailed for just £4.

On November 15, Bob confirmed that chancellor George Osborne would waive VAT on the record, with all the money raised going towards the cause. He also confirmed in interviews that iTunes was not taking a cut of the 99p download cost.

In many ways it was like 1984 all over again but in so many more, it wasn't.

This is shit.

It made me really angry for a few days and then I just felt sad. I was genuinely surprised by how much of an effect it had on me.

The cause was worthy.

The artists great.

You couldn't knock it as a stand-alone gesture of support for a really worthy cause.

But Band Aid 30?

For me, it devalued everything that had gone before. Those amazing lyrics.

The constituency of compassion.

Gone.

The bands and artists could have been in it as much for self-promotion as for the cause itself. I watched an interview where one of them struggled to know who Bob was, let alone what the record was all about and why they were doing it.

There was also a media backlash.

Bob trying to mirror the personality and practices of the 1980s seemed to piss people off. His criticism of Adele for not answering his calls was the last straw.

A piece by Bryony Gordon in the Telegraph told everyone why Adele was right and he was wrong.

'Band Aid singers gave up a few hours of their time on a weekend.'

Bryony had a point and I shared it.

In the video, everyone looked pleased with themselves, seemingly unaware that in a world now obsessed with social media, someone might just look into their charitable backgrounds. Some within Band Aid 30 were accused of shirking taxes and not giving real donations to the Ebola crisis.

Bob's angry reply that it was all 'bollocks' went down badly with critics, who said Band Aid's credit-to-effort ratio was much higher than NGOs such as Medicines Sans Frontiers, whose staff risk not their reputations or precious time, but their very lives.

Eyebrows were also raised about the lack of African singers on the record. Most were white and Anglo Saxon, which gave the single a distasteful colonial feel. This was reported on UK News, along with the fact that they had depicted the whole of Africa on the Band Aid logo, when Ebola only affected a handful of countries within the continent.

It wasn't good and for the first time ever I didn't feel so proud of the organisation that had inspired me.

Public reaction focused on 'the tackiness, condescension and hypocrisy of the single' as well as the fact that they had 'wheeled out the same song again.'

A song for the most part irrelevant to the cause.

Bob said he'd received a call from the UN that Ebola was getting out of control. Having worked at the UN, I knew the emergency telephone didn't go straight to him. The United Nations favoured joined-up inter-governmental action first and foremost.

Thirty years on the amazing record that started a chain-reaction in which I played my part, should not have ended like this.

Things had moved on - or had they?

Why were pop stars rising up to sing a song that somehow managed to dehumanise the very people it was supposed to be helping? Even the hashtag '#E30LA' felt crass.

For me, sport was still a far better vehicle than music for demonstrative action.

Ethiopia and Sudan had some of the best athletes in the world and it was one of them who took the lead centre-stage in Sport Aid and showed Africa could actually help itself.

Omar Khalifa, the man who represents what Africa could be, given half a chance.

But, here we were again. Us rich kids over here helping those poor unfortunate bastards over there.

Surely we had moved on.

What happened to Paul Vallely's 'from charity to justice' - the very slogan taken up by Live 8?

What happened to Live 8?

Why this Bob?

Why?

It really pissed me off.

That Christmas was a difficult time. I'd hear the single on the radio but there was no singing along this time. No kids in the back seat, smiling and laughing.

No gut-wrenching desire to help at whatever cost.

Had my 20 million runners been forgotten?

It was September 2015 and it was my birthday.

I was 61 years old and when I looked in the mirror my dear old Dad looked back at me.

I turned on the BBC news and something incredible happened.

On the screen was a heart-breaking photograph of a dead three-year-old boy. His body had been washed up on a beach in Turkey.

"Aylan Kurdi and his five-year-old brother, Galip, drowned after their overloaded boat capsized off of the coast of Turkey."

Aylan's body had been discovered on one of Turkey's beaches in the Bodrum Peninsula. Images of the ghastly find, photographed by Nilufer Demir from Turkey's Dogan News Agency, had been shared on social media and on the front pages of newspapers around the world, particularly in the UK and Europe.

The image of a distressed Turkish gendarme carrying the lifeless body of little Aylan was too much and I just sobbed and sobbed.

The tears ran down my cheeks uncontrollably and, as much as I tried, I could not stop them. Everything that had happened had just been magnified a million times in that single moment. The tears were not just for Aylan. They were born from something else, a profound connection with everything that had gone before.

I stared through my watery glaze and was suddenly transported back in time. I was standing shoulder to shoulder with 70,000 people in Wembley Stadium. I was watching a small African child in a refugee camp. Her tiny famine-ravaged body trying simply to stand up.

As I looked around, everyone was crying with me.

The mist slowly cleared and the image of young Aylan returned. The dark-haired toddler wearing a bright-red T-shirt and blue shorts, lying face down in the surf not far from Turkey's fashionable resort town of Bodrum.

That was it.

That was the moment I decided to write this book.

I would tell the story of Sport Aid and the journey behind it all.

What 130 kids in a London office and 20 million people around the world really did.

What we achieved and more importantly . . .

What **must** be done now.

I would write a book for my children, my grandchildren and anyone else who wants to help change the world in which they live.

If I inspire just one, it will be worth it.

Our world is so different now.

The internet has more than 6 billion pages.

You can find any organisation you want with a simple mouse-click. Everyone has an email account or can set one up in minutes. You don't have to send a telex or letter and wait days or weeks for a reply.

We have mobile phones that fit into our pockets and don't hang round our necks like a lead brick. We can call any country in the world in an instant.

We can communicate with millions of people from a single laptop at home, or in a coffee shop, and receive news from all over the world, as it happens.

Our phones are also cameras that can take high quality pictures and video. We can edit that video ourselves and show movies to anyone we wish, on YouTube, by email or by sticking it on a cloud.

More than one billion people are now active daily on Facebook and some 330 million have a Twitter account.

Almost a quarter of the world's population have one or the other.

In the USA, nearly 80 per cent of all internet users are on these platforms and because social networks feed off interactions, they become even more powerful as they grow.

Thanks to the internet, every person in the world, whatever their view, can now see that he or she is not alone. When they find one another via social media, they do things - create memes, publications and entire online communities that bolster their worldview and eventually break into the mainstream.

The balance of power has shifted from the hands of a few, to those of the masses.

It's a different world to the one I and my beloved Sport Aid grew up in, but is it a better world for it?

Has social media killed real activism and just replaced it with 'slacktivism'?

Sport Aid's millions got off their arses and physically demonstrated that they cared enough about something to demand change. They took their message to the doorstep of the United Nations and called for action from our policymakers.

And they got it.

As I write this Greta Thunberg, who started a school strike for climate change outside the Swedish Parliament building, is now regarded across the world as a model of determination, inspiration and positive action.

National presidents and corporate executives are lining up to be criticised by her, face-to-face. Her *skolstrejk för klimatet* (school strike for climate) banner has now been translated into dozens of languages.

I like this girl.

The teenager's lone protest has developed via social media into a powerful global movement challenging politicians to act.

She wants to change the world.

In 1992 at the UN Earth Summit in Rio de Janeiro, Severn Cullis-Suzuki, who was only 12 at the time, demanded the same of policymakers:

"Adults you must change your ways."

The environmental activist was called 'the girl who silenced the world for five minutes.'

Severn has since spoken around the world about environmental issues urging listeners to define their values, act with the future in mind and take individual responsibility.

Like Greta, her message was angry, powerful and passionate, delivered at a time before social media.

Do you remember her?

I doubt it.

Greta wants policymakers to listen to the science and act as if their house is on fire.

Her argument has divided opinion.

Maybe because to truly beat climate change we must all try to put out the fire.

We all live in the same house for fuck's sake!

It has been argued that Greta is part of a generation that wants a TV in every room, that spends all day and night on electronic devices, who don't walk or ride bikes to school but prefer a bus or private car. That she is part of a generation of consumers who like trendy things, foreign holidays, the latest smart phones, gadgets and fast food made from beef, processed foods and wrapped in plastic or polystyrene containers.

Her generation is also part of the problem.

Rallying global support for any cause is an incredible challenge and we must not forget Greta is only 17.

Ask the scientists who have been trying to engage with us on climate change for years.

Ask me how difficult it was more than 30 years ago.

She has done well.

But now engaged, the call-to-action should not be to simply blame someone else for not listening to the science.

This is an opportunity of a lifetime.

Don't waste it.

Don't run the risk of disenfranchising as many people as you engage with organisations like Extinction Rebellion.

Instead, use your constituency of compassion wisely.

Explain to your supporters why we are **all** part of the problem and empower **everyone** to become part of the solution.

Of course force our governments and corporations to do their duty, but don't hide behind them.

Governments are there because we elected them.

Companies exist because we buy their products.

Show all your supporters how just a few changes by every man, woman and child can help put out the fire.

All of us united, affecting the world in which we live.

Get a message to the millions with whom you now engage - we **all** need to listen to the science - we are **all** part of the problem.

We **all** need to change.

So, here's an idea.

A new Sport Aid for a brave new world.

Another truly global event, providing a participation platform for everyone who cares enough to affect the world in which they live.

An event that harnesses the best of 21st Century communication technology.

At its heart a Sport Aid app.

In 1986 people bought an 'I Ran the World' T-shirt.

This time everyone can buy a branded step tracker bracelet. You've seen them. Fitbit, Nubands, Letscom and others.

Let's make one branded 'Change the World'.

It will look good on your wrist - like many of today's charity bands - but this one will have a function, a real purpose.

The tracker will link to the Sport Aid app and a special Sport Aid website.

People can buy the tracker and all proceeds go to the cause. Alternatively, just download the app and link it to a mobile phone or gps device.

When you get a tracker, you'll log on via the app and set up your profile. Add your name, birthdate, gender (however you identify), nationality, profession (if you have one), sports club (if you have one), gym (if you have one), school, college or university (if you've been to one). Add a company (if you work for one), a group of friends if you want, simply by creating it in your profile. You'll be able to design your own or group avatar on the app, and then do something very special indeed.

For one week in a month of a year to be decided, a global network of participating gyms, health and fitness clubs, local authority parks, schools and recreation centres can open their facilities to the public. This network of partners could include big organisations such as Virgin Active, David Lloyd, Bannatyne's, David Barton, MVP, Wellbridge, Equinox and Golds as well as smaller gyms in schools and private locations all over the world.

There are more than 6,000 health clubs in the UK alone, with 2.4m members. More than eight million adults in the UK have a private gym membership. There are 46 million members in European health and fitness clubs. There are about 36,000 gyms in the USA and thousands more across Africa, Asia and Oceania.

Every venue engaging with potential new customers simply by opening their doors and embracing change.

Facebook and Twitter could help promote it.

Every country in the world can be involved and if there is no gym, people can simply walk or jog anywhere. Like in 1986 - if you couldn't get to an official race you just ran around your block or your garden.

Why?

To make a big fucking point and send a huge message to our policymakers that we will do our bit and the world demands action.

Every person's avatar will carry a virtual flame from their home town and country to the doorstep of the United Nations in New York.

The home of our policymakers.

Where people shape our lives.

Every mile you walk or run will be downloaded and your journey recorded and displayed on the Sport Aid website.

With every step, your flame and your message getting closer to the UN.

Each participant can run or walk as an individual or as part of a team, school, club or university, as well as a company, village, town, city or nation.

Graphics will display a plethora of statistics in real-time on the Sport Aid website.

Virtual flames leaving each home town in every country of the world will be tracked as they make their way to the United Nations building in New York.

In New York those virtual flames will become actual flames as real torches are lit each time a person, team, group, school, company, town, city, nation arrives.

A massive screen will show the names and avatars of individuals and teams and groups as they arrive in real time.

Every person, every flame, a call to action to effect change.

The first school to arrive, the first girl, the first boy. The first club, country, town, city. The first doctor, scientist, plumber, electrician, aid worker. The permutations are endless and each statistic a real-life petition in itself.

TV can follow the events in each country with celebrities doing their bit in gyms, parks, schools, universities, wherever - endorsing the message that we can all make a difference.

Where people can't afford trackers, sponsors can support them with each tracker branded with that company's name and that name incorporated into the avatar.

I love BBC's *Children in Need, Comic Relief* and *Sport Relief* - the latter probably spawned from Sport Aid. I am envious of the massive airtime they enjoy.

Give this project just half of that and use it for advocacy. Show billions of people how they can truly make a difference to the world in which they live.

It would be huge and more importantly, significant. Why do it?

Because it will unite people in a common cause - everybody doing the same thing at the same time for the same reason. It will once again empower people all over the world to take control.

Unlock ears.

Demand action.

Make a difference.

Help change the world in which we live.

Because we must.

I agree with Greta.

Our policymakers need to listen to our scientists. More importantly, they need to act now.

The evidence for rapid climate change is compelling. The planet's average surface temperature has risen about 1.62 degrees fahrenheit since the late 19th Century, a change driven mostly by increased carbon dioxide and other human-made emissions into our atmosphere. Most of the warming has occurred in the past 35 years, with the five warmest years taking place since 2010.

Our oceans have absorbed much of this increased heat. Global sea levels have risen about two hundred millimetres in the last century and the rise in the last two decades is nearly double that.

Warming has caused the Greenland and Antarctic ice sheets to decrease in mass. Data from NASA's Gravity Recovery and Climate Experiment show Greenland lost an average of 286 billion tons of ice per year between 1993 and 2016, while Antarctica lost about 127 billion tons of ice per year during the same period. The rate of Antarctica ice mass loss has tripled in the last decade. This only serves to increase temperatures as the earth's ability to reflect heat from the sun diminishes.

Glaciers are retreating everywhere around the world including in the Alps, Himalayas, Andes, Rockies, Alaska and Africa.

Satellite observations have revealed that the amount of spring snow cover in the Northern Hemisphere has decreased over the past five decades and that snow is now melting earlier.

The number of record high temperatures in the world is increasing, while the number of record low temperatures is decreasing. Many parts have also witnessed increasing numbers of intense rainfall.

This is the result of humans emitting more carbon dioxide into the atmosphere. More is being absorbed by our oceans.

The amount of carbon dioxide absorbed by the upper layer of the oceans is increasing by around two billion tons per year and yet our oceans ability to process it has been damaged. We dump eight million metric tons of plastic waste into them each year and fish them beyond sustainable limits.

The oceans are the lungs of our planet.
We are slowly destroying them.
Fact!
It's really happening.
Listen to the science.
We need governments to listen.
We need people everywhere to understand.
We **all** need to act **now** before it's too late.

As this book nears its publication date, the COVID-19 pandemic has become a global health and societal emergency that has demanded effective immediate action by governments, individuals and businesses.

Press attention has been unprecedented.

The reaction of governments unprecedented.

The response has been dramatically different to anything provoked by repeated scientific warnings about climate change. The many organisations that declared climate emergencies throughout 2019 and 2020 have so far done nothing on the scale and speed of action to limit the spread of coronavirus.

Ironically, action on COVID-19 has lowered CO_2 emissions drastically, with flights suspended and factories closed in many parts of the world.

The big question now is how do we continue the environmental benefits once the COVID-19 epidemic ends? And how can we learn from one crisis response in the pursuit of another?

One thing's for sure: governments and people can make huge sweeping changes in a crisis.

In circumstances of immediate life or death most of us will, given the opportunity, take action to reduce our risk.

Climate change, on the other hand, while potentially bringing about the end of the world as we know it, does not affect us with the same urgency.

We need to change this mindset.

If our world is still here by the middle of the century, Africa will still have its problems too.

Soaring birth rates mean that by 2050 around 2.2 billion people could be added to the global population and more than half will come from Africa. According to a new UN population report, the continent will account for the highest growth spurt with an additional 1.3 billion people.

Much of that boom will come from Nigeria, currently the world's seventh most populated country. By 2050, the same report predicts, Nigeria will become the world's third most populated country, one of six nations projected to have a population of more than three hundred million people.

But this rapid growth poses massive challenges for many African governments. How will public infrastructure, much of which is already substandard, keep pace with its rising number of citizens.

Nigeria already struggles to cater for the further educational needs of its millions of high school pupils. Between 2010 and 2015, of the 10 million who applied for entry into Nigerian tertiary institutions, only 26 per cent gained admission.

The UN report underlines the problems.

In the 47 countries (33 of which are in Africa) designated by the United Nations as least developed, population is expected to nearly double from 1 billion in 2017 to 1.9 billion in 2050. This population growth, the UN believes, will make it even harder for the governments in these countries which are already struggling with reducing poverty and hunger.

The continued growth is related to the age structure of the continent's population as Africa is home to the majority of the world's youngest generation.

Beyond 2050, Africa is expected to be the only region still experiencing substantial population growth and its share of the global population could rise from 17 per cent at present to 40 per cent by 2100.

Where will all these people go?

You've seen it already.

Thousands of refugees fleeing from north Africa into Europe - and this is just a trickle compared to what it will be if we do not change things.

How many more baby Aylans do you want to see?

But this issue needs billions in investment and a global commitment to effect change. It is the policymakers of our world who must provide that for Africa and we need to get to them.

It worked in 1986 and I believe it will work again.

Maybe better.

More than 30 years ago Sport Aid's millions took to the roads around their towns and cities and it seemed for a moment in time the whole world came together. There was a sense that all things were possible, that if humanity put aside its differences, it could achieve anything.

Fitbit, you listening?

UNHCR, you listening?

UNEP you listening?

Samsung?

Garmin?
Apple?
Huawei?
Facebook?
Twitter?
Branson?
Ballantyne?
Celebrities?
Television?
Everyone?

When 'social distancing' ends, let's all come together and do it again.

Pick up my torch and Run the World.

CHAPTER 22
What you did

It was never possible to tell you how the funds raised by the Sport Aid projects were spent given circumstances explained in this book.

It's really bugged me for years.

If you are one of the millions of people who ran the world, not only did you force governments to change, not only did you help make UNICEF's Silent Emergency less silent, but this is who you helped with the money that you raised.

I trawled through many historic files to produce the list of beneficiaries set out in this chapter. To the best of my knowledge it is accurate.

On behalf of all the charities and NGOs listed, I thank you all from the bottom of my heart.

1986
(from Sport Aid)

Ethiopia and Sudan

Band Aid Trust
Projects to alleviate suffering from the African Famine.
US$ 17,500,000*.
Ethiopia and Sudan.

United Nations Children's Fund
Projects to alleviate suffering from the African Famine.
US$ 17,500,000*.
Ethiopia and Sudan.

* I was told by UNICEF that US$35m was raised by Sport Aid and divided equally between the Band Aid Trust and UNICEF. I never received the actual final figures.

1987
(from Sport Aid '88)

Belize

United Nations Children's Fund
Project relating to the assistance of disabled children.
£23,500

Sudan

United Nations Children's Fund
Project to benefit children.
£37,500

Ethiopia

United Nations Children's Fund
Project to provide emergency assistance.
£16,500

Zimbabwe

The British Red Cross
Child Alive, Primary Health Care - a project to improve both the knowledge of primary health care through an educational programme as well as making provision for basic sanitation.
£8,710

The British Red Cross
A project consisting of the building of an orphanage.
£18,067

Botswana

The British Red Cross
A project relating to the provision of physical education facilities for children.
£45,000

The IAAF
The Bristol Outdoor Pursuits Centre, which required a safety boat for their water activities.
£500

The IAAF
A project consisting of the building of a multi-gym at the Mill Hill Youth Centre in Bristol.
£1,600

The IAAF
Funds allocated to Sea Mills boys and girls club in Bristol to enable them to refurbish an outdoor floodlit games area.
£1,600

The IAAF
Funds allocated to the Newcastle Park Tennis Association to help provide organised tennis coaching and competitions for children from deprived backgrounds.
£1,680

The IAAF
Funds allocated to clubs based on St. James Church in Benwell, Newcastle who needed minor items of sports equipment.
£1,000

The IAAF
Funds for The Percy Hedley Centre in Newcastle, who required a sports wheel chair for training purposes to help children with cerebral palsy.
£940

The IAAF

Funds allocated to 14 different YMCA Youth Centres in Leeds with pressing needs for a considerable amount, and variety of minor items, of sports equipment to enable youngsters to participate in sport.

£10,000

The IAAF

Funds allocated to Sports Leagues in Derby who operate in Sports Halls in the inner City to enable children to participate in games.

£5,000

The IAAF

Funds allocated to the British Sub-Aqua snorkel training scheme for physically handicapped children in inner city areas throughout Yorkshire and Humberside.

£10,000

The IAAF

A project to develop two Community Centres as Recreation Centres in Derby with particular emphasis on helping young people to participate.

£5,000

The IAAF

Funds allocated to a sports centre for sports equipment in Leicester which was refurbished as a result of self-help by a Youth Association.

£4,000

1988
(from Sport Aid '88)

Bolivia

Project Tomorrow
Project Qharuru, a project providing health care, educational and vocational training and sport and recreational elements for street children in Bolivia.
£12,500

Guatemala

Project Tomorrow
"La Novena", a project providing health care, educational, vocational training as well as sports and recreation elements for street children in Guatemala City.
£5,405

Belize

The British Red Cross
Child Alive, Primary Health Care, a project to develop maintainable maternal and child health activities within the capability of resources of the National Society, and which will effectively and appropriately meet the needs of the community served.
£19,000

Kenya

The British Red Cross
Child Alive, Primary Health Care, a project to train 100 community health workers in Nakuru and Nyahuru, Kenya.
£20,000

UK

The British Red Cross
Notts. Visual stimulation facilities, Surrey. Asian play scheme, Mid Glam. Minibus for Youth Activities Programme, Powys. Minibus for Youth Activities Programme, Northumbria. Minibus for Youth Activities Programme.
£36,712

Philippines

The British Red Cross
A project providing portable water facilities for depressed areas in the Philippines – thirty-two schools were assisted.
£10,000

The British Red Cross
A project consisting of the training of Youth Motivators in the Philippines Red Cross Healthcare Programme.
£7,200

Zimbabwe

The British Red Cross
A Community Rehabilitation Programme which consists of the training of local staff in rehabilitation and physiotherapy techniques in Zimbabwe.
£8,419

Mali

CARE USA
Macina Child Health Programme. (the following is the detailed report of CARE USA).
Mali suffers some of the highest child death and illness rates in the world. Over 20 percent of all children born alive do not live to see their fifth birthday. Health conditions are even worse in the villages of Maliís Macina Circle, and before CARE arrived, malnutrition was widespread, there was poor access to medical care, and little understanding about disease causation and prevention. CARE's Macina Child Health Project (MCHP) successfully worked to

improve the health of mothers and children over seven-year period (1986 through 1993), providing preventive primary health care for 144,000 people in 90 villages in Macina Circle. CARE worked in close collaboration with its partner, the Malian Ministry of Public Health (MOPH), providing logistical and outreach support for diarrheal disease control, immunisation, hygiene and sanitation, nutrition, and maternal health. The MOPH hailed CARE is Macina Child Health Projects as one of the most effective child survival projects in the country. A cornerstone of the project was the role of local Malian women as "health promoters to reach out to the rural poor. These women, graduates of Mali's nursing and midwife schools, were not hired by Mali's health services because of budget cutbacks. CARE gave them special training on how to live, work, and teach in the poorest rural areas. They also learned to ride mopeds, change flat tires, and make other mechanical repairs so they could travel independently to remote villages. Each promoter lived in an assigned village and was responsible for project activities there and in neighbouring communities.

Project Accomplishments:
From July 1989 through June 1991, the period of Sport Aid '88 funding, the project worked in 18 villages in three sub-districts: Sarro, Saye, Monimpe and Kolongo. During this period, the project achieved the following:
Mother-Child Immunisation: CARE worked with the MOPH to immunise thousands of women and children against seven deadly diseases: diphtheria; tetanus; whooping cough; polio; tuberculosis, measles, and yellow fever. CARE provided key support in the areas of immunisation promotion and education, as well as logistical support to cover fuel and maintenance costs of the immunisation teams.
Oral Rehydration Therapy (ORT):
The project trained MOPH health workers to educate mothers on how to prepare and administer oral rehydration drink out of a home-made sugar and salt solution. Breast-feeding, good diet and proper hygiene were also taught.
Mother-Child Health and Nutrition:
The project organised maternal/child health education sessions on topics that included the following: Prenatal and postnatal care; safe delivery practices; birth spacing; growth monitoring; and mother-child nutrition. The project also worked in coordination with

CARE's Agricultural Development Project to help families improve their diets through the establishment of small gardens. An evaluation of the project carried out in 1993 revealed the following three-year accomplishments: An increase in child immunisation rates, from 51 percent to 90 percent; An increase in the number of mothers who consistently used oral rehydration therapy to treat diarrhoea, from 28 percent to 50 percent. A fall in child malnutrition rates, from 44 percent to 20 percent; and an increase in the use of modern family planning methods, from three percent to 13 percent.

Personal Accounts:

The following personal accounts were told to CARE staff by two Macina Child Health Project participants. Forty five year old Kassim Diarra is a farmer and father of four children. He talked about the changes the project had made to the lives of his fellow villagers.

"When CARE first came to Macina, our people were suffering from famine. CARE came with corn flour and helped us dig wells for drinking water. After that, health workers arrived who taught us about the importance of vaccination, and how giving children rehydration to drink when they were sick with diarrhoea could save their lives. Before CARE came, many children would die each year of tetanus, diarrhoea and other diseases. During an epidemic, several people in one family would die. Thanks to CARE, that rarely happens anymore." Mariam Katile, a mother of three children, had this to say about CARE's project:

"My baby was malnourished and I didn't know what to do. A CARE health worker came and taught me I needed to continue to breast-feed, and to give my child other foods to eat. Following CARE's advice, and with time and patience, my child got better. I also learned that there are clinics nearby where I can get myself and my child vaccinated, or where I can bring her when she gets a cough or diarrhoea. My husband and I can't thank CARE enough. Without the health workers, many of our children would die."

Expenditure Report:

During July 1989 through June 1991, the Sport Aid '88 contribution of £52,371 was spent in its entirety in support of Macina Child Health Project implementation.

Conclusion:

Mothers and young children living in the villages of Macina Circle in Mali, West Africa, are beset by a host of health problems that

each year take hundreds of lives. CARE's Macina Child Health Project worked to establish a community health system that served the health needs of even the most isolated villages and improving their quality of life.
£52,371

India

The British Red Cross
Partnership Nutrition Project, £47,629 - July 1989 - June 1991
Of an estimated 190 million children in the world who are moderately or severely malnourished, at least 73 million (40 percent) are in India. Furthermore, one out of every eight children born in India dies before his or her fifth birthday. Diarrheal diseases, acute respiratory infections, poor postnatal care, and vaccine-preventable diseases all contribute to India's high malnutrition and infant/child mortality rates. In India, for every 100 babies born alive, 12 die before reaching their fifth birthday. While the primary killers of children are pneumonia and diarrhoea, malnutrition is a contributing factor in that it increases a child's susceptibility to disease and decreases the chance of survival when she falls ill. Women also suffer from poor health and nutrition, especially during pregnancy. For 15 years (1981-1996), CARE-Partnership Nutrition Program worked successfully to improve the health and nutritional status of up to 14 million impoverished women and young children, especially girls (see below). CARE's partner in these efforts was the Indian government's Integrated Child Development Service (ICDS) program and its national network of anganwadi childcare centres (AWCs). ICDS was established in 1975 and is organised to serve only the poorest of the poor. CARE-supported ICDS health activities included immunisation, control and prevention of diarrhoea and acute respiratory infections, prenatal care, family planning, provision of food supplements, and health and nutrition education. Through ICDS, CARE regularly provided food and health services to 8.3 million of these participants in 140,000 AWCs, or 50 percent of all centres. Each year, CARE delivered more than 185,000 tons of food to the centres, a process that it closely monitored to ensure the food was reaching its intended beneficiaries. CARE also helped ensure sustainability by training thousands of ICDS staff in food

logistics, management, monitoring, and health and nutrition education.

Project Accomplishments:

In 1992, the National Institute of Public Cooperation and Child Development completed an extensive survey of the ICDS project. The survey revealed the positive impact of the ICDS program on mothers and children:

The infant mortality rate was 20 percent less in ICDS areas than in non-ICDS areas; Fifty percent of children under three years old in ICDS areas were immunised, compared to only 32 percent of children in non-ICDS areas; Non-ICDS mothers had between two and three times the number of low birth-weight babies as in ICDS areas; and overall, the infant and child malnutrition rates were approximately 13 percent lower in ICDS areas than in non-ICDS areas. Lower malnutrition rates mean two to three times fewer infant/child deaths.

Donor Expenditures:

Between July 1989 and June 1991, the Sport Aid '88 contribution of £47,629 was spent in its entirety in support of CARE-India's Partnership Nutrition Project activities in Mayurbhanj and Keonjhar Districts in Orissa State.

Conclusion:

Impoverished women and children in India suffer some of the worst health conditions in the world. CARE's Partnership Nutrition Project has helped improve basic mother and child health and nutrition services, thereby significantly reducing illness rates and saving lives among vulnerable populations.

£47,629

Mozambique

UNICEF
Rehabilitation of basic health services programme
£20,000

Yemen

UNICEF
Girls' education programme
£31,000

Burma

UNICEF
Iodine deficiency disorder control programme.
£23,850

1989

Lesotho

Africa Self-Help Quick Action Relief

Quick Action Relief Project No 41 for general relief feeding of children suffering from malnutrition as a result of continued crop failure and famine.

£10,000

Craigavon

Playboard Northern Ireland

Integrated Playground Committee - Pinebank Community Centre to provide finance to enable the building of play structures for physically handicapped and able-bodied children.

£5,000

Duncairn

Playboard Northern Ireland

Play Scheme and Youth Club - Inner City Belfast - to provide a mini-bus to enable children to be taken out of trouble zones and to provide access to integrated play facilities and opportunities.

£10,000

Dove House

Playboard Northern Ireland

Play Project - Inner City Derry - to provide a mini-bus to enable children of both sexes to be taken out of trouble zones and provide access to integrated play facilities and opportunities.

£10,000

Swaziland

The IAAF

A project consisting of the building of a Multi Sports Centre in Swaziland to be used by all schools in various championships.

£12,000

1994
(from Sport Aid '88)

Tanzania

UNICEF
Street Children and Aids Prevention Programme.
£65,000

Vanuatu

UNICEF
Early Child Development Programme.
£25,000

Chechnya

British Red Cross
Warm Winter Clothing for displaced children. The conflict in the region plus the severe political and social turmoil since the collapse of the Soviet Union caused great humanitarian need in 1995. BRC initiated the only submittal relief programme in the region at that time. The bombardment of the capital caused considerable devastation: the conflict caused around 260,000 civilians including children to become displaced from their homes in Chechnya itself, with more in the surrounding region. Many of those displaced were taken in by family and friends but their needs soon outstripped the ability of hosts to provide for them. Others sought refuge in public buildings where the Red Cross supplied food and protection from the harsh winter conditions, in the form of plastic sheeting, blankets and warm clothing. The cold coupled with the lack of water and electricity made living conditions for those displaced, especially the children, very difficult. The Sport Aid '88 grant was used to purchase and transport 790 sets of winter clothing for children 0-12 years old. Each set consisted of a winter coat, sweatshirt, jogging pants, T-shirt, hat/cap, pair of socks and a set of underwear. The clothing was purchased and transported to the operations base at Nalchik, Russia, within the first quarter of 1995 from where it was transported to Chechnya and distributed.

The clothing supplied warmth and protection to some of the most vulnerable group of children caught up in the bitter conflict. £17,536

1995
(from Sport Aid '88)

Uganda

British Red Cross
Youth mobilisation and Training Programme

The Uganda Red Cross Society initiated the Youth Mobilisation and Training Programme in April 1995 in five branches (Kisser, Palissa, Soroti, Moyo and Kabarole) supported by the British Red Cross Society through Sport Aid '88. Project goals were: Reduce the vulnerability of young people and increase their capacity to respond to their own community's need for development; mobilise youth, particularly those who are out of school, providing training in leadership skills, practical skills and project identification as well as support for six community projects in each branch over two years - to be run by the Red Cross Youth links. A recent review of phase 1 found that the project had successfully mobilised the youth. They were active in this project with community activities and played a major part in other URCS programmes. It was clear that many youth links were formed and well organised. They had elected committee members in line with project guidelines and had recommended officials. Many links met regularly and reported carrying out numerous activities including cleaning wells, Red Cross dissemination and recruiting members. The URCS relies on the youth to implement many of its programmes. For example, they were used to distribute food and non-food items during recent food shortages in the east of the country. The first phase of the project has achieved 72% of its targets and resulted in the establishment of 43 youth links, the training of youth leaders and trainers in each branch, plus the establishment of 11 community projects. Targets for the recruitment of members and establishment of community projects proved to be too ambitious. Also, fewer joint meetings between each branch's Youth Council and Board were held than planned, 21 were held out of the planned 40. Phase 1 of the YCDP successfully mobilised and trained a large number of youths who are committed to work to address their needs and to work in the community.

The commitment and enthusiasm of the youth is clear. In addition, the ability of branches to mobilise youth to carry out all its activities is a huge benefit to the URCSS. Furthermore, the activities of the youth in the community are changing the community's view of the URCS from one of an organisation concerned only with large international emergencies to one which is concerned with problems of local communities. BRCS contributed 50% of its own funds to match the Sport Aid '88 contribution for the implementation of the first Phase of the programme.
£31,808

Ethiopia

The British Red Cross
The Gulele Street Children's project implemented by the Almaz Children and Family Support Programme (ACFSP) has been running since 1994, providing support to street children and young women in some deprived and run-down slum areas of Addis Ababa in Ethiopia. The funding provided has enabled orphaned numbers to be increased in the programme's shelter and educational project as well as significantly upgraded training facilitates for street girls. Forty five full time orphans receive shelter and education in Gulele while an additional 85 receive support through a foster care programme. The programme employed a donor liaison officer in 1995, which has significantly upgraded the projects management and reporting ability and further attracted donor funding in 1996 and 1997. Support enabled the complete upgrading of shower and toilet facilities within the project compound and also facilitated the establishment and equipping of a training room aimed at providing employment opportunities for young street girls. Typewriter and sewing machines have been used to train and have provided a number of girls with employment. The programme itself has employed four of the past students as trainers.
£22,616

The British Red Cross

Psycho-Social Support to Children in Mozambique. 'Healing Through Play' Programme. In 1992 a peace agreement was signed to end 16 years of civil war; the war's effects are long lasting. Many thousands of children have suffered psychological trauma as a result of the violence they experienced or witnessed, and many were orphaned as community and family groups were torn apart. The Healing through Play programme started in mid 1993 and extended to over 20 Districts in the six provinces of Sofala, Tete, Manica, Zambezia, Niassa and Gaza over 1994-96. The programme worked with children aged four to 16 including orphaned children and those reunited with their families or with foster families, those repatriated or returning to their area of origin. It was funded in 1995 by UNICEF and BRC through the donation from the Sport Aid '88 Trust.

The objectives of the programme aimed to alleviate and prevent the effects on children of violence war and other adverse social situations, stimulating their normal psycho-social development and strengthening family ties, as well as providing community and family members with knowledge and skill which enable them, through play and expressive activities to respond to the problems of traumatised children. The activities of the programme were carried out by trained Mozambique Red Cross volunteers, in a 2-phase course:

1. Providing skills to give more individualised assistance to the children.

2. Providing general skills needed to help children.

In 1995 25 new activists were trained in Sofala Province and 175 activists were given second phase training in the six provinces and 175 activists were given second phase training in the six provinces. The total number working in six provinces in 1995 was 951. The activists were supervised in their work by occasional visits from national headquarters Social Programme staff and by trainers from the Chimoio Training Centre. They also receive a manual on how to deal with children with Psycho-social problems. The activists, who don't get a salary, receive some incentives through the year, including shoes, blankets and some locally bought items, such as soap, oil, beans and maize meal, depending on local need. Some equipment for the children's activities was also distributed

including balls, toy kits and exercise books. The total number of children helped in 1995 was 9,499 through 89 centres in six provinces.
£40,000

Lesotho

The British Red Cross
Funding for a day care centre provides educational services, primary health care and protection to children under the age of five, while parents are at work. The day care centre programme aimed to build five centres after consultation with the local communities. Two have been built and the balance of funds was forwarded to the National Youth Programme. Two day care centres were completed and opened by the end of 1996. Semonkong Day-care centre in Maseru District and Muela day care centre in Leribe District. Semonkong centre has one classroom for 35 children, whilst Muela has two Classrooms of 70 children. Children aged between two and five years old are taught from 8am until 12 while their parents are at work. Lessons are aligned with national schools and by qualified teachers who attend early development courses. There is also a schools committee to oversee the teaching in the centres. Muela is also beginning handicraft activities for North, South and Mountain Districts Day Care Services to Children under 5 The National Youth Programme Lesotho. There had been a decline in the number of youths involved with the Lesotho Red Cross, many programmes rely on a consistent pool of youth volunteers. The youth programme aims to empower and motivate the youth, by identifying and training youth leaders to learn to provide community services to communities through long and short-term development programmes and activities, such as first aid and AIDS awareness, exchange visits and work camps. Funds were allocated to this project, covering youth leadership training, community service activities, exchange visits and monitoring support.
£16,050

The British Red Cross

Special Needs School: children with learning difficulties and physical disabilities. The Montserrat Red Cross special needs school, Dagenham, Monserrat, was set up in the early 1990s to cater for children with physical disabilities and learning difficulties. On the academic side, the school focused on reading, writing and mathematics and on the vocational side art, sewing, basketry, domestic tasks and typing. At the beginning of 1995, Sport Aid '88 donated £25,000 to the BRC for physiotherapy equipment for physically disabled children. Chalkboard and exercise books for children with learning difficulties; assistance with extension of building; part-payment of salary for the helper of the physically disabled. Due to the volcanic activity, the school was closed down. The money has been spent on on-going projects in Montserrat. The BRC sent two representatives to the island to quantify how the Sport Aid '88 donation could best be spent on children. £25,000

1996
(from Sport Aid '88)

Ethiopia

The British Red Cross
Sport Aid '88 donated £16,990 towards the second year of the water and sanitation programme in North Gondar, North West Ethiopia. The overall goal of the project is the reduction of the levels of morbidity related to inadequate water and sanitation through the establishment of a water and sanitation unit.

The specific objectives:

1. Increase local understanding of illness and preventive health through raising awareness of personal hygiene and sanitation for the prevention of disease.

2. Rehabilitate existing non-functioning small-scale water distribution systems in rural areas.

3. To involve elected local communities in the design, implementation and maintenance of small scale water schemes.

The activities carried out are:

Spring maintenance.

Spring protection.

Shallow well construction.

Construction of six seat latrine in schools.

Construction of incinerator in schools.

Development of pipeline construction.

Construction of ferro cement tank for rainwater harvesting.

Contraction of water storage tank.

Five springs were protracted, five were rehabilitated, five shallow wells dug and equipped with hand pumps, three six-seat pit latrines constructed, 17 school floors were cemented, rubbish incinerator constructed and an animal drinking trough built benefiting 27,000 young people. Community magnet structures have been implemented to ensure sustainability. The work of WSU is now being modelled in other parts of Ethiopia.

£16,990

CARE USA

Health Sector Support Project, Northern Guatemala

Guatemala is one of the poorest nations in Latin America, with more than 50 percent of the rural population living in abject poverty. In many impoverished areas, more than half of all children under the age of five are moderately or severely malnourished. The Guatemalan Ministry of Health services reach less than one-third of the country's population, with poor rural communities severely under-served. Widespread malnutrition, limited health care knowledge, and poor access to basic health care services contribute to Guatemala's high child mortality rate, where one out of every 14 children born dies before his or her fifth birthday. Countless other Guatemalan children become sick each year from vaccine-preventable diseases, such as measles or diphtheria, or from treatable diseases such as diarrhoea or pneumonia. CARE's Health Services Support Project, working in collaboration with the Guatemalan Ministry of Health (MOH), helped improve the health of 52,100 impoverished people in 103 Guatemalan rural communities. The project targeted the most vulnerable members of the population; 14,800 children under five years old and 15,300 women of childbearing age (15 - 49). The project worked in four departments/districts of northern Guatemala: Alta Verapaz (Cahabon); Baja Verapaz (Purulha); Huehuetenango (Coatan); and El Quiche (Zacualpa). The three-year project ended on September 30, 1996. The overall project accomplishments are provided below. Project interventions included the following: strengthening of local partners; increased vaccination coverage; diarrhoea prevention and treatment; nutrition education and growth monitoring; and maternal health. The project's acute respiratory disease prevention and treatment program and family planning components are not included here since responsibility for these activities was largely with the MOH and other agencies. Increased vaccination coverage: 24 vaccination campaigns carried out in 103 communities; 432 village health workers (VHWs) trained in vaccine administration and education/promotion; 7,119 mothers attended education sessions; and 40 percent to 60 percent increase in total vaccination coverage between January and June 1996.

Diarrhoea Prevention and Treatment:

439 VHWs trained in the prevention and treatment of diarrhoea; 86 Community oral rehydration units were established and provided services; 5,177 mothers attended health education sessions; and 11 percent increase in the number of mothers who treated their sick children with oral rehydration solution.

Nutrition Education and Growth Monitoring:

232 VHWs trained in infant-child nutrition and growth monitoring; 655 mothers with children under two years old attended nutrition education sessions; and 36 communities conducted monthly infant child growth monitoring.

Maternal Health:

422 village midwives equipped with birthing kits made up of scissors, thread and other materials; and 168 village midwives participated in four workshops to improve their birthing techniques.

A personal account:

Mrs Alicia Caal lives in the village of San Juan in Santa Maria Cahabon, Alta Verapaz. She is married and has two children, Jose, four years old, and Maria Victoria, who just completed her first birthday. This is her story of how CARE changed her life. "In our village of San Juan, the month of May is a mixed blessing. It brings rains to water our crops, but also diarrhoea that kills our children. That's why we call it the Month of Death. Last May, my daughter, Maria Victoria, began running a high fever with diarrhoea and vomiting. I was scared because my husband was away from home and wouldn't be home until the next day. Maria Victoria was getting worse and worse. She was so quiet, her eyes were sunken and dry, and anything I gave her to eat or drink would come right back up. What could I do? I felt so terribly alone. I knelt down by my child's bed and asked God for help. Suddenly, I remembered that Don Agustin, our local health promoter, kept packets of rehydration solution at his home. All you had to do was mix it with clean water. For someone with diarrhoea, it could save that person's life. I rushed over to Don Agustin's house to get a packet, but to my horror, he wasn't there! I thought to myself, if I wait for Agustin to get back, my baby will die. Then I made the best decision of my whole life. I would make the oral rehydration solution myself. Augustin had taught me how to make the solution from sugar, salt and boiled water.

I hurried home, mixed eight teaspoons of sugar and one teaspoon of salt in a litre of boiled water, and gave it to my daughter a little at time. Thanks to CARE, I was able to save my child's life. I help Augustin with his health talks. I tell mothers my story and show them how to prepare the life-saving drink. I also encourage them to wash their hands after they use the latrine, and to take their children to the health clinic for their vaccinations."

Conclusion:

CARE Guatemala's PASS Project helped to improve the health of tens of thousands of impoverished children and their mothers in 103 rural communities. Through the establishment of a community-managed health system capable of providing basic health services, and by creating linkages with government health services, CARE also helped ensure that activities would continue long after the project had come to a close.

£97,500

Indonesia

CARE USA

Village maternal - Child Health Care

The rural poor of East Flores, Indonesia, face a host of health problems which every year takes the lives of thousands of infants and young children. For every 1,000 babies born, more than 75 die before their fifth birthday. One of the most common killers of young children is pneumonia and other acute respiratory diseases (ARIs). CARE's Control and Prevention of ARIs project is working to reduce ARI-related death and illness among children under five years old in 79 villages and sub-villages in three sub-districts of East Flores. CARE works to improve ARI case management by training health workers and village midwives to diagnose, treat and, where necessary, refer patients to the appropriate medical facility. The project works at both clinic and community-based levels. The project also educates mothers about how they can protect their children from ARIs through proper ventilation, good nutrition and immunisation, to recognise signs and symptoms, and to seek help from the local health workers or medical professionals as soon as possible.

Health workers are trained in ARI, to diagnose, treat and follow up ARI cases, and to monitor this process using a special patient card developed by the project for this purpose. Project staff and counterparts currently tabulate and analyse patient information manually, however a computerised data management system is being developed that will significantly improve this process. The project works in conjunction with five health centres (HCs), 17 health sub-centres (SCs) and 21 village maternity huts (VMHs). Project counterparts include provincial and district government health departments, the local Development Planning Board and local non-governmental organisations (NGOs). The project works to strengthen the capacity of local NGOs to work collaboratively with government and community health authorities in reducing ARI child death and illness. The project was launched in September 1996 and continued through June 1999.

Project Accomplishments:

During this reporting period (September 1996 through June 1997), the project achieved the following:

Data Collection:

CARE carried out a baseline survey among mothers of children under five in 30 sub-villages that served to determine the status of mothers' knowledge, attitudes and practices regarding the causes, prevention and treatment of ARIs before project activities began. The information collected was then used to monitor project effectiveness at the end of the first year (see examples below).

Government Collaboration and Coordination:

The project conducted an orientation workshop for local government officials from the district Ministry of Health, Planning Office and Office of Information, as well as local government and private health workers, NGOs representatives and community leaders. The event served to inform local counterparts about project objectives and strategies, inspire commitment, and define roles and responsibilities.

Improve ARI Case Management for Children Under Five Years Old:

CARE trained 54 government health workers in ARI case management, 36 (67%) of whom were able to demonstrate full knowledge and abilities in diagnosing and treating ARI. This surpassed the project's annual goal of 60 %.

A total of 255 children under five with ARI were identified and treated using the patient card system. This number is expected to increase as more health workers are trained and case detection and monitoring improves.

Provision of Antibiotics (Cotrimoxasole):

The project procured and distributed 55,000 cotrimoxasole antibiotic tablets to all government and community-based health facilities. This is expected to fill the gap until district health authorities are able to independently provide the medication. At the same time, the project helped bring together district health offices and local planning boards, strengthening their ability to work together to determine the amount of cotrimoxasole needed in a given area and time period, make budget allocations to cover medication costs and logistics, and supply HCs, SCs and VMHs in a timely manner.

Community-Based ARI Education and Treatment:

Ten community health workers from each of 21 villages (210 health workers in all) were trained to carry out the following activities: diagnose children with ARI (fever, rapid breathing, etc.); refer patients to the nearest HC or SC for treatment; educate mothers through health talks and home visits; follow up ARI cases; and properly fill out the patient monitoring card. The project formed groups of between 20-30 mothers with children under five in each of the 58 sub-villages. Community health workers were assisted by village midwives and CARE staff. Videos as well as posters and other visual aids were used to enhance the learning process. Other aspects of good health, such as nutrition and hygiene, were also taught. An assessment carried out by project staff in May-June 1997 revealed that the work of community health workers was having a favourable impact on patient referrals and mothers' education. Of the 255 cases treated, community health workers referred 53 cases to a health facility. The project's education component was having a positive impact on its intended audience. Of the more than 2,100 mothers who attended the sessions, 90% demonstrated improved knowledge and understanding the causes surrounding ARI, how it can be recognised and prevented, and how to seek medical help.

Local NGO Capacity Building:

The project trained supervisory and field staff from two local NGOs in ARI case management and education. To enhance NGO effectiveness even further, CARE hired nine staff members (seven field officers, two supervisors) on a 50% part-time basis. One of the NGOs works in villages outside the project areas, a fact that will increase the number of people reached by the project.

Conclusion:

Every year in East Flores, Indonesia, pneumonia and other ARIs take the lives of thousands of young children. CARE is making a difference by strengthening the ability of government, NGO and community health workers to detect and treat sick children and enabling mothers to take an active part in safeguarding the health of their children. CARE thanks Sport Aid '88 Trust for its very generous assistance in helping to make this possible.

£44,000

Nicaragua

CARE USA
Child Survival in Nicaragua

Due in large part to the political turmoil and severe economic crisis in Nicaragua over the past decade, the standard of living has declined and essential social services such as health care have deteriorated. Women and young children are the most vulnerable members of the population and therefore the ones who suffer most. For every 100 children born, eight die before reaching their fifth birthday. The principal causes are preventable, and include pneumonia, diarrhoea and low birth weight. Many impoverished women suffer from poor health, especially during pregnancy. The major causes of death are haemorrhage, post-partum infections, miscarriages and high blood pressure (toxemia). The high maternal death rate is attributed to a lack of prenatal and postpartum care, deliveries by untrained village midwives, and a lack of family planning services. Matagalpa Department, a mountainous region in north-central Nicaragua, is one of the areas most affected.

CARE NICARAGUA'S CHILD SURVIVAL PROJECT aims to reduce mother and child death rates among a population of 25,404 women of childbearing age (15-44 years) and children under five years old in 65 rural communities in Matagalpa Department. CARE's strategy for carrying out these interventions involves the training and supervision of village health workers (VHWs) and village midwives in coordination with the Ministry of Health (MOH), and local and international non-governmental organisations (NGOs) and the formation of village health committees. Their participation is essential and will help ensure that project activities continue after CARE leaves. The projects are scheduled to operate for three years, from 1 January 1995 to 31 December 1997. Project Accomplishments:

During this reporting period (January - June 1996), the project accomplished the following:

Inter-Institutional Cooperation:

The project co-ordinated efforts and shared information with the MOH and numerous local and international nongovernmental organisations (NGOs) through various meetings and workshops during this period.

Individual accomplishments included:

A meeting with the MOH as well as PROFAMILIA, the Matagalpa Women's Collective, and other NGOs, to create an inter-agency committee to facilitate information sharing and avoid duplication of effort. A meeting attended by other agencies working in child survival to examine the ways different institutions work to guarantee quality of care. A meeting of the UN Population Fund (FNUAP) to examine training and educational materials developed by FNUAP, and to plan a workshop for NGOs working in maternal health and family planning.

Vaccination:

The project worked to increase the number of women and infants being vaccinated through training of VHWs and family education. In January 1996, Matagalpa health officials reported that, with CARE's help, they had achieved an over 95% vaccination coverage rate for children under one year old.

Individual accomplishments included:

509 VHWs trained in vaccination education and promotion; 3,363 women taught about the importance of vaccinations for them and their children; 18 vaccination campaigns carried out in coordination with the Dario, Sebaco and Matagalpa municipal health departments.

Diarrhoeal disease prevention:

The project trained VHWs to educate women about good hygiene practices, and to teach them how to prepare and administer life saving oral rehydration drinks for their children who fall ill with diarrhoea. The project also established Community Oral Rehydration Centres staffed by trained VHWs who used oral rehydration salts (ORS) to treat children with severe diarrhoea or referred them to a health facility, depending on the degree of severity.

Individual accomplishments included:

403 VHW's trained in aspects of diarrhoea prevention and the preparation and administration of ORS; 2,142 women taught about the importance of good hygiene and to prepare and administer ORS for their sick children; 694 children under two years old treated with ORS; 47 community oral rehydration units created and functioning and/or supported by the project (all six centres are now up and running).

Control of Acute Lower Respiratory Infections (ALRI):

VHWs learned to recognise the danger signs of ALRI, educate mothers how to prevent colds and other simple respiratory infections from becoming ALRIs, and refer ALRI cases to a medical facility.

Individual accomplishments include:

403 VHWs trained in the management of ALRIs; 1,302 women taught about the dangers of ALRIs, how to prevent them, and how to treat simple respiratory infections.

Nutrition Education and Growth Monitoring:

The project worked to improve the nutritional status of women, infants and children through nutrition education, and by monitoring the growth of children under two years of age. The project also worked with families to improve agricultural production to ensure good health and increase family income.

Individual accomplishments included:

509 VHWs trained in nutrition education and growth monitoring; 3,163 women taught the basics of good maternal-child nutrition, including breast feeding; 2,787 children under five years old received vitamin A supplements; 403 VHWs trained in various agricultural techniques, including family gardens, preparation of organic fertilisers and insecticides, seedbed management and crop diversification.

Maternal Health and Family Planning:

VHW strained by the project the previous year educated women about the importance of prenatal care and birth spacing. They also referred interested couples to PROFAMILIA, the local family planning agency, for contraceptive material and advice. CARE and project partner staff plan to train village midwives to provide basic prenatal care and to diagnose and refer high risk pregnancies. Individual accomplishments included:

1,593 women taught how to maintain their health and the health of their unborn children during pregnancy; 1,049 women taught about family planning and how to access contraceptive material and information through PROFAMILIA.

Conclusion:

In Matagalpa Department, Nicaragua, thousands of poor women and young children fall ill or die each year from diseases and conditions which could be prevented were it not for the lack of easily accessible, quality health services. CARE's Child Survival Project is helping improve the health of more than 25,000 impoverished women and children through the creation of a community-managed health system with links to governmental and non-governmental health, nutrition and family planning services.

£18,500

India

Save The Children Fund

Leh Nutrition Project in Ladakh, India was established in 1978, covering 70 villages (pop. 15,000). The project focuses on themes of health, rural development and training. The scheme is now trying to build up skills and strengths in the community so they are able to support themselves, focusing on children and women and to benefit the most isolated, disadvantaged and marginalised communities. Its most recent project was to attempt to involve children in the decision making of village life, setting up children's village committees. As a result of these committees children felt much more included and adults gained a wider understanding of children's views. The LNP is in the process of setting up womanise groups in the villages of the region in order to increase income through a range of activities such as selling tea and vegetables and knitting. The women have been given training in basic book-keeping out of the 15 villages supported by LNP 13 have their own community health worker, the workers receive extra training each year and this year's focus will be AIDS awareness and health education The Sport Aid '88 donation has been used to fund health and education work.

£25,000

Save The Children Fund

Garwhal Project (BMA), Northern India, Utter Pradesh

The project has been working in the Garwhal region for several years. Focusing on mother and childcare, health services and education. The project has been running two primary schools and 57 nurseries caring for a total of 1000 children. Children are taking an active part in development activities. groups of 20 children have been acting as peer counsellors, promoting hygiene and tree planting. Girls have been generating income by knitting and vegetable gardening. There have also been literacy classes for girls and increased emphasis has been placed on women having a say in running the community as men seek work away from the villages. The project is a health programme concentrating on safe motherhood, hygiene and clean water supplies. The project also run a number of local health clinics which they are in the process of handing over to the government, freeing resources to build up community services such as mobile midwives and doctors. The project has also forged strong links with local government, hopefully this will lead to the experience gained by the project being written into policy and planning decisions. The Sport Aid '88 donation has been used to fund health and education work, supporting the nurseries and running health clinics.

£40,000

Kenya

Save The Children Fund

Starehe, the only free school in Kenya, has 1164 boys living and studying there, 867 of whom are from very disadvantaged backgrounds. These boys rely totally on the school for residential care and free education. Save the children has provided for many of these children.

Pupil breakdown

Primary 222

Secondary 845

Post-secondary 97

At post-secondary, accountancy and computing are offered. Nominations come from all over Kenya, competition for places is stiff. Pupils are awarded a place according to their need, irrespective of background and ethnic group. Many arrive at the school unable to share a common language.

Academic results:

The school came third in the national results of the Kenya Certificate of Education and 182 of the 206 leavers were offered places at university.

Other achievements:

Took part in the 1997 National Swimming Championship, the Nairobi Province Football Athletics and Cross Country Running Championships. It also performed well in cricket, hockey, badminton and basketball. 621 boys are currently participating in the president awards scheme (like Duke of Edinburgh's); 141 boys have qualified for their gold award. Many boys from the school take part in a holiday voluntary service scheme choosing to volunteer in organisations rather than have a summer holiday. last year's placements were 181 in hospitals, 230 in clinics, dispensaries and health centres, 61 in commerce, industry and agriculture. All the boys learn first aid and many of the boys work in a small clinic run by the school. Save the children is gradually withdrawing its support to the school and to compensate for this a trust fund has been set up to allow 100 free places a year for the foreseeable future. Our donation was used to purchase text books and stationery, sporting equipment and recreational facilities. Purchase was for 12,000 children and included text books (in all subjects and at all levels), exercise books, geometrical instruments, scientific and workshop equipment, sport and recreational equipment including bats, balls and nets as well as sportswear for activities including hockey, basketball, handball, cricket etc.

£35,000

UK

Save The Children Fund

Deptford Project London

The fund run a family resource centre at the Pepys estate Deptford SE London. The centre provides day long child care with a playgroup from 9am to 4pm. There is a drop-in centre, mother and toddler sessions, language classes and translation services. The surrounding council estates house 17 different ethnic groups although the predominate ones are Vietnamese and West African. The charity is in the process of handing the centre to other organisation and the local community. Specialist work has also been carried out with the Vietnamese community the project aims to provide a community base to support Vietnamese families until they can use mainstream services. The focus is on healthcare and literacy especially in the young. The aim is to train the community to help itself. Areas covered include advice and information services in Vietnamese, Creche and mother and child groups, home support through outreach, family literacy project to encourage parents and children to learn together. Literacy skill for mothers, and childcare and play to help the children develop new and different skills and lobbying other agencies locally and nationally to make changes to help Vietnamese and other children in the area. The Sport Aid '88 donation of £50,000 was used to support four child care workers who ran a variety of activities at the centre during 1996 and 1997.

£50,000

UK

The Sport Aid Foundation

The Sport Aid '88 Trust donated £100,000 to establish a Sports Award Fund for Disabled Youngsters.

£100,000

1997
(from Sport Aid '88)

Afghanistan

UNICEF
Control of Diarrhoeal Diseases
£50,000

Rwanda

UNICEF
Peace Education
£50,000

1998
(from Sport Aid '88)

Sri Lanka

The International Childcare Trust
The Makandura Village Project for 100 Street Children. Since its establishment in 1986 this project has been delivering a range of vital support to many of Sri Lanka's most deprived and marginalised people, in particular distressed children who have become homeless as a result of family problems, endemic poverty and the continuing civil war. The contribution of the Sport Aid '88 Trust is being used specifically to support child war victims - Street Children. The support has provided education, food, clothing and recreation for 100 children for one year. 100 x £245 per child.
£24,500

UK

The Centre for Brain Injury Rehabilitation and Development
The Centre for Brain Injury Rehabilitation and Development is based at Broughton, near Chester as a treatment charity for brain injury. 90% of the 2,000 patients treated have had their quality of life improved. The Sport Aid '88 Trust provided a grant of £10,000 for the treatment of mentally and physically handicapped children.
£10,000

UK

The Welsh Centre for Conductive Education
The Welsh Centre for Conductive Education spends 96.3% of its annual donations on specialised support for children suffering from cerebral palsy. The Sport Aid '88 Trust established a Bursary fund of £20,000 to support approximately 100 children aged between six months and five years with cerebral palsy.
£20,000

338

Churchtown
Together with a small dedicated staff team and young international volunteers, Churchtown established a centre of excellence, unparalleled in Europe, providing personal development programmes for around 1,200 disabled youngsters, their families and carers each year. The Sport Aid '88 Trust donated £10,050 to enable the building of a specialised Adventure Ropes Challenge Course for disabled children. This facility benefitted thousands of disabled children from all over Europe, throughout its lifetime.
£10,050

UK

The British Institute for Brain Injured Children
The British Institute for Brain Injured Children is based in Bridgewater in Somerset and has achieved amazing results in improving the quality of life for brain injured children. The Sport Aid '88 Trust established a bursary fund to assist brain injured children in 1998.
£10,000

UK

The Royal School for the Blind
Two transfer trolleys and stretchers for hoisting disabled children to the hydrotherapy pool. One hoist with sling. One bobath for disabled children in wheelchairs.
£9,188.25

1999
(from Sport Aid '88)

Zimbabwe

Tjewondo Primary School
The Sport Aid '88 donation funded the purchase of a complete range of sports equipment for Tjewondo Primary School in Maphisa, Zimbabwe. The equipment included soccer, netball, volleyball, athletic and tennis equipment and Z$10,000 was allocated to purchase musical instruments and choir uniforms.
£3,000

Albania

Hopes and Homes for Children
The Sport Aid '88 Trust funded the building and refurbishment of a children's orphanage in Albania.
£10,000

India

VSO
A Sport Aid '88 Trust donation enabled the placement of Jeanette Parry into the Rural Organisation for Social Action in Tamil, Nadu, India. Her work provided quality pre-school facilities for disadvantaged children and thereby met their educational needs.

Gambia

VSO
The Trust funded the placement of nutritionist Clare Levi in the Gambia. Clare operated in a very unstructured work environment providing specialist services in child nutritional care. Her main activities included surveillance, breastfeeding, lecturing at health institutions, the prevention of micronutrient deficiencies and the treatment of diabetes. All of these activities are to ensure that the nutrition of children in the Gambia is improved.

VSO

The Trust also funded the placement of Doctor Emma Lim - a paediatrician - on the Pacific Island of Vanuatu. Emma addressed the health needs of children. She was employed as national paediatrician for Vanuatu and worked for the majority of her time at Vila Central Hospital in charge of the children's ward and nursery. Emma was responsible for all paediatric patients admitted to the hospital, regular outpatient clinics and service training for medical personnel.

Total for all VSO projects £30,107

U.K

The British Blind Sport Association

The Sport Aid '88 Trust donated £6,500 to the British Blind Sport Association to fund a special holiday for visually impaired children.

£6,500

India

Care Council

The Sport Aid '88 Trust donated funds to Care Council - a private school catering for the needs of disadvantaged children in Gingee, Taluk. The donation purchased a five acre games and sports centre for more than 3,000 rural children, providing for all equipment and staffing needs.

£15,500

2000
(from Sport Aid '88)

UK

The British Deaf Association
The Sport Aid '88 Trust donated £10,000 to the British Deaf Association to benefit deaf children in the UK
£10,000

China

The Save the Children Fund
There are few facilities for children with disabilities in China, and most schools do not accept disabled children. A number of social and economic factors contribute to a large number of disabled children being abandoned or placed in institutions. Children who are brought up in institutions are isolated from community life and do not receive the care they need to develop to their full potential. The Sport Aid '88 Trust donated £30,000 to the Save the Children Fund to help find alternatives to institutional care for children with disabilities in China and to encourage their integration into mainstream schooling.
£30,000

Mozambique

The Save the Children Fund
The Sport Aid '88 Trust donated £39,470 to the Save the Children Fund to construct three primary schools in Mopeia District in Mozambique. Mopeia district in Zambezia province in the Zambezi valley was very badly affected by the 16 years of civil war that commenced after independence in 1976 and finally came to an end in 1992/3. Save the Children has been working there since 1986, running a broad programme to improve social welfare, and the quality and accessibility of health and education services. The Sport Aid '88 Trust funding relates specifically to the building of three schools. Each primary school will have two classrooms, accommodation and offices.
£39,470

The English Federation of Disability Sport

The Sport Aid '88 Trust donated £30,000 to the English Federation of Disability Sport to enable a Football Development Programme for special schools. The main objectives of the scheme was to establish pathways for young people with special educational needs to existing community clubs and teams to ensure access to football opportunities and to improve the quality of life among these children.

£30,000

Sudan

IAAF

The Sport Aid '88 Trust donated £81,496 to the International Amateur Athletic Federation to support street children in Khartoum.

£81,496

UK

The Sports Aid Foundation

The Sport Aid '88 Trust donated a further £35,000 to the Sports Aid Trust to assist disabled youngsters.

£35,000

Cambodia

The Save the Children Fund

The Sport Aid '88 Trust donated £19,085 to the Save the Children Fund to renovate a primary school in Cambodia.

£19,085

Ethiopia

The Save the Children Fund

The Sport Aid '88 Trust donated £21,313 to the Save the Children Fund to purchase school furniture for eight primary schools in Ethiopia.

£21,313

Lao

The Save the Children Fund
The Sport Aid '88 Trust donated £3,125 to the Save the Children Fund to provide teaching materials (blackboards and text books) for schools in three provinces of Lao PDR.
£3,125

Nepal

The Save the Children Fund
The Sport Aid '88 Trust donated £3,000 to the Save the Children Fund to supply toys and play equipment for Bhutanese refugee children in Nepal.
£3,000

Pakistan

The Save the Children Fund
The Sport Aid '88 Trust donated £23,900 to the Save the Children Fund to fully equip a Child Resource Centre in Pakistan.
£23,900

Sierra Leone

The British Red Cross
The Sport Aid '88 Trust donated £105,153.24 for a child advocacy and rehabilitation programme in Sierra Leone.
£105,153.24

Guinea
The Save the Children Fund
The Sport Aid '88 Trust donated £27,838 for a child development programme in the Republic of Guinea to improve the physical wellbeing of children from both the indigenous and refugee communities.
£27,838

If you could change the world, would you?

Printed in Great Britain
by Amazon